CRIMSON SKY

The Air Battle for Korea

CRIMSON SKY
The Air Battle for Korea

JOHN R. BRUNING JR.

POTOMAC BOOKS, INC.
Washington, D.C.

First The History of War edition published in 2005

First paperback edition 2000

Copyright © 1999 Brassey's

Map on p. vi by Molly O'Halloran

Library of Congress Cataloging-in-Publication Data

Bruning, John R.
  Crimson sky : the air battle for Korea / John R. Bruning Jr.
    p. cm.
  Includes bibliographical references and index.
  1. Korean War, 1950–1953—Aerial operations, American. I. Title.
  DS920.2.U5 B78 1999
  951.9049248—ddc21

                                                                98-43110
                                                                CIP
                                                                r98

1-57488-296-1 (alk. paper)

1-57488-841-2 (paper)

Potomac Books, Inc.
22841 Quicksilver Drive
Dulles, Va. 20166

10 9 8 7 6 5 4 3 2 1

Printed in Canada

For Phyllis and Jane,
who taught me what it means
to be an American

—◆—

Contents

Map   vi
Preface   ix
Introduction   xii

PART ONE. THE SHOESTRING AIR WAR
1   The First Jet Kills   1
2   The Birth of Combat SAR   11
3   Fighting 53 Goes to War   22
4   Into the Tiger's Jaws   39
5   Home by Christmas   57
6   The Finest Kind of Honor   63

PART TWO. FROM STRANGLE TO STALEMATE
7   Carlson's Tigers   75
8   The Bridge Busters   82
9   The Battle of Carlson's Canyon   88
10 The Dam Busters   93
11 Night Intruders   105
12 A Fighter Pilot's Heart   116

PART THREE. MISSION TO NAMSI
13 Prelude to Black Tuesday   127
14 MiG Trap   133
15 Death Ride to Namsi   142
16 Horizontal Flak   150

PART FOUR. THE FIGHTER PILOT'S WAR

17 Payback   167
18 More Guts than the Law Allows   180
19 Stalemate in the Air   190
20 The Edge of Disaster   195
21 The Soviet Riddle   203
22 The Hybrid War   208

Glossary   213
Notes   215
Bibliography   219
Index   221
About the Author   232

Preface

The Korean War frequently has been called the "Forgotten War." Not only has it been forgotten by the American public at large but also by the military. Even worse for the historian, the lack of attention to this war extends to the military archives. In Montgomery, Alabama at Maxwell Air Force Base, the USAF Historical Research Agency has some of the best-organized World War II records anywhere. Conversely, the Korean records are very disorganized. Wading through them is a nightmare.

The National Archives in Washington, D.C., presents an even greater challenge. Recently, hundreds of boxes containing documents from the Korean War era were transferred to the National Archives from various Air Force repositories. The boxes are disorganized and generally uncataloged. There is faint hope for seeing this collection accessioned anytime soon because the Archives and the Air Force are fighting over who should pay to have the work done. As a result, information that could prove of immense value to historians is currently almost inaccessible. When I was at the National Archives during the summer of 1997, I waded through many of these boxes. Thousands of pages of documents had been randomly thrown into ragged cardboard packing boxes.

Compounding the situation is the fact that, throughout the Korean War, the squadrons doing the fighting frequently did not keep thorough records of their combat experiences, unlike the usually meticulous efforts by their World War II counterparts to do so. Some of the available documents from Air Force squadrons deal more with routine matters than they do with combat operations. Discussions of important missions sometimes consist of only a paragraph or two.

Because of the lack of accessible records, all this meant that the memories of those who fought the war were critically important to this book project. In fact, I could not have written the book without the generous assistance of

Harold Carlson, Bob Wayne, Paul van Boven, Dick Heyman, Charles Darrow, Charlie Mitson, Ed Laney, Al Dymock, Nate Curry, Dave Rowlands, Tom Hudner, Eben Dobson, Joe Conley, Doug Evans, Fred Beissner, Emil Goldbeck, Jim Kirkendall, Warren Lawyer, Sumner Whitten, and Robert Dewald. Lil Booker gladly told me about her husband Jesse's experiences and sent me much information on his career.

Special thanks go to Dick Heyman and Bill Runey, who spent many lunch hours with me at the Hungry Duck and set me straight on various aspects of air combat. Bill, a veteran of the 8th Fighter Squadron during World War II, also provided much help in tracking down names and information.

Don McKeon, a superb editor, deserves as much credit as I can give him. *Crimson Sky* would have remained just a dream without his assistance. A big thank you must also go to my agent, Elisabet McHugh, who sold this project only three months after I signed with her agency.

I'm indebted to the gracious Ms. Ann Webb, archivist, who runs the reading room at the USAF Air Force Historical Research Agency. She provided much support and assistance during my whirlwind trip to Maxwell Field in the summer of 1997. Archivist Archie DiFante also lent a hand while I was there.

My wife Jennifer deserves much credit. Her dedication to this project has been a source of continuous inspiration. While checking through the final manuscript, she actually began having contractions. We thought for sure we'd be parents within hours, but it proved to be another false alarm. Our daughter Renee arrived four days later.

Lindsay Johnson, Shawna Yost, Nick Kelley, and Jason Carver transcribed interview tapes. To each of them, I offer a hearty thanks.

Independence, Oregon Mayor Tom Ritchey, Commissioner Warren Lawyer, and Councilor Jim Kirkendall all provided input and comments in an effort to keep me on the historical straight and narrow.

Doctor Laura Archer provided much support by editing and commenting on the manuscript.

Jarrett Jester, Gary Stottlemyer, Steven Hill, Randy Dersham, and Scott Rudi of Dynamix Inc. supplied both support and the opportunity for me to finish this project. Russ Francis, former San Francisco 49er tight end and pilot extraordinaire, gave me vivid descriptions on how to fly the F-51 Mustang. Russ and his flying experiences merit a book of their own someday. Damon Slye broke me of some bad habits I picked up in grad school. He taught me how to make history interesting.

Thanks are also in order for Jack Cooke, Robin Puccetti, Judy Bruning, Billy Kay, Marge Taylor, and the rest of the folks at Taylors, Stacey McCarthy, Bob and Jake Archer, Terry Gregson, and Dana Baily. John Bruning Sr. also deserves credit for sending me down the historical path in the first place. I know of no one else with whom I could have a three-hour debate over weapons placement on the Ki-61. We always made Thanksgiving dinner interesting, eh, Pop?

I also owe a great deal to Scotty Girard and El Agena of the Independence, Oregon Pioneer Museum. They gave me an office in the basement of the 110-year-old museum building, where I wrote most of *Crimson Sky*. For years, folks in our little town have been convinced that the museum is haunted. After spending many late nights there, I became a true believer. Check it out if you're ever in our part of Oregon.

Introduction

Korea: The word conjures up images of mud, trench warfare, defeat, and demoralization for generations of Americans. The Korean War was a fierce, frustrating conflict that, despite increasing numbers of U.S.-led United Nations victories, did not end in outright victory. Instead, a political solution allowed the war to taper off into a long and uneasy truce. Incredibly, though the solution to the war was political, none of the political leaders, including Dwight D. Eisenhower and Mao Zedong, signed the Panmunjom Accords. As of late 1998 the front lines in Korea remain in virtually the same state in which they existed when the fighting ceased in July 1953. Americans still patrol their hilltop fortresses and occasionally take fire from their North Korean counterparts a few hundred yards away on the next ridge line. The shaky truce of 1953 has lasted more than forty-five years, but news from Korea in recent years, for instance the North Korean commando assault by submarine during the summer of 1996, indicates that the threat of war is far from over.

Above the muck and mud through which the infantry slogged for three years, the Korean War gave rise to a new type of aerial warfare. Born at the end of World War II, the jet engine revolutionized air warfare to a degree that nobody could understand until East and West clashed in the skies over North Korea. The air war fought over the suffering, miserable armies was long and costly, but most postwar accounts do not make that fact clear. Far from being just a joust between North American F-86 Sabrejets and Soviet MiG-15s, as is so often presented, the air war was far more diversified and complex. It was in Korea that jets first flew from aircraft carriers into battle and, in the process, demonstrated how unsuitable the World War II flattops were for this new generation of aircraft. The hard-won lessons of the Korean War gave birth to the modern supercarrier, complete with angled deck and steam catapult.

Korea also witnessed the first widespread use of the helicopter. Helicopters had been almost totally ignored by the U.S. Navy and Air Force during the

National Archives

Aerial formation including (*left to right*) a Lockheed F-80 Shooting Star, a North American F-82 Twin Mustang, a Lockheed F-94 Starfire, and an F-86 Sabrejet.

late 1940s. The Korean War, however, changed that attitude when the spindly little Sikorskys demonstrated their many abilities on such support missions as medical evacuations and search and rescue (SAR). By the end of the first summer of the war, both the U.S. Army and Navy were screaming for more helicopters to use in Korea. The U.S. Air Force went so far as to strip most of its other commands of their helicopters so they could be thrown into action around the Pusan perimeter in August 1950.

At the end of the war, the Army concluded that helicopters would remain a critical component of their fighting capacity. Rather than depending on the Air Force's helicopter units, the Army established its own permanent rotor squadrons, thus setting the stage for their massive employment in Vietnam a decade later.

On the ground as well as in the air, the United States was humbled by the Korean War. Emerging from World War II as the undisputed victor and most powerful nation on earth, the United States entered the postwar era with a cockiness about the quality of its military personnel and equipment. This overconfidence cost the lives of thousands in the early days of the Korean War. Combat against the North Koreans and Chinese soon showed how poorly trained and equipped the infantry units in the Far East were by 1950. Bazooka shells bounced off Soviet-built T-34 tanks, artillery proved inadequate in both amounts and effectiveness, and the average GI had little motivation, training, or experience.

As bad as things were on the ground during the first year of the war, the U.S. Air Force and Navy received a terrible shock in November 1950 when the Chinese and Soviet air forces intervened in the war. Riding high on the prestige garnered by the incredible air victories secured in Europe and the Pacific five years before, both the Navy and the Air Force had failed to realize just how far behind most of their aircraft technology was in comparison to the recent innovations of the Soviets.

They learned that lesson when the first MiG-15s swept down from Manchuria and engaged Air Force F-80s and Navy Panthers and Corsairs. Both services suffered heavily at the hands of this fearsome new Communist weapon, but it could have been much worse had the Red pilots been better trained. Time and time again, many American pilots were able to save themselves in the midst of apparently hopeless situations by falling back on their training and combat experience and using them to their advantage. In the end, only the F-86 Sabrejet could stay in the air with the MiG. Postwar accounts stress the amazing 7:1 kill ratio that the sleek American fighter scored over its Communist counterpart. Recent scholarship, however, has shown that this alleged walkover did not actually take place, and the ratio has been revised downward several times since the war. Some accounts pin it at barely 2:1 when all UN losses to MiGs are included.

While the air war in Korea set the stage for modern jet warfare, it also was one of the oddest crossroads of aviation history. Korea represents the only war in which three distinct phases of aerial evolution met in one place at the same time. Over MiG Alley, the latest and best jet fighters clashed in strangely sterile and remote dogfights. The fighting over MiG Alley represented the pinnacle of Western technology pitted against the best that the Soviet Bloc had to offer.

South of MiG Alley, the bulk of the air war was fought by World War II holdovers. Douglas B-26 Invaders prowled for trucks, tanks, and other targets of opportunity. Navy Vought F4U Corsairs, made famous by Greg "Pappy" Boyington and his men in 1943, struck daily at troop concentrations and fortifications a full ten years later. The North American P-51 Mustangs, so common in the skies over Germany in 1944–45, appeared again five years later, with a new designation of F-51 Mustangs.

Finally, as if to mock the technological marvels that America was just beginning to produce during the early 1950s, the North Koreans and Chinese began raiding UN bases with ancient Polikarpov Po-2 biplanes. First built in the late 1920s, the Po-2 saw service in Korea as a night heckler; the crew tossed out hand grenades and light bombs as the plane buzzed over airfields and supply dumps at a clunky 90 mph.

Over Korea at night, thanks to the Po-2s, technology developed during World War I began to clash with the first evolution of the jet age. Starting

U.S. Air Force

Funeral services at an air base in Korea. Aircraft pictured include F-86s, B-26 Invaders, Convair PB4Y Privateers, and Douglas C-47s.

in 1952, the U.S. Air Force (USAF) attempted to intercept these nighttime prowlers with its latest all-weather fighters. In scenes repeated throughout South Korea, Lockheed F-94 Starfires swooped down on the Red biplanes with their gears and flaps down to keep them from overshooting the museum-piece targets. The results were surprisingly bad for the USAF. Several F-94s stalled out and crashed, killing their crews. At least one F-94 actually flew through its Po-2 target, which caused the destruction of both planes. In the end, shooting down a wood-and-fabric plane with a 100-horsepower engine proved to be more difficult and more dangerous than it was worth.

The technology gap was not always one-sided. Over MiG Alley, the Chinese and Soviet MiG-15 formations frequently cut into UN formations flying totally inferior aircraft. MiGs fought Mustangs, Corsairs, and, most notably, the famed and feared Boeing B-29 Superfortresses. The latter, the symbol of postwar American power, suffered terribly at the hands of the MiG pilots on several occasions. If anything, their demise as effective daylight bombers demonstrated to the world's air forces how quickly aviation technology had progressed during the five years following World War II.

Because the Korean air war marked an evolutionary crossroads, the air battles themselves are some of the most interesting to be found in the annals of combat aviation history. Despite this, little has been written about them. Most historians have focused their energy on World War II and ignored Korea altogether. Few have devoted their careers and efforts just to Korea, and the number of books on the subject would hardly fill a shelf in an average bookstore. It is significant that hundreds of memoirs have been published by World War II aviators, but fewer than a dozen from Korea have ever set their memories down on paper in published form.

Although little has been published about the Korean air war, significant and fascinating events occurred that deserve a place in aviation history. Based mainly on the recollections of those involved, this book sets out to tell the story of the men who fought those battles. For their legacy, this book was written.

Part 1 | The Shoestring Air War

1 | The First Jet Kills

The North Korean air force struck at 5:00 P.M. on June 27, 1950. Four Yak-7Bs swept over Seoul Airfield on the deck, strafing the tiny Republic of Korea (South Korean) air force's North American T-6 Texans parked around the field. When the Yaks cleared the area, seven of the ten T-6s had been damaged in the attack.

At the same time, Kimpo Airport also drew an attack. Two Yaks shot up the base control tower and set fire to a gasoline dump. North Korean pilots also put holes in an American Douglas C-54 transport trapped on the ground when the attack commenced.

The air war had begun.

The North Koreans started the war with about 150 combat aircraft in their nascent air force. Established only a few years earlier, the North Korean air force (NKAF) consisted of a single air division composed of a fighter regiment, a ground-attack regiment, and a training regiment. Soviet factories produced the equipment used by each regiment. The fighter regiment flew a motley collection of Yakovlev Yak-7s, Yak-7Bs, Yak-3s, and a few Yak-9s— about 70 altogether. The ground-attack regiment used the Ilyushin Il-10, the latest version of the World War II Il-2 Sturmovik. To round out the service, the training regiment flew a few Polikarpov Po-2 biplanes and some twin-engine light transports designated as Yak-18s.

With no tradition to build on, and little time to train properly, the NKAF was an untried and relatively brittle force when it went to war in June 1950. Nevertheless, its pilots were young, highly motivated, and eager for a chance to test themselves in battle. They were to get that chance, not just against the ill-equipped South Koreans but also against the first-line U.S. Air Force and Navy.

Meanwhile, in Japan, the U.S. Fifth Air Force was making preparations should orders come to lend air support to South Korea. Word of the first attack by the North Korean People's Army had been received by Headquarters Far East Air Forces (FEAF) at 9:45 A.M. on June 25, 1950.[1]

In the event of war in Korea, FEAF's contingency plans stated that its first priority would be to evacuate all American nationals from the peninsula. Once word of the North Korean attack reached FEAF headquarters, that plan was put into motion. By noon on June 25, orders had been cut to prepare for the evacuation missions.

The plan was to cover the evacuation with the 8th Fighter-Bomber Wing (FBW) based at Itazuke Airbase, the Japanese air base closest to Korea that was used by FEAF's Fifth Air Force. The 8th's commanding officer, Col. John M. ("Jack") Price headed the air task force needed to execute the evacuations, and he would use his own outfit's Lockheed F-80C Shooting Stars to cover the transports as they made runs into and out of Korea. Later, as the situation developed around Seoul, 8th FBW pilots not only provided cover for the transports but also flew patrols over refugee-laden merchant ships fleeing Inchon.[2]

On June 25, while FEAF and the Fifth Air Force prepared for the air evacuation mission, events in Korea were swiftly moving ahead. At first, it appeared that the Republic of Korea (ROK) army might hold on the frontier, but the news turned progressively worse as the day wore on. In Seoul, American Ambassador John Muccio fielded repeated telephone calls from Syngman Rhee, president of the Republic of Korea. Desperately worried about North Korea's superiority in tanks and aircraft, Rhee implored the American ambassador to send him ten North American F-51 Mustangs that could be used to bomb and rocket the North Korean T-34 tanks grinding southward. Muccio passed on the request through channels. The 8th FBW was also assigned a job, and the stage was set for its entry into the Korean War.

-◆◆◆-

During the early hours of Sunday, June 25, 1950, First Lieutenant Robert E. ("Bob") Wayne of the 35th Fighter-Bomber Squadron, 8th FBW, was playing bridge in his off-base quarters. He and his wife had been battling a fellow pilot and his wife throughout the night and into the morning. All-night bridge games were a popular diversion at Itazuke, and this session was one of the better match-ups. By mid-morning on Sunday, however, everyone was running out of energy and getting ready to grab some sack time.

The phone rang. When Bob picked it up, the squadron's intelligence officer said, "Bob, don't go anywhere. The North Koreans have invaded the south."

Stunned but excited, Bob hung up and broke the news to his guests. The more he and his friend talked about the news, the more anxious they were to get into the fight. To his regret, Bob had missed World War II. Now, he thought, he'd get a chance to fight his own war. He and his pilot guest headed to squadron ops (operations) to await the word that would send them over Korea.

Nearby at Itazuke's base gas station, Bob's good friend and flight mate, Robert ("Slick") Dewald, was taking inventory. Armed with pencil and clipboard, he looked more like a clerk than a fighter pilot on the verge of his first combat sortie. While going through various boxes stacked in the supply room, he first heard the news breaking from Korea. He quickly wrapped up his paperwork, discarded his clipboard, and headed to squadron ops, where he joined Bob Wayne and the rest of the pilots from C Flight. Together, they settled down and impatiently waited for orders.

At first glance, Bob Wayne was an unlikely fighter pilot. A native of The Bronx, New York, his early obsession in life was football, not flying. In fact, he hadn't even thought about aviation as a career until December 7, 1941. On that fateful day, he was watching a semipro football game when news of the Pearl Harbor attack was announced over the stadium's loudspeaker system. Moments later, a Curtiss P-40 Kittyhawk appeared overhead and performed stunts to the delight of the crowd. Walking out of the stadium that afternoon, Bob was convinced that flying was for him.

He chose the U.S. Military Academy as his entry into the military and won an appointment after high school in 1943. He played football for three years and developed into a tough and gritty tackle and end. At five feet, eleven inches and 188 pounds, Bob was not the size of a typical football player of the era, but he showed such fight on the field that the coaches put him on both offense and defense.

He carried his love of the game with him long after he left West Point in 1946 as a freshly minted second lieutenant. The following year, in fact, Bob returned to the Academy as an assistant football coach. He had trained to be a fighter pilot and had been assigned to a Mustang outfit, but the coaching job suited his interests perfectly. He spent two falls scouting for and working with the Academy's team before heading to Japan in January 1949 as a replacement pilot for the 35th Fighter-Bomber Squadron at Miho Air Force Base.

Whereas football dominated most of Bob Wayne's early years, aviation was Slick Dewald's obsession. The son of Protestant missionaries, Slick had spent four years of his childhood in Honduras while his parents established a congregation. After his family moved back to the States and settled in Atlanta, Dewald saw his first airplanes. It was love at first sight. Throughout his childhood, he built models, read all the aviation magazines of the era, and followed the careers of his favorite air heroes—Roscoe Turner, Charles Lindbergh, and Jimmy Doolittle.

After he graduated from high school in 1942, Slick joined the Army Air Forces and became a fighter pilot, but the war ended before he saw combat. In November 1945, he left the service to enroll at Georgia Institute of Technology. He stayed in school until 1948, when he rejoined his old service with a new name, the U.S. Air Force. After refresher training, the Air Force sent him to Japan, where he also joined the 35th Fighter-Bomber Squadron in early 1949. Assigned to C Flight, Slick struck up a friendship with his flight leader, Bob Wayne.

After spending six months with the squadron, Bob Wayne was getting pretty good at knowing where to get the choice assignments. As the first day of the Korean War drew to a close, Bob became bored with the lack of activity at the squadron ops shack and slipped away to wing headquarters. He knew that he could eavesdrop as the "straight scoop" came in from the Fifth Fighter Command. Bob's timing could not have been better. Moments after he arrived, Headquarters Fifth Air Force ordered the wing to restore its cast-off F-51s to combat readiness. Although the 8th FBW now flew F-80 Shooting Stars, each squadron in the group still had a couple of leftover Mustangs that it used for towing target sleeves during aerial gunnery practice. The Fifth Air Force wanted guns reinstalled in these target tugs and the Mustangs flown to South Korea, where they would be turned over to the ROK air force. Rhee was anxious to acquire the Mustangs because he hoped to use them against the North Korean T-34 tanks grinding their way southward toward Seoul.

Once Bob understood the nature of the mission, he hurried back to his buddies at the 35th Squadron's ops shack and spotted his commanding officer, Major Vince Cardarella. Bob and the rest of the men liked Vince and found him to be a quiet, steady sort who always remained calm in the midst of a crisis. Perhaps he'd learned that from his days of flying fighters over Germany during World War II.

Bob struck up a conversation with Vince and proposed a deal. "You fly the first F-80 mission," he said, "and I'll fly the first F-51 mission." Vince thought about that for a minute, then agreed.

The phone rang almost immediately after the bargain was struck. Grinning from ear to ear, Bob watched Vince's jaw tighten when he learned that the wing needed an F-51 pilot to make a run into South Korea.

"And I went on that mission," Wayne recalled later, "That ticked Vince off at first, but he was such a super guy, he just laughed it off."

The next day, June 26, Bob went with the group commander to the flight line, climbed into one of the refitted F-51s, and flew into Suwon. The flight proved uneventful, but it was the first mission of the war for the squadron. Later that afternoon, a Douglas C-47 transport picked up the fighter pilots at Suwon and returned them to Japan. Although Wayne and his comrades

National Archives

A North American F-82 Twin Mustang.

made it unscathed into Korea and back, the danger to them was real. Throughout the day the North Koreans had been running fighter sweeps and ground attack missions into South Korea. Slightly after 1:00 P.M. that day, a flight of North American F-82 Twin Mustangs were bounced over Inchon by a single NKAF fighter. It made a pass, then swept away, leaving the F-82 pilots behind. The incident is all but forgotten today, but it showed the Americans that the North Korean pilots might be willing to fight if the situation proved advantageous.

At the squadron ops shack the next day, Wayne teamed up with the rest of C Flight, Ralph ("Smiley") Hall, Captain Ray Schillereff, and Slick Dewald, for their first mission together. Schillereff was the second element leader that day, although he was the squadron's ops officer and technically outranked Wayne.

The 35th Fighter-Bomber Squadron had been scheduled to protect Kimpo Airfield that day, so Vince Cardarella planned to have at least one flight over Kimpo all day long. C Flight was the third flight from the squadron over Kimpo that morning. The four fighter pilots circled overhead and watched as the C-47 and C-54 transports flew in to pick up evacuees. The scene was one of chaos. Fortunately, no North Koreans attempted to interfere with the evacuation mission on C Flight's first watch.

The flight had just returned to base when the North Koreans attacked Kimpo. Coming in at 10,000 feet, five Yak-7s appeared over the airport, but before they could get to the transports on the ground, a flight of F-82s intercepted them. Three of the Yak-7s fell in flames before the others scattered for home. Lieutenant William ("Skeeter") Hudson scored the first kill of the day for the first American victory of the Korean War.

Clearly, the airspace over Korea was heating up. When Wayne took C Flight back to Kimpo later that afternoon for its second patrol, he and his men were ready for anything.

The patrol started out just as the first had begun. Wayne and Hall, his wingman, began a 40-mile-wide circuit pattern around Kimpo. Schillereff and his wingman Dewald detached from Wayne's element and patrolled separately. Wayne kept one element always heading north so that over Kimpo, the two-ship formations would pass each other as they flew in opposite directions. That way, he hoped to cover as much sky as possible with only four F-80s. Forty minutes into their patrol and with Schillereff's element nearly forty miles to the east, Hall called out a bogey (unidentified aircraft) to Wayne.

Wayne later remembered, "Man, I looked and looked, and I couldn't see anything. So I told Smiley, 'OK, you've got the lead. I'll get on your wing.'"

Hall's F-80 bounded ahead, pointed at the mysterious black dots northwest of Kimpo, as Wayne slipped over to the right and tucked in next to his wingman's fighter. But as quick as the dots appeared, Hall lost sight of them. Wayne scanned the sky for them. As his eyes passed over Hall's F-80, he spotted a formation of planes at nine o'clock and level with the F-80s at 5,000 feet.

"Smiley!" Wayne called out, "I've got seven of 'em at nine o'clock. Do you have them?"

Silence greeted Wayne's question as Hall twisted his head around and searched for the planes. Finally, he replied, "No. I don't see them."

"Get back on my wing," Wayne ordered, as he throttled up from his 250-mph cruising speed.

The planes Bob had seen were flying in a long echelon left formation, heading south toward Kimpo Airfield. He watched as the formation passed behind his left wing, as he and Smiley continued heading north. Soon, the dots were all behind them as they continued on their southern heading.

With their speed approaching the F-80's maximum, they were ready to engage. Wayne led Hall into a gentle 180-degree turn, which put them dead astern and a few miles out from the bogies. As they closed, Wayne formed a quick plan.

"Smiley, you get the last one. I'll get the next-to-last one. Then we'll make a 360 and get the rest."

Since the planes were in echelon left, Wayne figured that the pilots all would be looking to the left as they kept their eyes tacked onto their leader. The far right pair could be dropped in the first pass, and the rest of the formation might not even notice. Of course, he was assuming that they were hostile, something Bob wasn't too sure about at the moment. As they closed, his doubts grew. During the morning briefing, the pilots of the 35th Squadron

A Lockheed F-80 Shooting Star.

had been warned to watch out for a British Fleet Air Arm unit flying Fairey Fireflies and operating from a Royal Navy carrier off the Korean coast. As Bob and Hall closed on the formation ahead, they both thought the planes looked like Fireflies. The long nose and two-seat configuration made it impossible to discount the possibility that they might accidentally kill friendlies if they opened fire.

"Oh, shit! Smiley, these could be Fireflies," Wayne warned over the radio. "Drop back and I'll go up and make a pass at them and see what they are."

With Hall trailing behind, Bob drove on into the formation, searching for any distinctive markings that could tell him if they were friend or foe.

He got his answer soon enough. Before Bob could react, a stream of tracers speared the sky and tore past his silver F-80, which he had named Penny Sue after his wife. Far from being Fireflies, the planes ahead were North Korean— Ilyushin Il-10 Sturmovik ground-attack bombers.

"Smiley, go ahead and fire," Wayne yelled, as he broke hard left to avoid the incoming machine-gun rounds. But Hall didn't have time to line up on any of the bombers. Instead, he overshot the Il-10s, twisted his F-80 into a 360-degree turn, and ended up trailing Wayne again as his element leader lined up on the lead Il-10.

Wayne's initial plan had failed, so now he just wanted to pick off as many of the ugly olive green planes as he could. Working from left to right, he selected the lead Sturmovik, which was poking along at less than 200 mph. With his F-80 at full power, he closed the distance in a matter of seconds and the bomber swelled in his gunsight. At point-blank range, he pulled the trigger and gave the Sturmovik a sharp, quick burst. At that range, it was enough. The Il-10 erupted into flames. Before he could get his F-80 out of the way, the North Korean exploded right in front of him and showered the sky with bits of debris.

One down, six to go!

Breaking hard left again, Wayne swung around in another wide, arching 360-degree turn again. When he came around for another pass, he saw that the Sturmovik formation had started to disintegrate as the North Korean pilots desperately maneuvered to avoid the two F-80s.

Wayne selected another Il-10 and closed on it rapidly. Again, he held his fire until he could practically count the rivets on the fuselage and then unleashed a withering hail of 50-caliber slugs that tore apart the Sturmovik's engine. It belched out a long tongue of black smoke. The F-80 swept past the crippled plane as it began a staggering descent toward the countryside below.

His fighting blood thoroughly roused now, Wayne pushed his Shooting Star into another 360-degree turn. He hoped to mirror his successes on the first two passes, but when he lined up for his third run, the Il-10s had disappeared. Running for their lives, the remaining North Korean pilots had ducked into the broken cloud cover at 7,000 feet.

Wayne assessed the situation. Around him, the sky was clear except for Hall, who had stayed tacked on his wing through every pass and covered his leader as he'd been trained.

"Smiley," Wayne called, "You got any?"

"I have you, but that's it," came his reply.

"Well, OK. We've got to get home. We're just about out of fuel."

Together, the two F-80s flew back to Itazuke, their pilots happy in the knowledge that those Il-10s would not be hitting Kimpo that day.

Just as Wayne and Hall left the battle area, the other half of C Flight arrived on the scene to look for action. When Wayne and Hall had first made contact with the Il-10s, Schillereff and Dewald were almost forty miles away as they patrolled on the southbound leg of their racetrack circuit. When Schillereff heard the element call out bogey, he and Dewald abandoned their pattern and sped northward. Although low on fuel, they were hot on the heels of the running Il-10s.

Dewald spotted the Sturmoviks first. At 10,000 feet, he watched as a single Il-10 skittered down the Han River valley southwest of Seoul, the pilot obviously hoping that he could get away undetected if he stayed under the cloud cover. Unfortunately for the North Koreans, the plane passed through a break in the overcast. Dewald keyed his mike and called out the bogey. At first, he couldn't reach Schillereff because the frequency was crammed with chatter.

Finally, Ray's voice burst through the background noise, "If you see him, go get him. I'll follow you."

By now, the Il-10 was almost directly below the F-80s, and Dewald was in a perfect position to bounce it. He rolled his silver jet inverted and tucked the stick into his stomach. Gracefully, he split-essed right down on the tail of the unsuspecting North Korean. Pushing the F-80's nose down slightly, he lined up the Sturmovik in his sights. At that moment, the Il-10's rear gunner woke up and began firing at him. Dewald held his fire a moment longer, than cut loose with a long burst—50-caliber rounds poured out of the F-80's nose and stabbed into the Sturmovik's fuselage. They hit the rear gunner, and riddled the canopy.

Dewald held the trigger down just a bit longer, then broke off his run. He zoomed past his target before pulling up for another pass. He looped the F-80 up and over the Sturmovik and again landed on his target's tail. This time, there was no return fire. The rear gunner was either dead or too seriously wounded to fight back. The North Korean pilot, probably aware that his comrade was incapacitated, played for time. He stuffed the nose down and ran for the deck, hoping he could elude Dewald by hugging the treetops.

But Dewald was not about to let him get away. His second pass damaged the Il-10 further but did not cripple it. Breaking up and away, he came around again and landed dead astern of the fleeing bomber. For a third time, he triggered his guns.

This time, Dewald's aim was perfect. He watched as his fire disappeared into the Il-10's cowling, tore into the engine, and blasted through the plane's oil reservoir. Oil began streaming back behind the Sturmovik, and the F-80 was so close that its windscreen was splattered with the stuff. Hardly able to see through the gooey stuff, Dewald broke off the attack. He climbed for altitude as the Sturmovik tumbled into the valley below.

"Hey, Slick," called Schillereff, "What's your fuel situation?"

That jarred Dewald. He had ignored his fuel gauge throughout the fight. Looking at his instruments, he realized that he'd cut deeply into his safety margin. He feared he might not even make it back to Itazuke.

He reported the situation to Schillereff. Together, they decided the best course was to head straight back to Japan individually. Schillereff had lost visual contact with Dewald just as the fight began and was no longer in the area. Without forming up, each pilot turned southward and nursed his thirsty bird home. Both of them made it to Itazuke without further incident. After they landed, Schillereff told Dewald how he had corralled another wayward Il-10 and dropped him near the Han.

At the debriefing, the four C Flight pilots proudly exchanged stories. Morale was sky-high when they discovered that they had flamed four of the seven Sturmoviks. Even better, these were the first kills ever scored by American jet fighter pilots. They had made aviation history.

The revelry would be long remembered, even through the later hardships and heartbreak that were to follow this first day of combat for the 35th

Captured Korean Il-10s.

Squadron. In the weeks to come, both Bob and Slick would lose many friends over Korea. But that was all in the future. For now, the men of the 35th fought and refought the day's battle until finally, one by one, they headed off to catch some sleep. Surely, they would be engaged again in the morning.

Bob Wayne said farewell to his comrades and slipped home. In the fading light of dusk, his wife Penny Sue, six months pregnant, and his two young daughters greeted him. It seemed an almost surreal end to a long and tension-filled day, but there was no better feeling than the moment he swept them all into his tired arms. For the Wayne family, though, the war was just beginning.

Some months later, Slick Dewald located the wreck of his Sturmovik and pried off a small access panel from the fuselage. Happily, he carried away his trophy, knowing that, in some small way, it was a true piece of aviation history. Almost fifty years have passed, but he still treasures that small reminder of a war now all but forgotten by most Americans.

2 | The Birth of Combat SAR

During the first hectic weeks of the Korean War, FEAF faced many difficult questions as to how its understrength and under-equipped units could fight effectively over and behind the battlefield. Questions of force strength, replacement planes and pilots, and the air defense of America's other interests in the Western Pacific all had to be solved by FEAF's staff as quickly as possible. In time, they would resolve all of these problems, but during that first summer of the war FEAF fought on a shoestring, frequently making do with ad hoc solutions and leftover equipment from World War II.

While the generals and staff officers dealt with these issues up at FEAF HQ, the pilots and crews fighting over Korea faced another problem. Early in the war, they clearly recognized that the skies over Korea were dangerous indeed. The North Koreans had built a powerful modern army complete with armor and anti-aircraft units. Consequently, aircraft losses mounted steadily throughout July and August of 1950 as pilots and crews ran afoul of flak and small-arms fire. The pilots began to wonder how they could be rescued if they were shot down behind North Korean lines.

The matter grew increasingly serious as the opposition increased and rumors of North Korean atrocities began to seep back to the fighting squadrons. Stories of torture and mutilation swept through the UN ranks within just a few weeks of the North Korean invasion. Such stories disturbed the aviators, who soon realized that, in this war, capture might not be preferable to death.

By midsummer, Fifth Air Force HQ and FEAF began looking for some way to save the pilots and crews shot down behind North Korean lines. For months, the Air Force experimented with different ideas, none of which survived the test of combat. Then, a small group of dedicated, all but forgotten men demonstrated that the solution lay not in conventional aircraft but in the helicopter.

In June 1950, the Fifth Air Force included only one small helicopter detachment composed of nine Sikorsky H-5As. Assigned as part of the 3d Air Rescue Squadron, the H-5s languished at Ashiya Air Force Base in Japan throughout much of the summer, unable to operate over Korea due to their extremely short range. It seemed that nobody really knew what to do with them.

Meanwhile in Korea, a real need developed for a small aircraft capable of evacuating wounded soldiers from the front lines. In July, the 3d Air Rescue Squadron sent a small contingent of Stinson L-5 observation planes to Korea to assess their effectiveness in such a role. It took only a few days to show the glaring problems with using these light, Piper Cub–like machines. Unable to operate in mountainous terrain or among the myriad of rice paddies found in South Korea, the L-5 operations were hampered from the outset since they just could not always get to where they were needed.

When the L-5s failed to fulfill the 8th Army's needs, the 3d Air Rescue Squadron decided to send a detachment of H-5s to Taegu. Ready to demonstrate their value, the first helicopters to serve in Korea arrived at Taegu on July 22, 1950.

Able to operate in even the most rugged terrain, the H-5s soon proved that they were the answer to the evacuation problem. In their first month, with barely a half dozen helicopters operational at any given time, the detachment at Taegu rescued eighty-three wounded soldiers and delivered them to rear-area hospitals. So successful were the copters that demand for their services grew. By the end of August, fourteen new H-5s were on their way to the 3d Air Rescue Squadron from U.S. Air Force commands throughout the world. From an all-but forgotten stepchild, the helicopter detachment now became an important part of support operations for the troops in the field.

Designated officially as Detachment F on August 30, the helicopter unit spent that first summer of the war expanding and refining its operations. Methods for evacuating the wounded were contrived and improved, and light supply missions were undertaken.

After examining these operations, Fifth Air Force Headquarters concluded that helicopters might also be the solution to the air rescue dilemma. If a pilot went down behind North Korean lines, couldn't an H-5 be sent out to pick him up? The idea had merit, but the limited range of these early helicopters combined with their total lack of defensive armament called into question the practicality of such missions. Would sending out an H-5 just result in two more crewmen lost to the North Koreans when the helicopter succumbed to ground fire?

While these questions needed answers, Fifth Air Force had enough confidence in the idea to establish a Rescue Liaison Office in the hope that Detachment

F might be used to extract pilots and crews shot down behind enemy lines. Though the H-5s were fragile and terribly vulnerable to enemy fire, Detachment F's pilots were more than willing to give this new venture a try.

-◆◆◆-

First Lieutenant Paul van Boven stood before his immediate superior, Captain Ray Costello, and listened intently as Ray related the news that an F-51 Mustang from the 35th Fighter-Bomber Squadron had gone down in flames near Hanggan-dong, just north of the Pusan Perimeter. The pilot had bailed out, landing in a rice paddy. His comrades circling above him had called for help. The Navy planned to send in a landing team to recover him, but that would take time and the Mustang pilot was surrounded by North Korean troops. He might be killed or captured before they could work the few miles from the beach to the crash site.

When he finished describing the situation, Ray said to Paul, "If you want to, you can go up and take a look, but I don't want you to cross the lines. We're not required to do that."

Costello hesitated for a moment, then added, "Well, you can make up your own mind about that."

Throughout July and August, Paul had been flying with Detachment F evacuating wounded troops from the front lines. It had been hazardous work. Once, after landing next to a British unit to pull out a wounded Tommy, mortar shells began bracketing his helicopter. Coolly, he ignored the explosions around him and waited until the young wounded soldier was loaded safely on board before taking off.

It would take similar courage to pull off this latest rescue attempt, but Paul never considered leaving the downed man for the North Koreans to kill or capture. He'd been under fire before—in fact, he had been a prisoner of war during World War II—and knew that he could not abandon a fellow American to that sort of fate if he had the power to prevent it.

Grabbing his gear, he headed off to find John Fuentes, his medical technician. He was going in.

-◆◆◆-

Fifty miles north of Detachment F, Captain Robert E. ("Bob") Wayne of the 35th Fighter-Bomber Squadron peered out from a manure pile and knew he was in big trouble. Minutes before, he had been strafing a North Korean troop column near an abandoned airfield outside of Pohang in his F-51 Mustang when his right foot suddenly felt as if it were on fire.[1] He had looked down and discovered that, well, it was. Flames were shooting out of the right side of the engine cowling, licking back along the fuselage toward the cockpit. At his feet, flames had already eaten through the firewall and were spreading around his leg.

All things considered, ending up in North Korean territory was the last way that Bob wanted to spend this September 4th. A few hundred miles away at the Osaka Army Hospital, his wife Penny Sue was ready to give birth to their third child. Trapped behind enemy lines was no place for an expectant father.

But with his F-51 in flames, he knew he had to get out, even if it meant capture and imprisonment. He jettisoned the canopy and prepared to jump. As the canopy blew clear of the fuselage, Bob tried to escape. Just then, the slipstream sucked the fire right into the cockpit, wrapping him in a sheath of flames.

Recalling the fire, Bob said, "I had third-degree burns on both legs and arms. I was bleeding and my hands and legs were just a mess. My hair was gone. So were my eyebrows."

Despite his injuries, he somehow managed to escape when the plane was at 400 feet. He had just enough time to pull the ripcord to his parachute and swing once in the harness before mushing right into a rice paddy a few hundred yards from the North Korean troops he'd been shooting up only seconds before.

The man who had scored the first jet kills of the war was now a few hundred feet from brutal captivity, at best. North Korean troops, especially those who had been on the receiving end of a strafing, generally did not treat downed pilots very well. Now, these angry soldiers, who moments before had been but distant targets in his K-9 sight, were stalking him on their turf. Watching them fan out around him, Bob realized his situation was close to hopeless.

Overhead, the other pilots of C Flight knew that he would not last long unless they could keep the troops pinned down. One by one, they made aggressive passes right down on the deck, their machine guns pouring fire into the North Koreans. For the moment, it seemed to be working. The North Koreans went to ground and could not move forward without exposing themselves to the Mustangs lurking above. It became a queer sort of standoff.

Bob took advantage of the lull to find a good hiding place. He began moving through the paddy, his eyes searching for some choice spot of dead ground that could shield him from the increasing amount of small-arms fire directed at him. As he slopped toward an embankment, he looked up for an instant and stopped cold. In front of him stood an enormous bull. The beast eyed the downed American warily, looking quite irritated that this brash human had dared to land in his paddy. It snorted, clearly angry, and set itself to charge.

"Oh, man," Bob thought to himself, "I don't like bulls."

Slowly, he moved away from the animal, looking for some avenue of escape. A nearby drainage ditch seemed to offer him a way out. He slid into it and wormed down it using his elbows to pull himself along. He climbed out a safe distance from the bull and crawled into another paddy. A few yards from an earthen dike he had discovered, he burrowed into the manure that had been used to fertilize the rice. Here, buried in insect-ridden manure up to his chin, with the dyke to protect him from small-arms fire, he felt safe for the time being.

With a sigh, Bob oriented himself so that he faced south. He figured that any rescue attempt would come from that direction. He knew there was a helicopter outfit operating out of the Pusan Perimeter, about thirty or forty miles south of his current location. If a helicopter didn't come to get him, he decided to try to make it to the coast, five miles away, when night fell. For now, though, he was trapped. With North Korean troops nearby, he wasn't going anywhere on foot until after dark.

The day before, Bob and the 35th had been on a mission when word came that an Australian pilot had been shot down near their patrol area. Hurrying to the scene, they spotted the pilot just as he ducked into a building. An hour and ten minutes later, a helicopter showed up and tried to get him out. The Aussie never emerged from the building, which led the pilots circling overhead to believe that the structure held North Korean troops who had captured or killed him.

Now it was Bob's turn to await a whirlybird. He knew it would take about an hour to reach him, so he kept one eye on his watch and the other eye on the ground around him, in case the North Koreans made a move on him. Overhead, his comrades continued to look out for him, and made passes at any North Koreans who showed themselves.

Trying not to think about all the things crawling around in the manure with him, Bob settled down for the longest wait of his life.

The Sikorsky H-5 noisily clattered northward from Pusan, with Paul holding it steady at 1,000 feet. As he flew toward the fury of the front lines, he might have recalled the day more than six years ago when he had been shot down behind the lines while piloting a Boeing B-17 Flying Fortress over Germany.

April 18, 1944, was that unforgettable day. Seven hundred B-17s strong, the Eighth Air Force had sortied against Berlin, the Nazi capital. Flying with the 385th Bomb Group, Paul's B-17 had been hit by flak somewhere over Germany, knocking out an engine. Soon after, more flak damaged the controls. Paul fought to keep the Fortress in formation as the bombers turned one more time and reached the Initial Point that signaled the beginning of the bomb run. Again, the flak thrown up at them was nothing short of awe inspiring.

They flew through black anti-aircraft bursts, clouds so thick at times that Paul thought it would take a miracle for any of the bombers to survive.

Paul's B-17 rocked as another hit ripped into one of the three remaining engines and knocked it out. Moments later, the Luftwaffe struck. Seventy-five strong, Messerschmitt Bf-109s dove down on the B-17s in a wide phalanx. They came at Paul's squadron head-on, spraying out bursts in tight, disciplined fashion. Paul and his crew braced for the destruction sure to come. They did not have long to wait. Cannon rounds smashed into a third engine and blew great holes along the wings and fuselage. Machine-gun bullets buzzed through the fuselage. A 20-mm cannon round exploded through the windscreen and blew off the top of the copilot's head. Seconds later, the flight engineer fell out of the top turret, his arm badly injured by a machine-gun round.

With three engines gone, the copilot dead, and a crewman hurt, Paul knew that he could not possibly get the B-17 home. Fighting the controls, he tried to keep the bomber steady so his crew could get out. The dying bomber wouldn't respond. Instead, it fell off into a shallow, spiraling dive. He ordered everyone to bail out. With the order given, Paul himself jumped clear of the B-17 at about 25,000 feet. Later, he discovered that everyone except the copilot had made it out alive.

He free-fell for 10,000 feet before pulling his D-ring that deployed his parachute. As he slowly drifted down from 15,000 feet, he had a panoramic view of the desperate fighting going on above him. He could see the 109s darting in and out of the B-17 formations as flak bursts scarred the skies. Every few minutes, he watched more of his brethren die as another B-17 caught on fire and tumbled out of formation. He never forgot those eternally long minutes as a helpless observer to a raid that cost 19 B-17s destroyed and 204 damaged.

Paul finally came down in a freshly ploughed field after narrowly missing some high-tension wires. He shed his parachute and Mae West and began to dig a hole to hide his gear. Working feverishly, he looked around for a good place to go and spotted a distant figure waving to him.

"Hot dog, it's the underground!" he thought to himself, "I'm really lucky," but that thought died quickly when he realized that the French underground wouldn't be twenty miles from Berlin. Now he knew he was in trouble and started running away.

Later, Paul recalled, "So here I was, running across this freshly ploughed field. It was just like I was running in slow motion. Then, the guy waving to me sent his Doberman after me. The dog came zooming up to me and bit me on the butt. I sat down and the dog just growled at me. Finally, the guy got over to me and said, 'For you za var is over!'"

Paul remained a prisoner of war at Stalag Luft 3 for a year. He was finally liberated on April 30, 1945, by the lead elements of General George S. Patton's Third Army, but he was nearly killed during the rescue when a firefight erupted between his captors and an American Sherman tank. Paul had just finished taking a shower—his first in nearly a year—when the Sherman rumbled by his bathhouse. His German guards began firing at the tank, which prompted the Americans to return fire. As Paul watched from a window, a cannon shell from the Sherman flew right past him, blowing a hole in the wall behind him. The shot left him unhurt, but outraged. "I was ready to go home," he remembered, "and here I was about to get killed by my own troops!"

Fortunately, he survived the exchange of fire and was liberated later that day. It had been the worst year of his life, and the memories that he carried with him back to freedom—images of being packed into cattle cars with fifty other men, cross-country marching through a blizzard, nearly getting shot by the SS on several occasions, and the psychological abuse inflicted by some of the guards—never faded from his mind.

Now, six years later over another foreign land in another foreign war, Paul was going to do everything possible to prevent another American from suffering as he had suffered. He pressed on over the front lines, heading for the crash site just outside of Pohang, unaware that at that very moment, he was flying into history.

Bob Wayne glanced at his watch again. Based on yesterday's mission when a helicopter from Pusan had tried to rescue the downed Aussie pilot, he guessed it would take about an hour and ten minutes for one to show up and get him out. An hour had passed since he had hit the silk. He was starting to get nervous. Overhead, no fewer than thirteen UN planes wheeled about, strafing the North Koreans who had by now completely surrounded him. Although the sight of so many planes bent on his protection eased his immediate fears of death or capture, he still had a gnawing fear that nobody would come to pull him out.

Time passed so slowly now, even the seconds seemed an eternity. Bob's badly burned right leg began to hurt, and the pain was becoming increasingly intense. His arms were bleeding into the manure. He stank of burnt hair and flesh. That, combined with the smell of the paddy, make it hard to keep from gagging.

He checked his watch again. Ten minutes had gone by. No sign of any helicopters. Above him, the strafing rose in intensity, which probably meant that the North Koreans were making another effort to move toward him. That was a really bad sign, as he didn't even have a pistol with him. Though most pilots carried some sort of sidearm, Bob had left his under his seat in the F-51 since the weapon poked him whenever he tried to wear it. So, at the very moment he most needed a weapon, he had exactly nothing. Nothing that is, except the machine-gunning Mustangs overhead.

An hour and thirty minutes went by, and the planes covering him began heading for home, one by one. Soon, only three or four remained in the area. One plane, Bob could see, was that of his wingman, Stan White. According to squadron lore, Stan had the best eyesight in the entire wing, an asset that would soon save Bob's life.

Bob glanced at his watch again, keeping his head low. He was taking some small-arms fire now, but he had selected his hiding place well. He had cover, and being in the manure made him hard to spot. His heart sank as he looked at the watch dial and realized he'd been down almost two hours. A wave of depression struck him as he thought, "Oh shit, they're not going to come and get me."

And then, he heard the unforgettable clap-clap-clap of a helicopter in flight. Someone was coming for him after all.

Paul van Boven swung wide around the crash site, deciding to come in from the north instead of the south. He figured the North Koreans would not be expecting a helicopter from that direction. It added a few minutes to the trip, but it seemed the safest way to handle the situation.

Two hours after takeoff, he and John Fuentes had spotted a pillar of white smoke rising from a rice paddy. As they moved closer, they could see the wreck of Bob Wayne's smashed and broken F-51 under the cloud of smoke. All they needed was a signal from the pilot—assuming that he was able to give one. Both pilots scanned the paddies below, looking for signs of the lone American.

The whirlybird was coming at him from the north. Bob had not expected it to come from that direction. Nonetheless, he sprang from his hiding place, unzipped his flight suit, and tore off his white T-shirt. Frantically, he began waving it at the approaching H-5. Without a radio or even a flare gun, the shirt was Bob's best hope for salvation. Yet, it almost cost him his life.

Not a hundred yards away, a North Korean officer rose from cover and began running toward Bob Wayne. Bob never saw him coming. Overhead, though, both the helicopter crew and Stan White noticed him simultaneously and realized that he was about to be killed.

Stan dove at the lone figure splashing toward his friend. He closed the range quickly, watching as the North Korean drew a revolver and pointed it at Bob, who was standing less than fifty yards away.

Stan cut the North Korean right in half with a long, deadly accurate machine-gun burst.

It had been that close.

Paul and John had no trouble finding Bob once he broke cover and began waving the shirt at them. Putting the H-5 into a sharp descent, Paul headed for the dike that Bob had used for cover. The helicopter was now taking small-arms fire, and several rounds hit home, tearing up the copter's fragile aluminum skin but doing no serious damage.

Paul put the H-5 right down on the dike. Bob sprinted toward the helicopter and reached it as more North Korean rifle and machine-gun bullets struck home.

As John Fuentes pulled Bob aboard, the fighter pilot cried out, "Take me to Itazuke!"

Within seconds, the helicopter bounded off the dike and into the air, this time heading south for Taegu and the new airstrip there. Behind Paul in the cargo area, Bob looked down at the wreck of his F-51. For the first time that afternoon, he began to relax. Perhaps he'd see his wife and newborn baby after all.

Within the hour, the H-5 touched down at K-2 airbase at Taegu. Still in pain from his wounds, Bob stumbled out of the machine ecstatic over his rescue. Standing near the helicopter, he regaled his two new friends with the story of how he ended up in the rice paddy. With sweeping hand gestures, he detailed how the fire and smoke got sucked into the cockpit after he had blown the canopy.

Colonel Edwin Lowe had been sent to the Far East by President Harry Truman some weeks earlier to keep an eye on General Douglas MacArthur and the operations in Korea. On September 4, he had been in a North American T-6 Mosquito, a forward air control plane. When Bob went down, the T-6 had come to the rescue and called in the other planes that had swarmed over Bob's head.

Lowe was so impressed with the rescue that he made sure that Paul received the Silver Star. That day on the tarmac at Taegu, the general confided in Paul that he had never before seen such a well-executed rescue. Perhaps Lowe's elation stemmed from the fact that he had just witnessed history in the making. Paul van Boven and John Fuentes had pulled off the first combat rescue mission with a helicopter. In later years, especially in Vietnam, such operations became commonplace. Hundreds of Americans avoided death or captivity when low-flying copters came to their rescue—missions that duplicated an event more than a decade earlier in a reeking South Korean rice paddy.

Bob spent the next few hours in a tent at K-2 banging down shots of bourbon with his wingman Stan White. Bob said, "Someone came and got me and said, 'Hey, there's a C-46 going back to Itazuke.' I said, 'Great, I'm still covered with shit!'"

That evening, Bob caught a ride on the Curtiss C-46 Commando, which turned out to be a mail transport. His wounds still hurt, but the bourbon helped take the edge off the pain. He crawled back among the mail bags and fell asleep, his slumber no doubt influenced by his bourbon intake. As he later put it, "I was probably half-bashed if you want to know the truth."

When he woke up a short time later, he went forward to ask the pilots how close to Itazuke they were. He nearly caused them to jump out of their skins. They had no idea that they had picked up a passenger, and here was one covered with burns, blood, and cow manure.

The weather was terrible over Itazuke. The pilots discussed the situation and decided they weren't going to be able to get through the overcast. Bob, however, talked them into trying at least once. He had been flying out of Itazuke for more than a year and knew just how to make an instrument approach to the field. Standing behind the two pilots, he talked them down into the runway without incident.

Bob spent the night at Itazuke and finally received treatment for his wounds. He remembered, "That night they took me down to the hospital and filled my butt full of penicillin and wrapped me all up."

Eager to see his wife, he caught a C-45 flight to Osaka the next morning. Unannounced, he appeared in the doorway of Penny Sue's hospital room. Looking up from her bed, she was startled at the sudden arrival of this walking mummy. Covered with bandages and burn salve, his hair missing in places, and his eyebrows nothing but a fond memory, Bob was hard to recognize. Worse, his burns had been oozing through the bandages, which caused him to have a particularly noxious smell.

She lost her composure for just a split second before it dawned on her that the mummy was, in fact, her husband. Then, the stoicism common to all great Air Force wives set in and her face went blank. Casually, without a hint of worry in her voice, she asked, "So, what happened to you?"

Bob shambled into the room, glancing down at his wife who held their new-born son in her arms. Smiling as he reached out for his boy, he replied with forced nonchalance, "Well, Hon, I had a little trouble refilling my Zippo."

3 | Fighting 53 Goes to War

When the Korean War began on June 25, 1950, the U.S. Navy possessed only one aircraft carrier task force in the Western Pacific that could respond immediately to the communist threat. Task Force 77, centered around the Essex-class carrier, USS *Valley Forge*, had been showing the flag in Hong Kong on June 25 when it received news of the North Korean attack.

Stunned by the initial North Korean onslaught, the U.S. Navy approached the new crisis with caution. Some members of the Pacific Fleet thought that this invasion might be the first step in a larger communist plan that could include recapturing Taiwan or moving into Southeast Asia. To defend against such a massive operation, the Navy stationed Task Force 77 at Buckner Bay, Okinawa. There, the ships would be out of range of Chinese or Russian bombers but close enough to Taiwan to counter any moves across the Strait of Formosa. The carrier force spent the last week of June sitting at anchor in Buckner Bay, waiting for the outbreak of what would have been World War III. All the while, the men on the *Valley Forge* steeled themselves for the conflict ahead, for at the very least they knew that combat awaited them up north in the Yellow Sea.

At the beginning of July, it became clear that the Chinese were not going to move against Taiwan anytime soon. That released the *Valley Forge* for duty off Korea. She was sorely needed. Everywhere on that miserable peninsula, the North Korean People's Army (NKPA) had thrown the South Koreans into retreat and disarray. The Fifth Air Force was doing everything it could to stem the Red tide, but it was fighting a war for which it was undertrained, understaffed, and equipped with the wrong types of aircraft. Any help, especially from a carrier off the coast, would be of immense value to the fighting men at the front.

National Archives

F-4U Corsairs aboard the USS *Bon Homme Richard*.

July 2, 1950 found Task Force 77 in the Yellow Sea, preparing for combat operations. That evening, the pilots and crews of the *Valley Forge*'s Carrier Air Group 5 (CAG-5) congregated in their ready rooms to receive their first briefings of the Korean War. For them to be effective over the front lines, they first had to destroy the North Korean air force. To do this, the *Valley Forge* planned a series of hammer blows against the airfields around Pyongyang, the communist capital. Once CAG-5 had eliminated the aerial opposition, the squadrons could be committed to the growing land battle to the south.

The first raid would hit Pyongyang airfields with a maximum effort on the part of all of CAG-5's squadrons. The air group's two jet fighter squadrons, VF-51 and VF-52, would go in first to sweep the skies of any NKAF aircraft. Just behind the jets would come the first blow—sixteen Chance Vought F4U-4B Corsair fighters and 12 Douglas AD-1 Skyraider attack bombers from VF-53 and VF-54. Laden with bombs and rockets, they would pound the airfields around Pyongyang and destroy hangars, fuel dumps, maintenance shops, and any aircraft unlucky enough to be caught on the ground.

In Fighting 53's ready room, Lieutenant (j.g.) Charles Darrow listened intently to the mission briefing. He'd been through all this before, having flown with Fighting Four off the USS *Essex* and Fighting Nine off the USS

Yorktown during World War II. To him, the scene was eerily familiar. He felt as if he were back in that last war and preparing for another war cruise.

Around him were a good bunch of pilots. Formed in August 1948, VF-53 included a number of combat veterans. Darrow had flown his first combat mission during the famous carrier raids on Tokyo in February 1945. He spent the rest of that spring fighting off kamikaze raids around Okinawa and scored one kill in the process. Lieutenant Carl E. ("Gene") Smith was an ace from the last war who had scored seven kills with VF-14. Lieutenants (j.g.) John Ford and Dick Downs also had World War II experience. And, their leader, Lieutenant Commander Bill Pittman, had fought at the Battle of Midway as a dive bomber pilot.

In addition to combat experience, many of VF-53's fourteen pilots had been with the squadron for almost two years, so the men knew each other quite well. Although training had been scarce in recent months—due to budget cuts they had been flying fewer than ten hours a month, barely enough to keep carrier qualified—the men of Fighting 53 were as ready as could be expected for the battle to come in the morning.

The Grumman F9F-2 Panthers tore across the North Korean countryside toward Pyongyang. Loping along behind the eight straight-wing jets were the sixteen Corsairs of VF-53 and VF-54, plus a dozen Skyraiders from VA-55. The war for the U.S. Navy had just begun on this cloudy morning of July 3, 1950.

Once over land, it did not take long for the Navy pilots to find trouble. As the Panthers closed in on the airfield, the pilots could see many Yak fighters scrambling off the runway. It was a confused scene. Some of the North Koreans took off from the same runway in opposite directions and narrowly avoided colliding.

Heading down the runway, VF-51 pilot Lieutenant (j.g.) Leonard Plog picked out a Yak just as it clawed its way off the ground. Before he could fire at it, another Yak made a pass at him from the port side. The North Korean missed, and one of Plog's comrades blew the Yak's tail off with a well-aimed burst of 20-mm cannon fire. Free from attack, Plog swung behind his original target and sent it crashing to the ground. These were the U.S. Navy's first kills of the Korean War.

Down on the deck, the rest of VF-51's Panthers thundered over the airfield strafing anything of value in their paths. When they pulled up from their runs, three more North Korean aircraft lay smashed and burning on the field—destroyed before they had a chance to fight.

Moments later, the strike aircraft arrived after flying through a storm front just off the coast. The ADs and F4Us rolled into their attack dives and selected their targets. Bombs fell and rockets flew as four hangars and several other buildings exploded in flames. The attack also left a nearby rail yard burning as they pulled off the target.

No American planes were lost during the attack.

Just as the raiders finished their strafing and bombing runs, Charles Darrow showed up over the target as escort for the Marine-piloted photo aircraft, an F4U-5P Corsair that CAG-5 used for reconnaissance and damage assessment. During World War II, Darrow had seen many photo planes get bounced by the Japanese just as the strike groups pulled off target. Remembering that, he had warned his Marine section leader to be extra watchful near Pyongyang. The last thing Darrow wanted to be was the war's first U.S. Navy casualty.

Smoke and flames rose from the airfield below as the two Corsairs arrived in the area and began their photo run. Keeping his head on a swivel, Darrow checked out the sky above and behind him.

Suddenly, from behind and off to his left, a tiny shape streaked into view. It swelled rapidly, taking shape as a North Korean Yak-9. It closed on Darrow from seven o'clock and executed a precise pursuit curve on the American F4Us.

Darrow called out to his Marine section leader but received no response. He tried again, calling out a warning. Still no response. Darrow glanced over to his right and saw the Marine looking down in his cockpit, ignoring the scene around him. He was a sitting target.

And so was Darrow. He glanced behind him again and there was the Yak, so close that "I could see the whites of his eyes," he recalled years later.

From dead astern, the Yak had a perfect firing position and was close enough to tear up Darrow's Corsair. For some reason, however, the North Korean did not fire. Perhaps his guns had jammed or he had already used his ammo on another target. Either way, the Yak's inaction gave Darrow just enough time to roll over and break hard left. He finished a 90-degree turn, then rolled the opposite way and broke hard right, coming right back at his Marine wingman. Darrow figured he and the Marine could start a Thach Weave—a World War II maneuver in which each pilot turned into his wingman, clearing each other's tails as they passed by. He watched the Marine, waiting for him to break hard and scrape the Yak off his tail with a head-on pass.

The Marine remained oblivious to the situation. As Darrow passed by him, he could see the man still looking down in the cockpit, totally focused on his photo run, and he hadn't even altered course or altitude. Now the Yak was behind him.

Fortunately, the North Korean must have seen Darrow's Corsair coming straight at him from off his port beam and decided discretion was the better part of valor. He eased off to the right and began climbing away. A thousand feet above them, the Yak leveled off and took station behind and just to the right of the Marine's Corsair.

Darrow swung alongside the Marine and tried everything he could think of to alert him to the danger lurking above. When nothing worked, Darrow finally eased over and used his wing to disrupt the airflow over the other Corsair's wing. That got the Marine's attention. He looked up and saw Darrow, just a few feet away, frantically waving and pointing back at the Yak, but he did not seem to understand. Perhaps his radio had failed, and he never realized the danger.

The North Korean never came down, though. He sat up above the two Corsairs in a perfect bounce position and trailed the Americans as they finished up their business and headed back to their carrier. As they came off target, the Yak finally turned away and headed home.

It had been a close call, but both Americans survived their initiation into the Korean War.

Later that day, Fighting 53 lost its first Corsair. While on a combat air patrol (CAP) mission over the task force, Ensign Bill Brown's F4U caught fire. He ditched the burning plane in the Yellow Sea after radioing his predicament. A destroyer fished him out and had him back on board "Happy Valley," as the crew called the *Valley Forge*, later that afternoon. It was the first of many mishaps that the squadron would experience during the coming weeks.

The next day, July 4, reality was driven home to everyone on board the carrier. The strikes laid on for that day all focused on the industrial areas of Pyongyang. Six Corsairs from VF-53 went along on the strike, led by Midway-veteran Bill Pittman—his first combat mission of the Korean War. Two hours after the Pyongyang strike had cleared Happy Valley's deck, VF-53 launched its first CAP mission of the day. Darrow, in Corsair number 304, joined up with the rest of the CAP that morning and spent the next four hours circling over the *Valley Forge* and her escorts.

An hour after the CAP was launched, Pittman's strike group returned. As the planes trapped aboard, one of VA-55's Skyraiders, damaged by flak during the raid, crash-landed aboard the *Valley Forge*, floated over the barrier, and careened into three of Fighting 53's Corsairs parked forward on the flight deck. All three F4Us were write-offs, which left Pittman's men with only eight Corsairs at the end of two days of operations.

If that wasn't bad enough, Darrow and the rest of the day's first CAP came down to land around noon. One by one, the pilots trapped aboard. For Darrow, however, this was no ordinary carrier landing (if carrier landings are ever ordinary). As he made his approach, his Corsair suffered hydraulic failure and one landing gear leg would not come down. He aborted the landing and triggered the carbon dioxide bottle that was supposed to blow down the gear in such an emergency. It didn't work; the gear remained stuck. He circled for a few more minutes and allowed his wingman, Keith Thomson, to land ahead of him. When Thomson was safely trapped aboard, Darrow swung around and made his approach.

"I decided to handle it like any other landing," he said later, "I just acted like both wheels were down."

He painted the Corsair right onto the deck, snagged a landing wire with his tailhook, and came to a sudden halt. When the plane lost forward momentum, it tipped over and the right wing crunched down as the prop made contact with the deck. Darrow emerged unhurt, but the Corsair would need new wing panels, a new prop, and an engine replacement before it could be used operationally again.

Although it was now down to seven out of twelve Corsairs, the squadron had scored well in celebration of the Fourth of July. Pittman's raid had destroyed a factory, chewed to pieces four locomotives, and scored hits on another industrial site.

That evening, *Valley Forge* and the rest of TF-77 pulled off station and returned to Okinawa for a short refueling and rest period. From July 6 through July 17, the men of CAG-5 remained away from the combat raging along the Korean peninsula. During the lull, the squadron's aircraft shortage was rectified so that the unit could return to Korea with its full complement of twelve Corsairs.

On July 18, Task Force 77 returned to combat. It proved to be an extremely busy day for VF-53, which flew no fewer than twenty-four sorties. Its first mission was to cover the landings at Pohang, a small port city just up the east coast from Pusan. Pohang was the site chosen for the U.S. 1st Cavalry Division to come ashore after a short transit from Japan. Fearful that the North Koreans would try to interfere, *Valley Forge* put up a series of target CAPs (TARCAPs) throughout the morning.

Later that afternoon, the pilots assembled in the ready room for the first strike briefing of the day. Most of the pilots, including Lieutenant Commander Pittman, Ensign Herb Riebeling, Thomson, Bill Brown, Darrow, and Ford, all had flown at least one TARCAP during the morning over Pohang. Although these missions passed without incident, the men were tired after spending several hours in the air.

Despite their fatigue, the afternoon briefing certainly caught their attention. About 150 miles up the coast from Pohang lay the strategic North Korean port city of Wonsan. Not only was Wonsan a major transportation hub for the northeastern section of communist-controlled Korea, it was also the site of the most important oil target of the war. Built in 1935 by the Japanese at a cost of some fifty million yen, the Wonsan Oil Refinery Factory by 1950 had become a joint stock company held by the North Koreans and the Soviets.[1] Intelligence reports estimated that the facility could produce five hundred tons of refined petroleum a day, more than any other facility in Korea. *Valley Forge's* air group would soon get a crack at this lucrative target.

At 5:00 P.M. on July 18, all twelve Corsairs of VF-53 lifted off from the carrier. Shortly afterward, VF-53 launched. Lieutenant Commander N. D. Hodson led his squadron, VA-55, into the air with eleven Skyraiders, each armed with a pair of 5-inch HVAR rockets, one 500-pound bomb, and one 1,000-pound bomb.

Pittman led the Corsairs into the target area first, with the Skyraiders trailing behind a short distance. Once they were over Wonsan, the oil refinery was not hard to find. Pittman reported later that it "stood out like a sore thumb. It was a tremendous installation, and we all recognized it immediately."

His first division, which included Charles Darrow as the second section leader, went into a shallow, gliding descent toward the refinery. Some pilots in the squadron thought the approach should have been made at a steeper angle to give the anti-aircraft guns more difficult shots. It was a moot point, however, as flak over the target was negligible. Virtually unmolested, the first division opened fire at 4,000 feet. Thirty-two HVAR rockets — more firepower than six World War II destroyer broadsides — sped toward the refinery as Pittman's men pulled up and away. Seconds later, the other two divisions opened fire and spewed out sixty-four more rockets.

Below them, the refinery exploded in flames as the HVARs slammed home. The rockets touched off secondary explosions in the stored stocks of gasoline and oil throughout the production site. Soon, huge clouds of black smoke roiled over the target.

The Skyraiders came in next with their bombs and rockets right on target and caused more damage. The entire air group then returned home late that afternoon, with all planes trapping aboard Happy Valley by 7:45 P.M. For the next four days, the refinery continued to burn and the CAG-5 pilots used the towering columns of smoke as a navigational aid.

Although the men of the *Valley Forge* knew they had hit the refinery hard, the flames and smoke had masked the severity of the destruction below. Not until October 1950, when UN ground forces secured Wonsan, did they learn just how successful the mission had been. Following close behind the fighting men was an inspection and assessment team that combed through the rubble of the Wonsan Oil Refinery Factory to examine the damage caused by the July 18 strike. The team also interviewed the firm's president, Cho Byung Kwi; his chief accountant; and four on-site engineers. All six men explained to the UN team that the refinery had been attacked five times before the *Valley Forge* strike on the 18th. No damage had been done on any of the prior raids—in fact, only three bombs had even landed within the facility's compound—but the attack by VF-53 and VA-55 had utterly destroyed the factory and the storage tanks. Fires caused by the raid burned the entire site to the ground and left the largest oil refinery in Korea nothing but a twisted mass of girders, broken concrete, and charred wreckage.[2]

The raid had destroyed twelve thousand tons of refined oil and gas. When some of the storage tanks were torn open by HVAR rocket hits, the streets throughout the plant were inundated with oil. In some places, two feet of oil flooded the streets. Other critical facilities, including the site's power plant, were completely demolished by the raid.[3]

The factory never recovered from the strike. Years later, many historians agreed that the Wonsan Oil Refinery raid on July 18 was one of the most successful air strikes of the Korean War.

There was no respite for the men of VF-53. The day after the Wonsan raid, the squadron flew a full strike against the city of Hungnam's industrial areas and caused much damage. Later in the afternoon, a division led by Lt. Carl ("Gene") Smith hit Wonsan again, this time focusing on the harbor area. While patrolling Wonsan looking for good targets, the four Corsair pilots discovered a gunboat tucked against one of the little islands in the harbor. The North Koreans had tried to camouflage the gunboat by covering it with netting and such, but it was still visible from the air.

Smith led the Corsairs on a strafing run toward the target. One at a time, they saturated the gunboat with 20-mm cannon fire. When the last Corsair, flown by Riebeling, pulled off the target, the gunboat seemed to be settling to the harbor bottom.

July 19 proved to be a solid day for the squadron. In addition to the gunboat and the damage inflicted to Hungnam, VF-53 destroyed no fewer than fourteen locomotives during their missions to Wonsan and Hungnam.

After a two-day break in operations, VF-53 returned to action on July 22. It flew fifteen sorties around Inchon as Task Force 77 renewed operations in the Yellow Sea.

As CAG-5 and VF-53 continued to scour the rear areas in search of enemy targets, the American troops on the ground made contact with the NKPA. Early in July, Task Force Smith, a combat group detached from the 24th Infantry Division, had encountered a North Korean armored attack at Onsan. The fierce professional assaults launched by the North Koreans completely surprised the Americans, and, within hours, Task Force Smith practically ceased to exist. Its survivors streamed south toward Taejon.

At Taejon, the 24th Infantry Division attempted another stand, but again combined tank and infantry attacks worked around the American flanks and struck the GIs from all sides. Defeated again, the disorganized American battalions tried to flee Taejon. Most of them made it, but many men were cut off and captured by the North Koreans, including eventual Medal of Honor winner Major General William F. Dean, the 24th's commanding officer.

As defeat followed defeat on the ground, a serious crisis developed. After Taejon fell, some planners wondered if the U.S. Eighth Army could even maintain a foothold on the peninsula. Clearly, to hang on until reinforcements arrived would require every bit of effort from all available ground and air units.

Accordingly, on July 23, Headquarters Eighth Army sent out a desperate plea to the Navy for help. In part, the message read, "Request information as to possible naval air employment in close and general support role in Korea . . . urgent requirement exists west coast Korea commencing 23 July. . . ."[4]

Before this message, marked with an "Emergency" prefix, arrived at Headquarters Seventh Fleet, the *Valley Forge*'s pilots had spent most of the month in shooting up targets, including airfields, gunboats, factories, and bridges, well behind the lines. But now, the nature of the war was to change for them. After July 23, close air support became their priority for the next two months.

The *Valley Forge* moved to a position off the east coast of Korea during the night of July 24 in order to strike the North Koreans on the morning of the 25th. At 8:00 A.M., Happy Valley launched its first close air support mission of the war.

Desperate times require desperate measures, and these early missions suffered severely as a result. Most of the trouble was caused by poor communication with the ground troops. Too few trained forward air control (FAC) parties had been allocated to the Eighth Army. The Navy had a well-trained FAC squadron, but it was heavily involved in plans for the Inchon invasion and could not be released for duty in Korea at that time. Consequently, the Corsair and Skyraider pilots had a tough time finding and putting their ordnance on the most important targets.

That first day quickly overwhelmed the Eighth Army's limited liaison capabilities. There were only two FAC parties in Korea—one assigned to the 24th Infantry Division and the other assigned to an ROK unit. Additionally, one Stinson L-5 observation plane was released for duty as a FAC aircraft.

These three FAC assets were incapable of handling the load required to get the bombs and rockets from each aircraft onto critical targets. Too few radio channels were assigned to the air controllers, and Navy and Air Force pilots soon overloaded every frequency with chatter. Worse, even when good communication existed, pilots often could not find the targets assigned to them. Korean names were difficult for the Americans to pronounce and many towns had similar names, so it was easy to get confused when communicating over jammed frequencies. Also, accurate maps were in short supply, which made coordination with ground units that much more difficult.

In the early afternoon of July 25, Vice Admiral Arthur D. Struble, Seventh Fleet commander, sent a dispatch to Tokyo in which he described the effects of the morning close air support missions:

> The results of the morning sweeps and strikes were very minor due to a dearth of targets. No rolling stock seen, only a few donkey carts plus men in rice paddies. On the whole, the area is one of peaceful agriculture. Seven trucks strafed did not burn. Four trucks strafed and burned. Will continue afternoon strikes, but under above conditions, the prospects appear poor. Consider it mandatory that proper communications be arranged. . . .[5]

The afternoon strike turned into a disaster for Fighting 53. Launched at 11:00 A.M., ten of the squadron's F4U-4Bs swept westward to look for good targets. Somewhere over a countryside of rice paddies and tiny villages, the squadron stumbled across a column of tanks and troops. Keith Thomson, who was Ensign Ed Laney's wingman that day, spotted the column as it marched northward. Since they were heading north, the Americans were unsure if they were friend or foe.

Passing over the column, Keith radioed his section leader, "I'll go down and check them out."

Thomson's Corsair rolled in on the mass of troops below. He buzzed over them, trying to get a good look, then started to pull back up.

"Don't shoot! They're friendly!" Keith called to his friend Ed Laney.

Seconds after that transmission, Thomson's plane shuddered as small-arms fire struck home. The "friendly" troops below were actually North Koreans. Marching northward to fool American pilots turned out to be a favorite North Korean trick.

"I'm losing oil," Thomson told his squadron mates. The ground fire apparently damaged the Corsair's oil system, and the engine rapidly began to overheat.[6]

He tried to make it to the coast, turning his Corsair eastward in hopes of going down offshore rather than in the middle of enemy-held territory. He didn't make it.

It took only a few seconds for the engine to seize up. Desperate now, Thomson looked for a place to land. His prospects were not good. He hadn't even cleared the troop column below. Then, he discovered a dry riverbed not too far away and pointed his dying Corsair's nose toward it.

Darrow was flying nearby with Pittman's division. He saw Thomson deftly mushing his Corsair right into the sandy river bottom. The plane kicked up a huge fan of dust before sliding to a stop.

Darrow heard Thomson call out, "How'd you like that landing?" Darrow remarked later that it had been a truly amazing display of skill from one of the squadron's consummate aviators.

Down unhurt, Thomson now could await rescue. But his situation did not look promising. He had landed close to the road on which the column was traveling, and now the North Koreans were fanning out to get him.

Overhead, Ed Laney watched as his downed wingman unstrapped himself and stood up in the cockpit. Seconds later, he doubled over. Ed thought he had been shot. A few minutes later, Darrow spotted Thomson standing next to his Corsair. If he had been wounded, he was still mobile.

The squadron stayed over Keith as long as it could. The pilots strafed the North Koreans repeatedly until Pittman led most of the squadron back to the *Valley Forge* when their fuel and ammunition ran low. They trapped aboard at 2:30 P.M., about sixty minutes after Thomson's crash.

Laney, Downs, and Ensign Arthur ("Art") Hanton stayed over their stricken buddy. Conserving fuel as much as possible, the three men protected Keith as best they could while waiting for word that a helicopter was on its way to rescue him. The *Valley Forge* had received the news of Thomson's crash at 1:42 P.M. and had flashed a message to Taegu in hopes the helicopter outfit there could get him out. By 3:30 P.M., however, no helicopter had reached the area. Reluctantly, the three Corsair pilots returned to *Valley Forge* on the dregs of their fuel supply.

Concern for Thomson grew as the afternoon sun began to sink in the western sky. At 5:00 P.M., Hanton took a Corsair to Taegu and personally investigated the situation. He came back on board three hours later and reported that a helicopter had been dispatched to pick up Thomson. The news heartened everyone, but, an hour before midnight, Taegu reported that the helicopter had gone down near Ponsong. Thomson would have to spend the night in the Korean countryside.

It had been a hard and frustrating day. The troops on the ground looked so much alike that it was almost impossible for the pilots to tell friend from foe. Communications had been a nightmare, and good targets were few and far between. In the end, the squadron claimed six trucks destroyed, ten trucks damaged, a train damaged by strafing, and a rail bridge damaged—not much to balance against the life of a buddy.

The next morning, a search flight left the *Valley Forge* and returned to the crash site. They found Keith's Corsair, but somebody—probably the North Koreans—had tried to camouflage it with sticks and branches. After circling the area and seeing no sign of life, the search flight strafed and burned the downed F4U and flew back to the *Valley Forge*.

Almost fifty years passed before some members of the squadron learned of Thomson's fate. Apparently, he had been captured that night and marched north into the hell of a North Korean prisoner of war (POW) camp. At some point, Thomson was tortured repeatedly in an attempt to force him to sign a communist-inspired document declaring that the United States was an illegal aggressor in Korea. Although the Russians later claimed he signed it, some members of the squadron still refuse to believe that he gave in to his tormentors. In January 1951, Thomson died in the POW camp.

—◆◆◆—

Through the final days of July, VF-53 participated in an increasing number of close air support missions. Following the directions of a FAC team (when one was available), the Corsair pilots patrolled an area until their ordnance was needed. If a target developed, the FAC team marked it with smoke fired from mortars. The Corsairs then made low, shallow passes and delivered their bombs or napalm right onto the smoke. It could be hazardous duty, as seemingly every NK soldier with a weapon shot back at them. The pilots ran the additional risk of missing their targets and killing friendly troops. This danger inspired much caution in the pilots.

Charles Darrow flew one particularly thorny close air support mission while supporting a Marine unit following the Inchon landings. He and his division had arrived on station and were waiting for a FAC team to give them a target. Somewhere below in the rugged terrain, one of the controllers called in a target and requested that Darrow and his men make their runs perpendicular to the Marine unit's front lines. Worse, the FAC team wanted the Corsairs to make their run from the North Korean side, which meant that any bombs or napalm canisters that fell long of the target would hit the Marines with high explosives and flaming jellied gasoline.

Darrow flatly refused. He would not run the risk of incinerating Americans. An argument with the FAC team followed, but Darrow had his way. He and his men made their runs parallel to the lines and totally destroyed their target. Ensign Al Frainier made the best run and dropped his load smack onto the spot requested by the FAC team. After his run the FAC team cried out, "Great job!"

Such were the problems encountered during these early close air support missions.

—◆◆◆—

On July 31, Task Force 77 steamed into Buckner Bay for a quick replenishment of its depleted ammunition and fuel stocks. While there, VF-53 received its first replacement pilots of the war. Since the squadron had been below authorized strength when it began the war, these new pilots were a welcome addition to the outfit and would help ease the mission load on them all.

Ensign Nate Curry was one of the new replacements. He had been flying with VF-113 out of San Diego, California, just a few weeks before. He didn't like the outfit, however, and volunteered for service with CAG-5, with whom he had served earlier in his career. When he came on board the *Valley Forge*, he later recalled, "It was just like coming home."

Nate Curry hailed from Lexington, Missouri, the youngest of nine children. Although his father had never been in combat—he had been a teacher and a farmer—his family had a rich history of military service. Nate's grandfather had served with General George A. Custer during the Civil War, and several other relatives had served in the Philippine Insurrection and with Theodore Roosevelt's legendary "Great White Fleet."

When the Japanese attacked Pearl Harbor on December 7, 1941, Nate's brother William died in action on board the battleship USS *Arizona*. Weeks later, his family suffered another tragedy when Wake Island surrendered to the Japanese. His brother Robert, who had joined the Marine Corps during the height of the Great Depression, was stationed at Wake. The family received no word from Robert until the end of the war, when he returned from four years of absolute misery as a POW of the Japanese. Nate would recall his brother's ordeal on a bitter autumn day in 1950 when he nearly was captured by the North Koreans.

Straight out of high school, Nate had joined the Navy's V-5 aviation cadet program in June 1943. World War II ended before he could see combat, however, but he liked the Navy and decided to stay in. Five years after the end of World War II, he was a regular officer with much experience and flight time under his belt.

On his third VF-53 mission, Nate looked over at his wingman, Captain Jesse Booker, and knew the Marine was in trouble. Talk about trial by fire, he thought. Both of his other missions had been uneventful CAPs over the *Valley Forge*—before landing in this mess.

Booker, who was called "Davy," was a tough-as-nails Marine who had flown Corsairs with VMF-218 during World War II. In 1946, he spent a tour with VMO-3 in China. When the Korean War began, he was the first Marine pilot to fly a combat mission. By August, he had flown twenty-five missions and destroyed seven trains with rockets while performing his photo reconnaissance duties.

All day long on August 7, CAG-5s had struck hard at the North Koreans as the Pusan Perimeter battles reached their bloody climax. The Corsairs, Skyraiders, and Panthers hit bridges, flak targets, troops, and tanks all around Seoul in an attempt to deny reinforcements and supplies to the North Korean units attacking the perimeter. At 3:30 P.M., Nate had launched from the *Valley Forge* as escort for Jesse, commander of the small

Marine photo reconnaissance detachment aboard ship. On this day, Nate and Davy had headed into Central Korea to locate and photograph a bridge that the squadron had tried to destroy on three different occasions. Jesse later related the mission in an interview with *The Hook* magazine:

> I went in for a photo run to try to determine where the stress members of the bridge were located. Talk about doing dumb things, I made three passes—*under the bridge*—lifting the wing each time to let the oblique cameras shoot the supporting members. The trouble was, on the third pass they were waiting for me.
>
> I was hit with something big which tore off half of my right wing and the oil cooler system. I couldn't climb but managed to keep it flying down the river bed for about a minute-and-a-half until the engine froze and I had to put it in.[7]

Overhead, Nate watched Davy's Corsair get hit and crash. He saw Booker alive on the ground, so he circled overhead and reported his position to *Valley Forge*. He stayed over the Marine as long as he could, despite losing all contact with Davy soon after he hit the ground.

In the end, Nate's nearly empty fuel tanks forced him to leave Jesse. He flew into Taegu on fumes. The next morning, trapped aboard *Valley Forge*, he was hoping to hear that Booker had been rescued. His introduction to combat had caused him much grief and sadness.

Davy Booker did not return to American lines until September 1953. Captured shortly after his plane went down, he was thrown into a cage by his North Korean guards and dragged through a village near the crash site. Old women spat on him. Men urinated on him. One of the North Korean soldiers mounted a sign on his cage that read, "I am a Capitalist Warmonger." Later, his captors beat him so badly that he suffered temporary paralysis.

Hauling him north after the Inchon landing, the North Koreans dumped Davy into a rice paddy with about a hundred other American POWs. Helpless, he watched as all but nineteen of the prisoners were machine-gunned to death. He and the other survivors were taken to a virtual death camp, where most died during the winter of 1950–51. Incidentally, Keith Thomson, VF-53's first casualty, turned out to be at the same camp. It was Davy who reported Keith's death after being repatriated in 1953.

When Lil Booker, Davy's wife of less than a year, learned that her husband's plane had gone down, she kept her faith hoping he had become a POW. Later, she learned that a former POW claimed to have seen Davy killed in the rice paddy massacre. Determined to learn everything he knew about Davy, Lil flew to California and talked with him. He was positive that he had seen Davy die under a hail of machine-gun bullets.

Despite this report, Lil refused to give up hope that her husband was still alive. A few months later, a photograph of American POWs caught her eye.

Examining the faces, she thought she recognized her husband among the sallow, hollow-eyed men. Her father was a Marine general, so she took the photo to him. He had the picture enlarged until they could positively identify Davy in the image. Now she knew her husband was alive.

Davy returned from captivity in September 1953 as one of the last POWs exchanged. He had remained in communist hands longer than almost any other American pilot.

Arthur Hanton went down next. Three days after Curry saw Booker go down near Seoul, he was again on another photo run, this time from Chongju to Suwon. Art Hanton was flying in the second division that afternoon, acting as John Ford's wingman. Curry was the executive officer's wingman that day in the first division.

Somewhere between Chongju, South Korea, and Suwon, Hanton's Corsair was hit. It burst into flames, forcing him to bail out. As he came down near the village of Chonnui, his plane struck a hillside and exploded. He landed in a tree, his parachute clearly visible to his comrades above.

As was becoming standard practice, the two divisions stayed over Hanton as long as they could.[8] When darkness forced them to return to the *Valley Forge*, they reported that, aside from the chute, they had seen no sign to indicate that Hanton was alive or that he was in enemy hands. In fact, they had seen no sign of life at all where Hanton had landed.

Curry trapped aboard with a damaged Corsair. Ground fire had hit his plane in both wings and in the fuselage. Fortunately, no critical systems had been hit, and the plane was ready for action by the following afternoon. Nate would fly 119 combat missions in two tours in Korea. He would return home with combat damage no fewer than 40 times. This was the first of a long, long series of close shaves for this son of Missouri.

The next afternoon, VF-53's executive officer, Lieutenant Commander Joe Murphy, revisited Hanton's crash site with a photo plane. He searched the area thoroughly, but saw no signs of Hanton. Even his parachute was now gone from the tree.

Years later, word of Hanton's fate surfaced. Like Booker, Hanton was captured by the North Koreans shortly after he went down. The North Koreans tortured him, then tied him to two vehicles and ripped him apart.[9]

The North Koreans got Nate Curry next. On August 27, Task Force 77 sailed up east of Wonsan to conduct strikes against that crucial port city. Fighting 53

launched eight Corsairs that morning with orders to bomb and rocket the docks and any shipping in the harbor.

Over the target area, the pilots discovered the overcast layer was so low that it restricted their maneuvering room. Instead of making steep diving attacks on their targets, they were forced to use shallow, vulnerable approaches in order to stay out of the scud layer. This left them exposed to anti-aircraft fire for a much longer period than if they could make the steep, almost 70-degree dives that they had been trained to execute.

Nate Curry arrived in the harbor area leading the second section of John Ford's division. Below them, Ford spotted a gunboat and ordered his men to attack. Line astern, they rolled in on the target in a shallow diving approach.

The gunboat threw up a surprising volume of fire at the onrushing Corsairs. Nevertheless, the Americans closed the range and strafed the vessel with their 20-mm cannon. The other division, led by Bill Pittman, followed suit. When all eight Corsairs pulled off target, the pilots could see that it had not been fatally damaged. Ford led his men down again, and this time as Nate opened up on the gunboat, his Corsair rocked violently as it took hits. He pulled up to assess his situation. The Corsair's engine was running rough, and a quick glance at the gauges showed that he was rapidly losing oil. Knowing he had but seconds left, he turned eastward and limped out to sea, determined to get as far from the North Korean coast as possible.

He didn't get far. About five miles off Wonsan, the engine caught fire. Flames erupted inside the cockpit, searing his legs, arms, and face. Desperately, he jettisoned the canopy and threw himself out of the burning Corsair. His chute opened, and he splashed into the Sea of Japan at 12:20 P.M. as his seven comrades watched from above.

Nate's troubles had just started. Though he managed to get into his life raft, he had been immersed in salt water. He lay exhausted in his raft, his body wracked by paroxysms of sheer agony as the salt water inflamed his second- and third-degree burns. Soon, the chilly water added to his misery because his cold-water "poopie suit" had been partially destroyed by the fire in the cockpit. Under the best conditions, a downed pilot in the Sea of Japan had only an hour or two before hypothermia killed him. With his injuries and the damage to his cold-water suit, he would be lucky to survive that long.

As his raft rose and fell in the heavy swells off Wonsan, salt water sprayed over the gunwales and lashed at his burned face and nose to torment him even further. He looked up at the Corsairs covering him. Eventually, he watched as, one by one, they headed back to the *Valley Forge*. By 3:15, all of the squadron had been trapped aboard the flattop.

They had left him. Alone now, he was but a few miles from captivity. His squadron had heard rumors about North Korean treatment of POWs, and the prospect of capture inspired terror in him. He recalled his older brother

Robert, who had been a shell of his former self when he returned home in 1945 after four years of brutal treatment by the Japanese.

But luck was with Nate on that day. He was not far from the USS *Holister*, a Navy destroyer. When his comrades had radioed his location, it was passed on to the *Holister*. As the ship came into sight, Bill Pittman directed her to Nate's tiny raft. Low on fuel, Pittman and the rest of the squadron returned to the *Valley Forge* secure in the knowledge that Nate would be picked up.

The destroyermen pulled Nate from the water and put him in the launch that the ship had sent out to retrieve him. Soon, he was aboard the *Holister*, having his wounds treated by the medical staff. Somebody gave him a hefty shot of morphine, which Nate greatly appreciated. For the first time since his ordeal began, his pain eased and he fell asleep. At 3:30 P.M., the destroyer radioed the *Valley Forge* to advise that her lost pilot had been rescued.

The next day, the *Holister* transferred Nate to the *Valley Forge*, where he spent four weeks in the skillful hands of Happy Valley's medical personnel. Amazingly, his third-degree burns required no skin grafts. Even the worst burns, mostly on his nose, healed quite well. Apparently, the cold salt water had actually helped his wounds, in spite of the pain it had caused. He had been very lucky.

Before his burns were completely healed, Nate Curry returned to action just in time to face VF-53's greatest challenges—Inchon and the Yalu bridge raids.

4 | Into the Tiger's Jaws

T he aviators in Carrier Air Group-5 soon realized during the summer of 1950 that the war in Korea had become a fighter-bomber pilot's war. The men who had joined the Navy in search of daring air-to-air dogfights, the likes of which they had grown up reading about and watching on the screens of their hometown theaters, were to be seriously disappointed in this new war. Far from the glamour of individual dogfights, the Korean War offered mostly the dirty work of close air support and interdiction. Flying at treetop level and shooting up troop columns, tanks, and trucks constituted difficult, hazardous duty. As unpleasant as these missions were, they turned out to be critically important to the UN cause.

The U.S. Navy turned out to be generally well equipped for this type of air war. While the U.S. Air Force's F-80 Shooting Stars and F-51 Mustangs could carry only a limited amount of ordnance — usually 2,000 pounds — the Navy's Corsairs and Skyraiders could haul aloft enormous bomb and rocket loads. On close air support strikes, the *Valley Forge*'s Corsairs could carry eight HVAR rockets, plus a 1,000-pound bomb slung under the centerline of the fuselage. The Skyraiders could carry even more. Typically, they catapulted off Happy Valley's deck with twelve rockets and three 500-pound bombs, but the load was often changed to reflect the nature of the mission. Frequently, the iron bombs were replaced with 150-gallon napalm tanks capable of burning out anything in a pear-shaped blast area roughly 275 feet long and nearly 100 feet wide.[1]

During the height of the Pusan Perimeter battles, Task Force 77's aircraft flew no fewer than 2,481 strikes against North Korean targets. Of these, 588 were true close air support (CAS) missions directed by forward air controllers. Most of the remaining missions were armed reconnaissance flown directly behind the lines in search of tanks, troops, trucks, and trains heading for the front lines.[2]

Such a frenzied flying pace could not have been maintained by CAG-5 alone. Starting in August, the first reinforcements arrived to help carry the war to the North Koreans. The fleet carrier USS *Philippine Sea* steamed into the theater on August 1, just in time for the climatic battles around Pusan. The escort carriers USS *Badoeng Straits* and USS *Sicily* also joined the fighting about that time. Each baby flattop carried one U.S. Marine Corsair squadron, whose pilots proved especially adept at the desperately needed close air support missions around Pusan.

By early September, the naval power assembled off the Korean coast had become formidable indeed. The carrier USS *Boxer* arrived in time for the Inchon landings on September 15. Additionally, the British Royal Navy deployed the HMS *Triumph*, a fleet carrier with two Fleet Air Arm squadrons equipped with Supermarine Seafires and Fairey Fireflies. In October, another *Essex*-class carrier, the USS *Leyte*, joined the fray after sailing halfway around the world to reach Korea.

With one British and three American fleet carriers, plus the two baby flattops, UN forces possessed a flexible strike force capable of inflicting serious damage on the North Koreans. It was about to be used to support the first UN offensive of the war—the Inchon landing.

As Task Force 77 swung around to the western side of the Korean Peninsula in order to begin softening up the Inchon area, the big question confronting the Seventh Fleet was how the Soviets would respond. With the Soviet air and navy base at Port Arthur just a few hundred miles away, tensions rose as the carriers moved northward to take up their new station southwest of Pyongyang.

On the morning of September 4, Fighting 53 launched two divisions of Corsairs against a rail bridge near the North Korean capital. They returned at 10:00 A.M. without loss, although Lieutenant Commander Joe Murphy's plane suffered flak damage in the left wing.

The second strike of the day was laid on at 1:00 P.M. Seven Corsairs, led by the undaunted Murphy, took off to hit another rail bridge, this time in Pyongyang itself. Just after the strike formed up over the *Valley Forge*, Dick Downs, Ed Laney, Leo Franz, and John Abbott left the carrier and began climbing out to serve as CAP for the task force.

Twenty-nine minutes later, the *Valley Forge* radar crew detected a suspicious contact inbound from the northwest. Sixty miles out, it was closing on the task force at 200 mph.

Shortly after it appeared on TF-77's radar screens, the contact split into two separate bogies. One of the mystery planes reversed course and headed back to the northwest, probably returning to Port Arthur. The other, however, continued to fly straight at Task Force 77.

Twenty-five miles out, Dick Downs looked down and caught sight of a dirty brown, twin-engine aircraft. Ed Laney, his wingman, spotted the plane as well. As far as the Corsair pilots could determine, the plane was either a Soviet-built Tupolev Tu-2 or an Ilyushin Il-4 medium bomber of World War II vintage.[3] Laney studied the plane but saw no distinctive markings, so he was unsure of its nationality.

Identified or not, the bogey had to be turned away from the task force. Downs reported contacting the bogey, and the *Valley Forge* ordered him to make an identification. Downs dove on the plane as he tried to get close enough to establish its nationality. The bomber pilot saw the Corsair arching down on him and put his plane in a steep dive. As the American plane closed, the bomber's rear gunner sprayed the sky around the F4U with tracer rounds.

Downs pulled up sharply and took station above the hostile bomber. He reported the situation to the *Valley Forge*. Within a few seconds, the VF-53 pilots gained permission to return fire. Laney wasted no time once he received clearance. Winging over in a shallow dive, he closed on the bomber from astern and slightly off to one side. The rear gunner opened fire at him, too. As tracers streaked by his Corsair, Laney held his fire until he was close and then gave a quick tug on his trigger.

The Corsair shuddered as its four 20-mm cannon churned out about a hundred rounds in a matter of seconds. The bomber disintegrated. Those 20-mm rounds exploded along the fuselage and the tail broke completely free and began spinning away toward the water. The shells walked forward, blowing a wing off and causing the bomber to burst into flames. Pieces of it fell into the sea, and when Laney looked down, the surface was strewn with wreckage.

But whom had he shot down? He and the rest of the division discovered the answer a few hours later after they landed on the *Valley Forge*. When the bomber crashed into the sea, a nearby destroyer had steamed to the area and combed the wreckage for survivors. Surprisingly, they found several members of the crew. Only the pilot was still alive, but he never regained consciousness before he died on board the destroyer. A search of the crew's personal effects proved conclusively that they were Soviets. According to Laney, the bodies were later returned to the Soviet Union. The Soviets explained the incident away as a training mission gone awry.

Training mission or not, VF-53 had scored its first, and only, aerial victory of the Korean War.

-◆◆◆-

Planning and preparation for the Inchon landing continued, but, following the attack on September 4, Task Force 77 put more effort into air defense planning in case the Soviets decided to intervene in the war.[4]

As the date for the Inchon landing approached—September 15 was the scheduled date—VF-53 continued to help pave the way for the troops who would hit the beach. The Seventh Fleet now had ten squadrons of Corsairs, three squadrons of Skyraiders, and four squadrons of Panthers with which to strike at North Korean positions. All were used effectively in the days before the landing.

To cloak the actual target of the planned landings, Task Force 77 devoted only 40 percent of its air strikes against the Inchon area. The remaining 60 percent focused on targets to the north and south of Seoul. Moreover, to convince the North Koreans that the UN landing would come farther down the coast at Kunsan, the Royal Navy, FEAF, and the Marine squadron on board the *Badoeng Straits* launched strikes around that port city. Bridges, power stations, and rail lines were hit to give the appearance that UN airpower was isolating Kunsan in preparation for the landing.

Fighting 53 would play a substantial role in the coming amphibious operation. By now CAG-5 was Task Force 77's most experienced and effective naval outfit serving off Korea. Within CAG-5, many of VF-53's men had served together in peace and war for almost two years. They had flown Corsairs for a long time, some had World War II experience, and all had learned lessons of survival in the summer skies over Pusan during the previous month. Fighting 53 would go into the final phase of its tour honed in combat and as effective as any that served during the war.

In contrast, the *Philippine Sea*'s CAG-11 had served in Korea for only a few weeks. Prior to its arrival in the theater, CAG-11 had not yet completed its jet transition training. It went to war that August with two squadrons of F9F Panthers whose pilots did not have adequate jet time.[5] Given some time and experience, CAG-11 would become as good a Navy outfit as any, but those first weeks in action were difficult ones as it went through its trial by fire.

Additionally, USS *Boxer*, with CAG-2 on board, had yet to arrive, so the *Valley Forge*'s pilots would form the backbone of Task Force 77's strike capability.

Following the September 4 incident, Task Force 77 sailed to Sasebo, Japan, for a quick rest and refit in preparation for the final Inchon support operations. During the break, the pilots and crews received their first briefings on the landings. Their Corsairs, Skyraiders, and Panthers were to clear the way for the troops to land safely in the harbor. Timing had to be precise, and coordination with the ground forces was imperative.

On September 12, Task Force 77 arrived in the Yellow Sea, just to the west of Inchon, for the final round of preparatory attacks. That day, VF-53 launched a full-squadron strike against warehouses in the Chinnampo area. Twelve Corsairs reached the target and burned out almost a dozen warehouses with napalm attacks. Two trucks and a village were also hit. All planes returned aboard ship without damage.

The next day, the squadron flew twenty-one sorties over Inchon, destroying a pillbox, an anti-aircraft battery at Kimpo Airfield, and two flak batteries around Seoul. One of the squadron's divisions found a truck convoy east of Inchon and destroyed six of the vehicles with gunfire and napalm.

On September 14, the day before the invasion, the squadron was again busy with bombing runs on the island of Wolmi-do. This island sat directly in the path the troops needed to take to the beaches at Inchon. As a result, it had to be first neutralized by air power, then taken in an early assault by U.S. Marines, who were scheduled to capture it about six hours before the main landings.

At 6:00 A.M., John Ford led a division armed with 1,000-pound bombs off the *Valley Forge*. Ford and his wingman, Herb Riebeling, dropped their bombs on Wolmi-do, but the second section, led by Charles Darrow, encountered a serious problem. When Darrow tried to drop his bombs, one of his thousand-pounders hung on the rack. Unable to shake it free, he could not land on the *Valley Forge*. Fortunately, he had enough fuel to get down to Pusan and land there.

While Darrow was waiting for his Corsair to be refueled, a U.S. Army officer pulled Darrow aside and told him "in strict confidence," that everyone in the perimeter would be "out of here soon." As Darrow left Pusan later that afternoon, he puzzled over the lack of security there. If the men were talking of the landing to complete strangers, in "confidence" or not, surely the North Koreans could pick up the information.

On September 15, the 230-ship assault force arrived off Inchon and the Marines went ashore at Wolmi-do. Overhead, the landing craft were protected by a web of Corsairs and Skyraiders that crisscrossed the invasion beach on their strafing and napalm runs. So low and close to the Marines were these big blue planes that some of the landing craft were pelted with 20-mm shell casings.[6]

Darrow remembered flying a TARCAP over Inchon that morning. Looking down, he could see scores of landing craft fan out from the assault ships en route to Wolmi-do. Fortunately, no enemy aircraft appeared to disturb the scene, and the Soviet planes at Port Arthur did not venture into the area.

Fighting 53 suffered a setback when Ensign H. C. Kuhlman's Corsair suffered complete engine failure twenty miles west of Inchon. He ditched the crippled plane and was picked up by the destroyer U.S.S. *Collett* within fifteen minutes.

VF-53 flew twenty-two sorties that day, costing the North Koreans twenty trucks, four machine gun emplacements, between fifty and one hundred troops killed, an ammunition dump blown up, and two gun emplacements damaged.

Thanks in part to the UN's complete mastery of the skies, the Inchon landings proved to be the single most successful UN operation of the Korean War. By the end of the day, some 13,000 UN troops had come ashore against moderate to minimal North Korean opposition. During the coming days, UN troops would move out toward Seoul and cut off the bulk of the North Korean army still locked in combat around Pusan.

For the next ten days, Fighting 53 supported the advance on Seoul. As the GIs and Marines battled their way from house to house inside the South Korean capital, VF-53 stalked enemy trucks and personnel just behind the front lines. The day Seoul fell to UN troops, the squadron suffered another tragedy.

On September 25, VF-53 was busy supporting the final effort to take Seoul. At 1:45 P.M., John Ford, William Ben Brown, Dick Downs, and Al Frainier left the *Valley Forge* on an armed reconnaissance mission between Seoul and Sariwon. The remaining North Korean elements in the area were fleeing northward, and the fighter-bombers of Task Force 77 were dogging them along every foot of their retreat. Already that day, the squadron had found several trains. It destroyed seven rail cars and damaged three locomotives.

Ford led the afternoon strike in search of any targets of opportunity. Somewhere around Sariwon, the four Corsairs ran into heavy ground fire. Ben Brown's plane was hit by either rifle or machine-gun fire. He tried to get out to sea, but his engine died, forcing him to crash land on a small hill three miles south of Sariwon. He came down in an area crawling with North Korean troops, who soon spread out around him. Brown crawled onto the nearly hill and waited for rescue, his .38 revolver in his hand.

For two hours, Ford kept the rest of his division over Brown. They did their best to keep the North Koreans away from him. In the meantime, the division learned that a helicopter was en route to pick him up.

At 5:40 P.M., Al Frainier trapped aboard *Valley Forge* to report the latest developments over Brown. Meanwhile, Ford and Downs stayed with their downed comrade.

The North Koreans were closing in. Surrounded, Brown kept his head down as his friends made repeated strafing runs. Despite their efforts, the volume of ground fire seemed to be increasing.

Another hour passed before the helicopter finally arrived on the scene. The pilot came in fast, the copter shuddering as the North Koreans peppered it with small-arms fire. Undismayed, the pilot reached Ben Brown's little hill and lowered the rescue belt.

On the ground, Brown raced for the sling even as the North Koreans began shooting at him. Pistol in hand, he reached the sling, then seemed to pause. According to Charles Darrow, Brown had actually started to get in the sling when the copter took several severe hits. He dropped the sling and waved the copter away. Stunned, his buddies overhead watched as he ran from his rescuers firing his .38 pistol at the North Korean soldiers closing in on him.

Badly damaged, the helicopter pulled out of the area and headed south. It later crashed due to the battle damage it sustained.

Ben Brown sacrificed himself to save the helicopter crew. He knew that had he not aborted the rescue, they surely would have been shot out of the sky and three men would have been down instead of one. His final act, witnessed by his squadron mates, was perhaps the most selfless and brave that anyone in CAG-5 would ever see.

Downs and Ford finally had to leave the area after being in the air for almost six hours. No American ever saw Brown alive again. A few weeks later, some GIs inspecting a cave came across his name, rank, and serial number carved into the wall, the only clue to his final fate. Somehow, somewhere, he had died or had been killed while a captive of the North Koreans.[7]

-◆◆◆-

Thanks to the Inchon landing, the war seemed to be coming to an end as Halloween approached. The once formidable North Korean army had crumbled and then collapsed as Lieutenant General Walton W. Walker's Eighth Army broke out of the Pusan Perimeter and pushed up the peninsula.

As the Eighth Army hammered at the fleeing North Koreans, Major General Edward M. Almond's X Corps (separate from the Eighth Army, it then included the 1st Marine Division and the Army's 3d and 7th Infantry Divisions) that had taken Inchon climbed on board seagoing transports once again and prepared for the second major amphibious landing of the war. It came ashore at Wonsan but only after the port had been liberated by advancing ROK units. The amphibious operation had been delayed by the heavy minefields protecting the approaches to the harbor. When the troops of X Corps came ashore, they were greeted by friendly troops, instead of machine guns and mortars.

Fighting 53 supported this operation by locating and burning a corvette and sinking a pair of gunboats in Wonsan Harbor on October 12. The pilots also flew several mine-spotting missions in support of the ships sweeping the harbor approaches. The squadron flew missions at a steady pace throughout October against rail targets, gun emplacements, coastal shipping, and troop concentrations. Yet the war seemed to be winding down. Few VF-53 planes suffered any damage, and, for the first time during its combat tour, the squadron didn't lose a single pilot during October. To everyone on board the *Valley Forge*, it seemed possible that they could be home for Christmas with a stunning victory under their belts. Morale soared and hopes were high that their final missions of the war were near.

Although the Fighting 53's pilots would get home for Christmas, they would not sail into San Francisco or San Diego flush with victory. Events on the ground were conspiring against that possibility.

The first of these events started at the end of October, just as General Douglas MacArthur, commander in chief, United Nations Command, ordered all UN forces to push toward the Yalu River, which bordered the Chinese region of Manchuria. Unknown to American intelligence, the Chinese had made the decision to intervene in the war, sending tens of thousands of "volunteers" across the Yalu and into the rugged North Korean countryside. With a light snowfall blanketing the ground, the Chinese struck fiercely at the ROK 1st Division, which was moving toward Kojang, a few dozen miles from the Yalu. At 11:00 A.M. on October 25, the ROK unit captured its first Chinese prisoner. From him, the UN Command learned that at least twenty thousand Chinese troops were deployed around Unsan and Huichon.

The North Koreans were no longer fighting alone. The arrival of the Chinese would soon greatly alter the entire shape and scope of the war.

Between October 25 and November 5, the Chinese attacked elements of the Eighth Army, decimated several units, and stopped cold MacArthur's advance to the Yalu. On November 6, the Chinese suddenly broke contact and disappeared into the North Korean countryside. For the moment, the front quieted down, but the Chinese assault unsettled nearly everyone in the UN camp and forced a shift in strategy.

On November 5, just before the Chinese had suspended their attacks, MacArthur had alerted FEAF that air power had to deliver the knockout blow to end the war. "Combat crews are to be flown to exhaustion if necessary," MacArthur announced to FEAF's commander, Lieutenant General George E. Stratemeyer.[8] Along with this pronouncement came orders to undertake a maximum-effort, two-week campaign directed mainly against the massive bridges spanning the Yalu River. MacArthur reasoned that if the bridges could be dropped, any Chinese troops in North Korean could be neither reinforced nor resupplied. The trick was to launch these attacks without hitting Manchuria itself. Accordingly, MacArthur ordered that the raids be directed against only the Korean side of the bridges.

Stratemeyer realized that such attacks so close to Manchuria could cause a massive diplomatic crisis. When he received his orders, he alerted Air Force Chief of Staff General Hoyt S. Vandenberg in Washington, D.C., three hours before the bombers were scheduled to depart.

As it turned out, MacArthur had ordered the bombings without the knowledge or approval of the Joint Chiefs of Staff (JCS). When news of the impending attacks reached the JCS and, subsequently, President Harry Truman, they reacted sharply against the idea. Truman felt that bombing the bridges would be justified only if there was an immediate and serious danger to American troops. After a hasty discussion of the situation, Truman and the JCS canceled the first round of attacks by ordering MacArthur not to attack any targets within five miles of the Manchurian border. This was the first time during the Korean War that MacArthur had issued a field order that was countermanded by Washington. Needless to say, he was not pleased.

For the next few days, MacArthur battled Washington over the Yalu bridge issue. "Men and material in large force are pouring across all bridges over the Yalu from Manchuria," he wrote to the Joint Chiefs, "This movement not only jeopardizes but threatens the ultimate destruction of the forces under my command."9

The argument raged back and forth until Washington finally compromised. The bridges could be hit, but MacArthur was ordered to bomb only the North Korean side of them. Also, the attacks had to be made in such a manner that they were not parallel to the bridges—the easiest way to attack such targets—but perpendicular in order to avoid violating Manchurian air space.10

The Air Force tried to hit the bridges first. Using 79 Boeing B-29 Superfortress bombers escorted by F-80C Shooting Stars of the 51st Fighter-Interceptor Wing, FEAF first struck the Yalu bridges on November 8. The first targets were the rail and road bridges at Sinuiju, which connected the temporary North Korean capital of Pyongyang to the Manchurian city of Antung. The bombers also struck downtown Sinuiju with incendiary bombs and burned out 60 percent of the city's center.

Nearby, the F-80s clashed for the first time with Chinese-flown MiG-15s that flew south out of Antung to intercept the raid. No UN planes went down in the world's first aerial battle between jet aircraft, but USAF Lieutenant Russell J. Brown caught a MiG in a dive and shot it down. It was the first of several hundred MiG-15s that would be brought down by American pilots during the Korean War.

Shortly after the firebomb raid, nine more B-29s arrived in the area and tried to hit the rail and road bridges from 18,000 feet. Flying through heavy flak, the 19th Bomb Wing's Superfortresses managed to damage the approaches to both bridges slightly but failed to close them to communist traffic.

The Air Force found the Yalu bridges to be tricky targets. Given the political restrictions placed on approach routes and angles of attack, the use of B-29s was problematic and their effectiveness greatly hampered. The mammoth four-engined bombers were designed to hit their targets from altitudes of 30,000 feet and up. Flying that high and following the twisting course of the Yalu River without violating Manchurian airspace was asking the impossible of their pilots. To bomb effectively from high altitude, the Superforts needed a long straight approach to their target from the initial point, which attacking downriver precluded.

Clearly, FEAF needed another means of destroying these difficult targets. It turned to Task Force 77 and asked that carrier planes destroy six of the critical rail and road bridges. Far from winding down their daily operations, the pilots and crews on board TF-77's flattops were about to execute the most important missions of the war to date.

-◆◆◆-

Fighting 53's pilots listened intently to the briefing on the morning of November 9. Their target was a particularly thorny bridge on Namson-Ni, about fifty miles upriver from Sinuiju, that the Air Force had found impossible to attack without violating Manchurian airspace. Spanning a bend in the river, the bridge was surrounded on three sides by Manchurian territory. CAG-5 was given the task of bombing it within the restrictions imposed by Washington.

The Navy pilots then received the bad news. The bridges were located in such a politically sensitive area that the Navy pilots would not have a free hand in the air during the strikes. It was drilled into them that, under no circumstances, could they violate Chinese airspace. This order included no chasing of MiGs in "hot pursuit" across the frontier, as well as no flying over the Chinese side of the Yalu during their approaches to the target area. Even worse, the anti-aircraft guns on the north side of the river were strictly off limits. By Washington decree, the Navy was forced to give their communist opponents a safe haven within a few hundred yards of their targets.

The briefing climaxed with the reading of a dispatch from Vice Admiral C. Turner Joy, Commander Naval Forces, Far East, to the pilots of Task Force 77. In part, it read:

> The hazards involved in employing aircraft in precision attacks on small targets protected by intense, well-directed anti-aircraft fire which cannot be attacked, as well as by enemy planes flying in the haven of neutral territory, except when the enemy chooses to attack, are tremendous. These factors were gravely considered by General MacArthur before he requested the Navy to take out the bridges. We all recognize that enemy reinforcements

and supplies are coming over those bridges now, and will continue to pour into North Korea until the bridges are down. Carrier aircraft alone can make these precision air attacks. Our Government has decided that we cannot violate the air space over Manchuria or attack on Manchurian territory regardless of the provocation. If such attacks were made, the world might be thrown into the holocaust of a third world war. Our naval pilots have been given a most difficult task. May God be with them as they accomplish it.[11]

Clearly, Admiral Joy recognized the unfairness of the situation and sought to explain its gravity personally to his aviators. Whether hitting the Manchurian side of the Yalu River would have triggered another world war remains an open question. What is questionable is the selection of the Yalu bridge targets in the first place. In retrospect, the flaws in the whole campaign became abundantly clear. On November 9, however, the only thing on the minds of VF-53's pilots was how best to accomplish this most difficult operation.

For the first mission of this new campaign, Fighting 53 would fly flak suppression. While their Corsairs shot up the south bank of the Yalu River to keep the enemy gunners off balance, VA-55's Skyraiders would hit the first span of the Namson-Ni highway bridge closest to Korean territory.

Sixteen Corsairs were launched from the *Valley Forge* that morning at 6:45. A short time later, eight Skyraiders armed with 2,000-pound bombs trundled aloft. The piston-engine aircraft formed up and flew westward together, across mostly hostile territory, to their target area almost 225 miles away. Fifty minutes later, CAG-5's two Panther squadrons were in the air, speeding westward to rendezvous with the strike force. Their job was to cover the attack and protect the prop planes from any communist MiGs that tried to intercept the raid.

Simultaneously, the other carriers in Task Force 77 also launched strikes. Slated to attack the two bridges at Sinuiju, the *Philippine Sea*'s air group ran into heavy opposition. Over Sinuiju, two MiGs flying out of Antung buzzed over the Yalu and struck at CAG-11. The escorting Panthers jumped in just as the MiGs made a run at the Corsairs and Skyraiders. The prop planes managed to evade the initial attack. Before the MiGs could come around again for another run, the Panthers of VF-111 engaged them. In the ensuing dogfight, Lieutenant Commander William T. Amen shot down one of the MiGs as it tried to climb away from him. It was the Navy's first MiG kill of the war.

While the fracas around Sinuiju developed, CAG-5 arrived over Namson-Ni about fifty miles to the northwest. Following the bends and turns of the river, the Skyraiders plunged toward the highway bridge as Fighting 53's Corsairs hit the anti-aircraft batteries scattered around the Korean side of the Yalu.

Ed Laney recalled the strike during a 1998 interview:

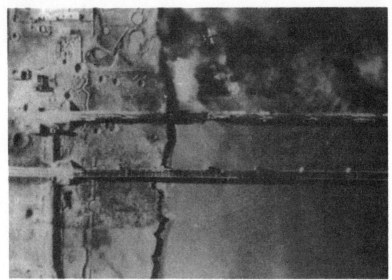

A strike on the Yalu River bridges.

We came in at about 27,000 feet or so. The whole air group—all the prop planes—rolled in simultaneously. The Corsairs were in there on flak suppression. Each one of us was assigned a particular gun to take out. The ADs each had three 2,000-pounders on them, and their job was to try to knock out the bridge.

We came down in a high-angle attack, probably around in a 70-degree dive. I remember I went down on my target with my wheels down. You did that in a Corsair for high angle dives in order to keep your speed down. Otherwise, you'd get up too much speed, and you couldn't use your flaps as the speeds were so fast you'd just blow them right off. The landing gear was designed to take the high speeds encountered in steep dives.

The flak was heavy, but the gunners weren't very good, as they didn't shoot any of us down. I remember dueling with one gun that I was assigned to hit. It was just a case of who was going to win. I won. We used rockets and guns to take out the AA positions. Our guns were our best weapons. We shot our rockets to try and quiet the guns, but the old HVAR rocket was just not much of a weapon.[12]

Charles Darrow, recalling those early flak-suppression missions, quipped, "I was one of the first Wild Weasels!" Using rockets and cannon fire, he and his division concentrated on forcing the communist gunners to abandon their guns and dive for their slit trenches. By watching for muzzle flashes on the ground, he could tell which guns were manned and which were not. Then, he'd focus on the ones still active. In many ways, he was right. These missions were very similar to the Wild Weasel SAM-suppression strikes flown during the Vietnam and Gulf Wars.

Despite the intense flak and the unusual approach to the target, all 16 of Fighting 53's aircraft returned from the first strike. In fact, amazingly, none of the Corsairs even had been hit. The Skyraiders all returned as well, and claimed several hits on the bridge. Later assessment of the strike gave the ADs credit for damaging the target but not destroying it.

Later that afternoon, five VF-53 Corsairs supported another AD strike against a highway bridge at Hysanjin on the eastern side of North Korea. The Skyraiders hit this bridge as well, inflicting some damage on the target. Although the pilots on board TF 77's flattops considered these missions successful, the political restrictions placed on them engendered considerable resentment. The fact that they had to endanger their own lives to avoid crossing some invisible line in the sky both outraged them and hampered the effectiveness of their attacks. As the bridge campaign continued, that situation would become only worse.

It did not take the North Koreans and Chinese long to figure out that the carrier planes were not allowed to attack any flak positions on the Manchurian side of the Yalu. They began pulling their anti-aircraft batteries off the Korean shore and placing them along the northern banks. Toward the end of the bridge campaign, the Chinese did not even bother to dig in or camouflage their flak batteries on the Manchurian side. The Chinese knew their guns were safe. For the attacking American pilots, the sight of so many anti-aircraft batteries blazing away at them from such exposed positions caused unbelievable frustration. Instead of being able to dive down and tear up the complacent Red gunners, the Americans had to grit their teeth and put up with the heavy flak until they pulled off target.

November 12 saw one of the biggest carrier raids of the Yalu campaign. Three air groups, five minutes apart, rolled in on the Sinuiju bridges. CAG-5 was scheduled to be the second group in, following the Corsairs and Skyraiders of the *Philippines Sea*'s CAG-11. CAG-3 off the *Leyte* would complete the attack, hitting whatever the other squadrons had missed.

Going into this massive attack, Fighting 53 was one of the most experienced squadrons in the fleet. Every one of Commander Pittman's pilots had at least fifty combat missions to his credit.[13] They were at the peak of their effectiveness, and this last big strike tested every ounce of strength and skill that they possessed.

Coming in on Sinuiju, the Panthers from VF-51 linked up with the rest of the air group and took station above and ahead of the piston-engine planes. As Pittman later reported, "At this stage in the war, we propeller pilots were increasingly thankful (and not a little envious) of the jets. They were our only protection against the MiGs."[14]

A Douglas Skyraider burns on a carrier deck after a 1951 landing accident.

Just prior to reaching the pushover point, Pittman spotted four MiGs lifting off the gigantic airfield complex at Antung. About the same time, Darrow, leading the second division that day, looked up and watched several MiGs buzz by a few thousand feet above the squadron. Fortunately, none of them came down to attack the strike group. Just being that close to the deadly jet fighters inspired caution and fear in the hearts of the outclassed piston-engine pilots. If the MiGs started intercepting in force, the coming weeks could turn into a real bloodbath.

Darrow had flown on the first bridge strike and had seen how foolish the political restrictions were. This time, instead of flak suppression, Darrow's division was supposed to backstop the Skyraiders and strike the bridge itself. To accomplish it, Darrow led his men down the length of the bridge—exactly what had been forbidden by Washington. Hitting the bridge from a perpendicular attack would have been almost impossible. Given the risk they were all running, with the flak and fighters whirling around them, Darrow wanted to do this one right.

He and his three men lined up over the first span on the south side of the Yalu. The sky around them was peppered with flak. They toggled their bombs and rolled their Corsairs until their wings were vertical. Pulling hard on their sticks, the pilots followed Darrow through a tight, 90-degree left turn that put them just inside Korean territory, nearly over the middle of the Yalu River. They had avoided Manchurian airspace by obeying the intent, if not the letter, of their rules of engagement.

Meanwhile, the other division raked the flak sites in the target area with 500-pound VT-fused proximity bombs. Three sites were destroyed before the air group pulled off the target to begin the long, cross-country trip back to the *Valley Forge*. Behind them, they left the bridge shrouded in smoke and flames. Between Darrow's flight and VA-55's twelve Skyraiders, one span had been dropped into the Yalu. It wasn't a great success, but there would be no Chinese trains crossing there that night.

For Fighting 53, the entire character of the war had changed by mid-November. It still flew CAS and armed reconnaissance missions, but the bridge strikes had soured some of the pilots on the way that the war was being conducted. The rules of engagement had given the Chinese just about every advantage in these fights. The Americans were so restricted that they were warned not even to fire their guns if there was a chance their bullets would land on the other side of the frontier. These conditions, combined with the complete superiority of the MiG-15 over all types of the Navy's aircraft, conspired to anger and embitter some of the squadron's pilots. As a result, they were eager to go home. But first, they had one last mission to fly.

On November 18, the air group again took part in a mass attack on the Sinuiju rail bridge. Task Force 77's other two air groups also joined in this attack, so that it was almost a repeat of the November 12th strikes. Over Sinuiju, the worst fears of the VF-53 pilots came true. From out of Manchuria attacked a formation of MiG-15s. Speedy, nimble, and far superior in every way to the Navy aircraft, the MiGs fell upon the vulnerable prop planes, with their pilots ready to initiate a massacre.

Fighting 52, flying F9F Panthers, threw itself desperately at the incoming MiGs. A violent dogfight developed around and over the Corsairs and Skyraiders. Though totally outmatched, the Panthers managed to stave off a potential disaster with brilliant flying and ice-cold resolve. These two factors, plus the better tactics employed by the Panther pilots, ensured that the Chinese would not get through in any numbers.

But a few got through. They waded into the heavily laden Corsairs, making lightning-quick gunnery runs. The F4U pilots broke into the attacks, maneuvering wildly to throw off their opponents' aim. Ed Laney, when asked how his fellow pilots avoided the MiGs, replied, "We did a lot of good jinking!"

Amazingly, the Corsairs emerged from the assault unscathed, nor had any other planes in CAG-5 been hit either. Obviously, the flying ability of the communist pilots must have been quite low. Later, one Navy pilot commented, "It is believed if [the MiGs] had been manned by pilots as aggressive and well trained as ours that [our] own pilot and plane losses would have been great."[15]

Nor did the MiGs get away unscathed. Lieutenant Commander William Lamb, skipper of VF-52, latched onto one MiG during the fight and chased it into a high-speed dive. As the communist pilot tried to escape, Lamb and another VF-52 pilot, Lieutenant R. E. Parker, managed to score hits on the MiG with their 20-mm cannon. The MiG escaped into Manchurian airspace, which forced the two Navy pilots to abandon their attack. Just short of Antung, the MiG began streaming a tail of oily black smoke. Seconds later, it exploded, and debris fell onto the north bank of the Yalu. The scene was witnessed by several pilots in the air group, who sighed heavily with relief as the Panther pilots proved that it took more than just a hot machine to win a dogfight.

With the MiGs behind them, Fighting 53's two divisions dove onto their targets. One group of four Corsairs struck at the flak batteries on the south bank of the river. By now, though, the North Koreans and Chinese had moved most of their guns to Manchuria where they could not be attacked. No matter what the Corsairs did, the volume of fire aimed at them was not going to diminish.

The other division dropped its loads on the bridge itself, as did the Skyraiders, and they damaged several spans. Laney recalled that at least one span had been dropped. In spite of these good results, the communists could rebuild whatever damage had been inflicted in a matter of hours or, at most, days, so long as the concrete pilings remained intact, which they did.

VF-53's Corsairs returned to Happy Valley, trapping aboard by 4:45 P.M. They were carefully tucked away below deck while the exhausted pilots headed down inside the ship for their debriefing and a hot meal.

Despite every effort that Task Force 77 and FEAF could muster, the Yalu bridges were never totally destroyed. Indeed, the whole point of the attacks had been to deny the Chinese the chance to move additional troops and supplies into Korea. By the time the bridge attacks started, more than two hundred thousand Chinese troops were already arrayed against the UN forces driving north. The attacks were launched too late to make any significant impact on the ground war even had the bridges been knocked out. Supplies continued to flow south across the bridges, and by the end of November, almost one hundred thousand additional troops had crossed the Yalu on the very bridges damaged by the raids.

Even nature mocked the bridge campaign. A few weeks after the first strike, the temperature dropped so low that almost all of the Yalu River froze over. American intelligence had learned from former Japanese officials that the ice on the Yalu was so thick during the winter that during World War II, temporary rail lines were laid across it. With or without the bridges, the Chinese would continue to get across the Yalu. The bridge missions had been a failure.

On November 19, Headquarters Seventh Fleet ordered the *Valley Forge* to return to the United States for rest and refit. Seven months after their peacetime cruise began, the men of Fighting 53 were finally going home. They were eager to get back. Many, including Darrow, had wives and children waiting for them in San Diego. Others were just burned out and needed a break. They had been flying combat missions almost constantly from July 3 until November 18, and their last missions had been among the most harrowing of the tour. Far from returning as conquering heroes, they were coming home from a war whose end no longer seemed at hand. Indeed, the outcome no longer appeared certain at all.

At the end of November, the Chinese struck X Corps and the Eighth Army with almost three hundred thousand men. Both UN formations disintegrated under the weight of the Chinese offensive, and thousands of American GIs died in the confused retreat or "bug-out" that ensued. So desperate was the situation that the *Valley Forge* received orders to return with all possible speed to the Sea of Japan and rejoin the fight. When this news reached the squadron, some of the pilots were quite dismayed—they had done their part and needed a break. In time, many of the men would go out on a second combat cruise, but that November of 1950, they had given everything they had to the war. To ask them to go back would have been too much. Fortunately for them, the *Valley Forge* returned briefly to San Diego, dropped off CAG-5, and picked up a new air group before heading back to Korea. The *Valley Forge* would stay in the fray, but a new contingent of pilots would carry the war to the communists.

From July 3 through November 18, 1950, VF-53 had flown 782 strike missions and 194 combat air patrols for a total of 3,292.7 combat hours. The squadron accomplished this with an average of fifteen available pilots and ninety-one enlisted ground crewmen. The pilots had fired 196,650 rounds of 20-mm ammunition, launched 2,430 HVAR rockets, and dropped 275 tons of napalm and iron bombs on communist targets from Pyongyang to Pusan. In the process, they had taken part in three of the war's most important events: the defense of the Pusan Perimeter, the Inchon landings, and the final drive to the Yalu River. They had destroyed 30 locomotives, helped to burn the Wonsan Oil Refinery Factory to the ground, blown up another 85 industrial targets, including factories and warehouses, destroyed 5 bridges and damaged 31 more. During the many armed reconnaissance missions, VF-53 had taken out 146 military vehicles, damaged another 91, and burned out 10 of the tough T-34 tanks deployed by the North Koreans in their armored regiments.

In many ways, their experiences mirrored those of the other Navy and Air Force squadrons deployed to Korea during those first hectic months of the crisis. They flew at a time when chaos reigned in the UN camp. Nothing came easy. Everything seemed both disorganized and ad hoc. More often than not, they went into combat with planes and equipment left over from World War II. In the process, they discovered that not only were their aging aircraft susceptible to ground fire but their weapons were not nearly as effective as they should have been. The old HVAR rockets, carried on so many missions, often lacked the accuracy needed to cause sufficient damage to the North Koreans.

Despite all these problems, morale had remained high until near the very end. Pittman's men simply did the best they could with what they had available. Until the Yalu bridge strikes, when they felt that Washington had chosen political expediency over their lives, they had gone into battle without complaint. This revelation left a bitterness that tainted their outlook of that first tour for the rest of their lives. Being let down by their leaders when they were putting their lives on the line in their country's name was almost too much to take. The unfairness and the display of disrespect constituted a travesty of the worst kind to these pilots.

Perhaps Ed Laney put it best. Almost a half century later, he said, "It is awful when politicians get involved in a war. If you're going to send us to fight a war, let us go win the war. Keep the politics and politicians out of it."

Almost five decades later, after two combat tours in Korea and four in Vietnam, Ed Laney, perhaps better than anyone, knows the wisdom of those words.

5 · Home by Christmas

Three hundred thousand strong, the Chinese came by night. Moving stealthily through the snow-covered countryside, they infiltrated UN units and struck simultaneously from three sides. Stunned and panicked, many UN units gave ground and stumbled into Chinese roadblocks as they retreated. Americans and South Koreans alike abandoned their heavy weapons when they realized that the Chinese had them surrounded. Thousands surrendered; others watched as their units were all but wiped out by repeated Chinese assaults. Across the peninsula, the UN Command was coming apart at the seams.

A few days earlier, on November 24, 1950, General MacArthur's "Home for Christmas" offensive had begun. The Chinese crushed it almost as soon as it began, striking the right flank of the Eighth Army and driving a wedge between General Walker's Eighth Army and General Almond's X Corps to the northeast.

The Chinese savaged the ROK corps holding the Eighth Army's flank and, in the process, exposed the U.S. 2d Infantry Division's right wing to attack. Under fierce Communist attack itself, the division suffered appalling losses as Headquarters Eighth Army rounded up every available unit to come to its rescue.

By November 28, it was clear that if the 2d Infantry Division did not move south soon, it would be destroyed in place. Because of the collapse of the units on its right flank, only one retreat avenue remained. This was a frozen dirt road that wound from Kujang-dong south to Kunu-Ri, then finally to Sunchon. To reach Kujang-dong, the 2d Division withdrew southwest along the Chongchon River valley, fighting off repeated Chinese attacks as it moved. Meanwhile, to the south at Kunu-ri, the Turkish Brigade struck out eastward in an attempt to restore the Eighth Army's decimated right wing and thus secure the road to Kunu-ri so that the Americans could get out of the Chongchon valley.

After an eight-mile advance, the Turks smashed into a massive Chinese force. Flowing around the flanks, the Chinese soon surrounded the Turks, who formed a perimeter defense and desperately resisted.

On November 28, Headquarters Eighth Army ordered a general retreat, which all units except the Turkish Brigade and the 2d Division were able to execute. The Army's reserve, the 1st Cavalry Division, was thrown into blocking positions northeast of Sunchon to augment the right wing

At all costs, the Turks and the 2d Infantry Division had to reach Sunchon. If they couldn't, they'd be destroyed.

On November 29, as the Turks were breaking out from their encirclement to the east of Kunu-ri, the 2d Division discovered a Chinese roadblock ten miles to the rear along its only escape route to Kunu-ri. A reconnaissance company was sent out to clear the roadblock but took heavy casualties and was stopped cold. Next, the 9th Infantry Regiment, down to less than an eighth of its authorized strength, tried to clear the Chinese position. With four hundred exhausted men, it futilely battered at the communists. In reality, two regiments of the Chinese 113th Division had taken up ambush positions along the seven-mile stretch of road. As the day wore on, it became obvious that only a full-division assault could clear the road. The 2d Division moved out along the road to Kunu-ri and left behind the 23d Infantry Regiment to act as rear guard.

What followed became one of the worst disasters in the history of the U.S. Army.

The division blundered southward, straight into a massive, seven-mile-long ambush set up by the Chinese 113th Division. Strung out along the road, its vehicles pressed almost bumper to bumper, the division lay horribly exposed to the small-arms and mortar fire the Chinese could bring to bear from both flanks. It looked just like a massive stateside traffic jam—with machine guns stitching through the trapped vehicles. As one historian wrote, the road became an "avenue of death and mayhem."[1]

Every time a truck or Jeep took fire, the men inside bailed out for the nearest cover, which forced every vehicle behind it to come to a grinding halt. Dead Americans littered the road. The living were too busy with sheer survival to worry about the corpses of their comrades.

To the north, the division's engineer battalion held two critical hills against repeated Chinese assaults. When night fell, the Chinese swarmed over both positions. On the northernmost hill, the engineers fought an epic last stand. All of them were either killed or captured. A few men from the second hill managed to struggle south to rejoin the column.

Along the road itself, the Chinese launched small-unit assaults against the column. Throughout the hours of darkness, the fighting raged around burning trucks, Jeeps, and artillery pieces. It was a nightmare of bayonet thrusts and rifles swung as clubs, the two sides interlocked, the brutal fighting silhouetted by the hellish light of burning vehicles.

Along that seven-mile stretch of road, forever after known as "The Gauntlet" to the men who fought their way south on it, at least four hundred UN soldiers died in action. By the time the division's forward units stumbled into Sunchon on December 1, almost five thousand men had been lost since the Chinese attack began on November 25. With one-third of its men lost and most of its heavy equipment smoldering in the snow along the escape route, the 2d Infantry Division was finished for the time being as a fighting force. The Eighth Army pulled it back to Seoul, far out of the battle.

During the entire ordeal, UN fighter-bombers provided the only relief. Air Force Mustangs and Shooting Stars scoured the terrain on the column's flanks, blasting any Chinese positions they could find. The Chinese quickly learned to stop firing their weapons the moment an aircraft began to dive on a strafing run. As soon as the plane pulled its nose up and began climbing for altitude, they opened fire again, which made it quite difficult for the pilots to pinpoint and destroy their targets.

Every FEAF plane that could support the beleaguered GIs flew during those frantic days following the Chinese attack, but this maximum effort was not enough. As it had in August, FEAF again turned to Task Force 77 for help.

At first, the Navy did not have much to offer. The *Valley Forge* had just gone home. This left only two fleet carriers, the *Leyte* and the *Philippine Sea*, off North Korea to conduct flight operations. They would have to shoulder the load in the midst of the worst crisis of the Korean War. Help would arrive soon, but in those first days of the Chinese attack, only a few squadrons were available for action.

Worse, the weather turned foul just as the ground troops most needed the dark blue planes. Out in the Sea of Japan, gale-force winds and blinding snow squalls buffeted the carriers and covered their decks with ice and snow. The carrier crews did their best to keep the decks clear and even went so far as to melt sections of ice with jet-engine exhaust, but no amount of dedication could get the planes airborne on November 25. The next day, as disaster unfolded on the right wing of the Eighth Army's lines, the Navy's planes still could not fly. Finally, despite huge swells and frequent snow storms, the planes struggled aloft on November 27 and swept the battlefields in search of Chinese targets.

As the 2d Division limped southward, the Navy's planes provided what support they were able to give. It proved to be little enough, indeed. The Mosquitoes had been withdrawn from the area, which left no airborne controllers to direct the Corsairs and Skyraiders to suitable targets. On the ground, the steady destruction of the 2d Division had caused the loss of nearly all its communication gear, as well as the deaths of many of the FAC teams. With the turmoil on the ground, the fighter-bombers tried their best to deliver their ordnance on whatever targets they found.

To help remedy the situation, the Navy started deploying its squadrons into the Kunu-ri area on armed reconnaissance missions. In the mission briefing, the pilots were each given a specific map area to patrol for enemy targets. If a controller was on the communications net, however, the planes would be diverted from their assigned areas to wherever the FACs needed them. These missions were long and dangerous. Flying nearly the width of Korea, most of which was now under hostile control, was taxing in the extreme.

Supporting the Eighth Army and its retreat soon became almost an impossible chore for the two air groups as the situation with the Marines and X Corps to the east suddenly deteriorated at the end of the month. By December 2, the day after the 2d Infantry Division reached safety, *Philippine Sea* and *Leyte*'s tired pilots were flying only in support of the UN troops trapped around the Chosin Reservoir.

While the Chinese were surrounding and chopping up the 2d Infantry Division, X Corps ordered the 1st Marine Division to strike out northwestward and cut off the communists from their supply lines. On November 27, the 5th and 7th Marines jumped off from Yudam-ni on the western shore of the Chosin Reservoir. That night, the Chinese counterattacked with no fewer than 120,000 troops of the Ninth Army Group.

The next morning, X Corps's situation seemed tenuous at best. Somehow, the Chinese had managed to infiltrate around the Marines at Yudam-ni and establish a roadblock along the only route to Hagaru-ri, the Marine supply and evacuation center. To the east, the three battalions of the U.S. Army's 7th Infantry Division on the other side of the reservoir discovered at dawn that the Chinese had completely encircled them. Also, far to the south near Koto-ri, Marine Corsair pilots reported sighting Chinese troops.

At Hagaru-ri, quick preparations were made for an all-round defense. It was a wise move. On the night of November 28, the Chinese attacked Hagaru-ri from the south and nearly penetrated the Marine positions. Fortunately, the Chinese were unable to exploit the gains they made, which allowed the Marines to clear their perimeter and thrust reinforcements into the gaps rent open by the attack.

To the south, Task Force Drysdale set out on November 29 from Koto-ri to reinforce Hagaru-ri along the only road connecting the two North Korean towns. Composed of U.S. and British Marines, plus a smattering of U.S. Army troops, Task Force Drysdale stumbled into a catastrophe.

Just north of Koto-ri the road passed through a narrow valley, later renamed "Hellfire Valley" by the UN troops who fought there. When Task Force Drysdale reached the valley the Chinese executed a perfect ambush. From all sides, they struck the convoy with machine-gun and rifle fire. As bullets rained down on them, the 921 UN troops in the column dove for cover. Somewhere in the middle of the strung-out convoy, a truck took a direct hit and caught fire. Every attempt to push the truck off the road was met by withering small-arms fire. Unable to get the truck off the road, the remaining vehicles behind it could not move forward.

At the head of the column, nobody had seen the truck get hit. Despite the Chinese fire, the vehicles in front of the burning truck moved forward and were soon free of the ambush site. In doing so, they abandoned the rear half of the column to a terrible fate.

The Marine and Navy fighter-bombers did what they could for the beleaguered men clustered below. They stayed overhead and executed precise rocket runs on the hills overlooking the road. While they remained overhead, the volume of Chinese fire pouring down on the UN troops declined. As night fell, however, the planes were forced to return to their bases, and the trapped elements of Task Force Drysdale were left to fend for themselves.

During the day, the rear part of the column had tried to turn for Koto-ri, but the Chinese hit several more vehicles and completely trapped the UN troops in place. The men took cover in the drainage ditches alongside the road and beside a narrow-gauge railroad embankment, but their efforts did little good. The Chinese held the high ground and could hit almost everything on either side of the road. Whenever the Navy and Marine aircraft left the area, no matter for how short a time, the Chinese blasted away with mortars, machine guns, and rifles. The exposed UN troops suffered terribly. More trucks, some of them loaded with the wounded, were hit and caught fire, which broke the column into four smaller groups.

When night came, the Chinese struck. After midnight, they swarmed out of the hills and onto the road. Hand-to-hand fighting raged throughout the column until, finally, the few UN survivors either surrendered or escaped southward to Koto-ri.

Of the 921 men who set out to reinforce Hagaru-ri, 321 were killed, captured, or wounded. Only about 300 made it to their destination. Seventy-five vehicles were also lost. Without the aid of the Navy and Marine "Airedales," as the aviators were called by the ground troops, the losses would have been much worse.

As the Chinese attack developed during the last days of November, X Corps's situation grew increasingly desperate. East of the reservoir, the 7th Infantry Division's trapped battalions attempted to break out of the Chinese vise and head toward Hagaru-ri. They ran into ferocious opposition, and many GIs were trapped on the road and shot to pieces. Still, the men fought their way south, as they pushed slowly through the opposition with the help of the ubiquitous blue Corsairs and Skyraiders.

On the way to Hagaru-ri, an Airedale's mistake caused discipline to collapse. While engaging some Chinese in front of the column, the GIs were blasted by an unidentified friendly aircraft. Napalm burst among the vehicles and men. Several men were killed and many others burned. Morale disintegrated at the sight of the carnage inflicted by a friendly aircraft, and the column gradually dissolved into a series of small groups, each doing their best to push on to Hagaru-ri. Wounded and dead men littered the scene. Those who could still walk tried their best to escape. In the end, most of those who made it to Hagaru-ri did so by moving off the road and crossing the ice of the frozen Chosin Reservoir. Of the 3,200 men who began the breakout southward, only 385 reached Hagaru-ri.

For the Marines at Yudam-ni, the debacle to their rear meant they were cut off and trapped fourteen miles from the nearest UN units. Their only chance was to fight through the roadblock to their south and push on to Hagaru-ri. From there, they could begin the long trek to the coast.

On November 30, the Marines began their withdrawal and took their dead and wounded with them. Unlike most UN units in the previous retreats, the Marines remained both well organized and highly disciplined. That paid dividends, for they reached Hagaru-ri largely intact on December 4. Although they had reached temporary safety, the worst part of their journey lay ahead.

On the day that the Marines reached Hagaru-ri, one of the most dramatic and heroic episodes of the air war took place amid this backdrop of catastrophe and retreat. Though practically forgotten now, the incident was perhaps the single greatest display of loyalty seen in the Korean air war.

6 · The Finest Kind of Honor

Lieutenant (j.g.) Tom Hudner stood on the flight deck of the USS *Leyte* and watched as the admiral boarded a helicopter that would transfer him to the USS *Midway* a few thousand yards away. The date was August 8, 1950, and Tom Hudner knew that something serious was happening. The commander of the Mediterranean fleet did not shift his flag on a whim. They soon discovered the cause for the shift: The *Leyte* had been ordered to Korea. They were going to war.

The news came as a surprise to Tom's squadron, VF-32, and to the rest of CAG-3 as well. Tom and his squadron mates had followed the news flowing out of Korea since June, but they never thought to be part of those headlines. Fighting 32 was an East Coast squadron attached to the Atlantic Fleet. That summer, it had deployed on board the *Leyte*, which joined the Mediterranean Fleet—about as far from Korea as a naval officer could get.

As the carrier steamed quickly to Newport News, Virginia, the shock of the forthcoming deployment began to wear off. Fighting 32 began to prepare for battle. Briefings were held on everything from Korea's political structures and history to the types of weapons and aircraft that they were likely to face.

Meanwhile, the squadron's mechanics and ground crew were modifying their Vought F4U-4B Corsairs by adding extra slabs of armor plating under the pilot's seat of each plane. Although the armor weighted down the Corsairs, the added protection from small-arms fire was greatly appreciated by every pilot in the squadron.

Toward the end of June, the *Leyte* reached Newport News and underwent a rapid outfitting for a war cruise. While the ship spent ten days in port, the men of VF-32 were granted a short liberty in order to say good-bye to their families.

Tom went home to Fall River, Massachusetts, to spend time with his parents. His father owned a local chain of markets in the Fall River area, a business started by his Irish-born grandfather who sold groceries out of a horse cart. Hard work and careful planning allowed the business to grow, and now the Hudner family enjoyed a comfortable existence that had allowed them to send its sons to the best private schools that New England had to offer.

Indeed, Tom Hudner benefited greatly from his early schooling. Born in 1924, he had enrolled at Phillips Academy at Andover, where he became acquainted with George Bush, future Navy torpedo bomber pilot and President of the United States. Toward the end of his academic career at Andover, Tom decided to apply for an appointment to the Naval Academy at Annapolis. Ever since he was a kid watching battleships and cruisers come and go out of Newport, Rhode Island (not far from his family's home in Fall River), he had wanted to join the Navy.

Upon graduation from Phillip's Academy in 1943, Tom received his appointment to Annapolis. During the next three years, he thrived at Annapolis and played football as a 145-pound halfback with future admiral and vice presidential candidate, James Stockdale. While there, he also met another future president, Jimmy Carter.

Graduation came a year early, in June 1946, as his class had its studies accelerated due to the war. Fresh out of the Academy, Tom joined the crew of the heavy cruiser USS *Helena* as a signal officer. For the next six months, he served on board the *Helena* as it patrolled the Yangtze River during the climax of the Chinese civil war. The ship's crew had several brushes with danger, including one incident during which Chinese communist riflemen sniped at the ship while it was anchored off Sing Tao.

In February 1947, Tom left the ship for shore duty at Pearl Harbor, but his desk job quickly bored and frustrated him. He recalled, "I was very dissatisfied because I wanted to have a Navy career rather than a clerk's career in a Navy uniform."

Finally, to escape the drudgery of his desk assignment, Tom's friends convinced him to apply for flight training. Although he had no special interest in flight, his friends proved so persuasive that he broke down and decided to apply. As he said later, "I wasn't going to be the guy who stood in the back saying, 'You guys go flying, I want to be on a destroyer.' So, I put my chit in for flight training. They almost shamed me into it."

In 1948, the Navy accepted Tom's application and he headed back to the States for flight training. He emerged from Pensacola, Florida the following summer with his wings of gold. Initially, the Navy assigned Tom to an attack squadron in Rhode Island. After he was there for only a few weeks, with his first outfit, however, the squadron was decommissioned and its pilots transferred to other duties.

National Archives
Jesse Brown, the U.S. Navy's first African-American aviator.

During the decommissioning process, two staff officers came down to write transfer orders for the squadron's pilots. While talking to them about his options, Tom recalled that one of the officers said, "Well, we have a slot for you in VF-32. What do you think about that?"

Nonplussed by the question and unsure of what the big deal was about that unit, Tom replied, "VF-32? What's that?"

Somebody else nearby overhead the conversation and asked, "Say, isn't that the squadron Jesse Brown's in?"

Tom had never heard of Jesse Brown, so the significance was lost on him. In a 1997 interview, he remembered, "Well, the name didn't mean anything to me at all."

A few days later, once his transfer to VF-32 had been arranged, Tom met Jesse for the first time and learned why the squadron was unique. During his first day with the squadron, he was taken on a tour of its facilities and told what the squadron expected of him. After completing this brief orientation and welcoming, Tom retired to the outfit's locker room when "in came Jesse."

Jesse was the first African-American naval aviator in American history. He had earned his wings at Pensacola a year ahead of Tom through a short-lived program called the Flying Midshipmen. In 1949, when Tom and Jesse first met, Jesse was the only African-American pilot who had graduated from flight training at Pensacola, which made him not only the first but the only black pilot on active duty. In fact, Jesse had started his training at a time when the other services were strictly segregated. Only months later did President Harry Truman issue his famous executive order integrating the military.

Becoming a pilot had been no easy task for Jesse. Born in Mississippi at the height of the Jim Crow era, he had been subjected to the cruelest humiliation imaginable. When he joined the Navy, that service's handbook for officers' wives (published in 1941) noted that African-American women made adequate maids, but they were prone to theft because they had to support "their usually lazy husbands and numerous off-spring."[1]

Though neither Jesse nor Tom knew it at the time, that day in VF-32's locker room set in motion a series of events that would inextricably link their lives together. At the time, however, Jesse stepped forward to introduce himself and cautiously offered his hand to Tom, who shook it in return.

Usually, as Tom later discovered, Jesse was not so quick to make an introduction. He had been snubbed so many times in the past that he was usually hesitant to offer his hand to a white stranger. Too often, he had stood before someone with his hand extended and a white person had refused to shake it. Perhaps Jesse sensed something out of the ordinary in Tom that prompted him to take a chance. They shook hands respectfully, and so began a special and unique relationship.

Although Tom was a lieutenant (j.g.) and Jesse was an ensign, the squadron had a policy of favoring experience over rank when flying. This was not uncommon in the Navy at that time because many units had adopted the policy during World War II. Jesse had considerably more flight time and experience than Tom. As a result, he became Tom's section leader. For the next year, as Tom flew on Jesse's wing, he learned not only how Jesse behaved in the air but who he was on the ground.

Tom discovered that Jesse was both modest and cautious. He had developed a strong sense of determination that saw him through the worst moments during his Pensacola training. He had real grit, but in a reserved and understated way. As Tom later put it, "Jesse was a very low-key guy."

Although they flew together for a year before the Korean War started, the two pilots did not spend a great amount of time together during their off-duty hours. Tom was single and spent his time with the squadron's other bachelors. Jesse had a wife, Daisy, and a baby girl, and he spent his off-duty time with them instead of with the rest of the outfit.

Yet, as they continued to fly together, Jesse and Tom developed a strong sense of mutual respect and rapport. Together, they would go into battle as a team—perhaps the most unusual one in the Navy at that time.

–◆◆◆–

The *Leyte* joined Task Force 77 just in time to support the drive on Pyongyang in mid-October. Beginning on October 8, 1950, Tom and Jesse flew many CASs and armed reconnaissance flights together. In early November, both men took part in the Yalu bridge strikes, always as a team with Tom protecting Jesse's tail.

When the Chinese unleashed their offensive at the end of November, VF-32 and the *Leyte*'s other squadrons flew constantly in support of the beleaguered UN troops. In early December, the flying pace increased as both the *Philippine Sea* and the *Leyte* threw their air groups into the battles around the Chosin Reservoir.

On December 4, 1950, Jesse and Tom were on a standard armed reconnaissance mission just north of the Chosin Reservoir. Here, on a frozen mountainside deep in enemy territory, the defining moment in their lives would be played out.

It was the cruelest kind of fluke. Somewhere on the frozen, snow-covered ground below, a Chinese soldier lay on his back, his white quilted uniform making him virtually invisible from the air. As the four Corsairs passed overhead with the throaty roars of their Pratt & Whitney engines echoing off the winter landscape, the soldier raised his rifle and pulled the trigger. His comrades did the same, throwing up a hail of bullets around the four blue planes.

What are the chances a rifleman could hit such a speeding target? And even if the tiny, 30-caliber bullet did connect with a Corsair, what damage could it possibly do? The F4U-4B was not only heavily armed but well armored to protect both pilot and plane from ground fire.

Yet that one round hit home, probably striking the Corsair's Achilles heel, the oil cooler.

There were eight Corsairs up that day from VF-32, divided into two divisions of four each. The divisions had fanned out from each other so that they could collectively cover more ground. Flying an armed reconnaissance mission north of the Chosin Reservoir, they were down low, around 1,000 feet off the snow-blanketed landscape, looking for any worthwhile targets. To the south, the final elements of the 5th and 7th Marines were staggering into Hagaru-ri, where they would begin the long march to the coast in two days.

"I think I've been hit," Jesse called over the radio, "I've lost oil pressure, and I can't maintain my altitude."

A quarter of a mile away, Tom had been flying in loose formation on Jesse's Corsair when he heard his Mayday. He glanced at Jesse's plane and saw that the F4U was already losing altitude.

Jesse Brown was in real trouble. His engine's temperature gauge soared into the red as his big Pratt & Whitney, starved of oil, quickly began burning itself up. Less than three minutes after he had been hit, his engine seized and he lost power so fast that he had no chance to make a run for the coast. Altitude, his lifeblood, bled away and left him no choice but to put his crippled bird on the ground. He was too low to bail out.

Tom and the rest of the division searched for a patch of level ground where Jesse could crash-land his Corsair. Below them, they saw only row after row of sawtooth, jagged mountains covered with thick forests—the worst possible terrain considering Jesse's situation. Still they kept searching until Jesse himself spotted a tiny, sloped clearing surrounded by trees just within his reach. He pointed his crippled Corsair toward the clearing and prepared for the crash. Above him, Tom recited the checklist for emergency landings—going through it step by step while Jesse completed each step.

Canopy open, tailhook down, Jesse's Corsair belly flopped into the snow, smashing into the ground with so much force that the fuselage bent 30 degrees at the cockpit. It skidded along the rocky ground, finally coming to rest a few hundred feet from the initial point of impact. Tom missed the actual landing, but as he swung around over the field, he could see the wreckage lying twisted and bent, partially covered with snow. He circled again and noticed that Jesse's canopy was now closed. It must have slammed shut on impact.

The radio filled with chatter. Most everyone who had seen the crash figured that Jesse couldn't possibly be alive. Most likely, the force of impact had killed him. They continued to circle, though, and prayed that their friend would show signs of life.

Tom came around in his circuit again, his eyes focused on the scene below. Then, surprising everyone overhead, Jesse cranked open his canopy and began to wave both arms to show his buddies that he was still alive.

But he hadn't climbed out of the cockpit.

That's when a thin tendril of grayish smoke started to coil up from under the cowling. Jesse's Corsair was on fire. Still, he didn't move from the cockpit.

He was trapped.

Though Dick Cevoli, the division leader, had called in a Mayday, the rescue helicopter, based at Hagaru-ri, was at least twenty minutes out. With a fire apparently brewing in the bowels of the engine, Jesse might burn alive before help could reach him.

Tom would not let that happen to his friend. He keyed his mike and announced, "OK, I'm going down after him."

The channel remained silent after Tom's transmission. Surprisingly, Cevoli did not try to stop him. Instead, all eyes focused on Tom as he headed down. He scouted the field on his first pass to judge how best to make a forced landing. When he came around again, he made a classic flaps-and-hook-down carrier approach—but with his gear up. Seconds passed, the field loomed large and then whoomp! The Corsair mushed into the thin covering of snow that hid the uneven ground. It struck with such bruising force that Tom would have terrible back pains for years to come.

After his Corsair slid to a halt, Tom unstrapped himself and ran the hundred yards or so to Jesse's plane. Along the way, he noticed a single set of footprints in the twelve-inch-deep snow. In the distance, a scattering of peasant shacks sat squat and dark against the winter landscape. Down in hostile territory, they were not alone.

Undeterred, Tom reached Jesse's Corsair, where he found his friend in bad shape. After the crash, Jesse had taken his helmet off, letting it drop inside the cockpit. He had tried to unstrap himself, but his gloves kept interfering. So, despite the near 0° temperature, he had taken off his gloves and fumbled at the straps. As he did, his gloves fell to the cockpit floor, out of reach and out of sight to Jesse, who was weak from his injuries. His fingers were already frostbitten.

Tom reached out to his friend, wrapping a scarf around his damaged hands. Jesse looked at him and said in a voice so calm and soothing that Tom would never forget it, "I can't get out, Tom. I'm caught."

From the wing, Tom leaned into the cockpit to see where Jesse was stuck. Because the fuselage had bent during the crash, he could see Jesse's knee crushed between part of the instrument panel and the side of the cockpit. As Tom studied the situation, he realized that he had no chance of pulling his friend from the wreckage by himself. He would need both equipment and help.

Realizing Jesse was also in danger from the biting cold, Tom pulled a sailor's wool watch cap from his jacket and brought it down snugly on Jesse's bare head. That done, he raced back to his own Corsair. Despite the jarring crash landing, his radio still worked. He called up to Dick Cevoli and asked that the helicopter crew bring a fire extinguisher and an ax to the scene.

Somewhere to the south, the helicopter crew received the news that now two pilots were down. The copter, a Sikorsky HO3S-1 from Marine VMO-6, turned back toward its base. Charlie Ward, the pilot, dropped off his crewman before heading to the crash site, knowing that his small helicopter would be hard pressed to carry out two downed pilots at such a high altitude. After a twenty-minute delay, the helicopter was en route again.

Back on the mountain north of Chosin, Tom returned to Jesse's Corsair. Jesse talked sparingly, but when he did, his voice remained even and unexcited. It could have been shock or the freezing cold's effect on him, but Tom believes it was due to his incredible self-control. Whatever the reason, Jesse's bearing helped Tom to remain calm.

Meanwhile, smoke continued to drift from beneath the cowling. Tom looked for its source but failed to find it. He tried shoveling handfuls of snow inside the cowling, hoping that might do some good. It didn't, but the smoke did not grow any more intense.

Jesse sat in the cockpit, his eyes closed. He was probably fading in and out of consciousness. Tom couldn't see any physical wounds on Jesse, but with all

A Sikorsky HO3S-1 from HU-1, stationed aboard the USS *Bataan*.

the layers of clothing they wore in combat, it was almost impossible to tell how seriously he had been hurt. Besides, the lower half of his legs could not be seen, let alone attended to if they were injured. Undoubtedly they were, given where the fuselage had bent.

In the distance, a clattering sound heralded the arrival of Charlie Ward's helicopter. It passed over the two downed Corsairs and swung back again. Tom stepped away from Jesse's plane and popped a smoke canister to help the pilot gauge wind direction.

Ward sat the chopper down and jumped from the pilot's seat, carrying an ax in one hand and a small fire extinguisher in the other. As he started toward the two pilots, a shock of recognition overcame him. Here were Jesse Brown and Tom Hudner, two of the pilots he had come to know on board the *Leyte* during the voyage to Korea. He hurried over to them, the frigid air already numbing his exposed face.

Together, he and Hudner set to work on the Corsair. Tom grabbed the fire extinguisher and shoved the nozzle into the engine cowling. The small bottle was used up in seconds with no visible effect on the smoke. Abandoning that, he and Charlie took turns swinging the ax against the fuselage, just under the cockpit.

The ax didn't even make a dent.

They kept trying, but the wing was so slippery now that the soles of their boots were caked with snow and ice and they could hardly keep their footing. Again, they tried to pull Jesse from the cockpit, but his trapped frame refused to budge. Jesse sat stoically through every attempt, possibly lapsing into unconsciousness every few minutes. He was so quiet and so calm that Tom couldn't tell for sure if he had passed out or not.

At one point, while they continued working on him, Jesse looked over at Tom. Knowing the score, he said to his friend, "Tom, in case I don't make it back, tell Daisy I love her."

Tom wasn't ready to give up. He hoisted himself up onto the top of the fuselage and straddled the cockpit, putting his feet in the canopy rails. He stood above Jesse and tried to pull him up and out of the cockpit. No luck. Jesse was hopelessly trapped.

Dusk was fast approaching. Charlie Ward looked around at the descending grayish twilight with trepidation. He called Tom over to a spot a few yards from the Corsair and related his fears. His helicopter had no night-flying instruments. Without those, even under the best conditions, Charlie would have trouble flying after dusk. But here, among the towering mountains of North Korea, flying that chopper at night would be near suicide.

They would have to leave Jesse behind.

Tom considered the situation and realized that he had no choice. No more help was available from any nearby UN base. Even if there had been, there just wasn't the daylight left to get it to Jesse. They couldn't stay the night with Jesse. With the temperature dropping to 35° below zero at night in the area, they would all freeze to death if they tried, since the helicopter carried no extra clothing or bedding for them to use to stay warm.

Tom knew what he had to do, but that didn't make it any easier. He would not just run out on Jesse without saying something. So, he trudged through the snow back to the Corsair, and climbed carefully onto the wing. "Jesse," he began quietly. His friend's expression remained blank, his eyes closed. Tom was not sure if he was still alive.

"Jesse, we can't get you out. We've tried everything. We're going to go and get help, so just hang in there and we'll be back."

Tom couldn't tell if Jesse comprehended or even heard what he said. Reluctantly, he eased off the wing and joined Charlie at the helicopter. Together, they climbed on board the Sikorsky and left behind one of aviation's true pioneers.

After spending the night at Hagaru-ri, Tom Hudner returned to his carrier the following day. When he arrived, the ship's skipper, Captain Thomas V. Sisson, called him to the bridge for a full report. A compassionate man, Sisson listened intently as his young lieutenant related the events of the previous day. Tom discovered that the captain was sympathetic, and he has highly regarded Sisson since that short talk.

When he finished describing what had happened on that frozen patch of ground, Sisson said that he wanted to send a helicopter back to retrieve Jesse's body.

"Captain, that's not the Jesse we knew. The Jesse we knew is gone," Tom protested. He knew how dangerous it would be to send another rescue crew out there. With the possibility of enemy troops in the area, the ruggedness of the terrain, and the altitude of the crash site in the mountains, the recovery of Jesse's body was not worth the risk. After hearing Tom out, Sisson agreed.

In such situations, it had become common practice to destroy any downed aircraft, if at all possible, in order to prevent the North Koreans from gleaning any useful intelligence from the wreckage. Later that day, the *Leyte* launched a division of Corsairs that returned to the crash site and incinerated Jesse's body and his Corsair with napalm.

Tom later wrote, "It was a funeral pyre for a beloved warrior."[2]

On Friday, April 13, 1951, Tom Hudner's family gathered at the White House Rose Garden to watch as President Truman awarded Tom the Medal of Honor, America's highest award for bravery. For Tom, as he stood before the audience, it was a bittersweet moment. He was proud of his actions and proud to receive so rare an award. Yet, as he stood to receive the medal, he could see Daisy Brown stoically watching the proceedings. It was a day of celebration for the Hudner family, but Daisy was there under trying circumstances—the death of her beloved husband.

Jesse Brown had served honorably and died honorably. In the course of his short life, he helped to change the Navy's treatment of African-Americans. Single-handedly, he had broken the color barrier at a time when America had yet to accept all of its sons and daughters as equals.

In 1973, the Navy commissioned a frigate bearing Jesse's name. Although it was recently sold to the Egyptian navy, Jesse's memory lives on. Each year on Memorial Day, he is honored in his hometown of Hattiesburg, Mississippi.

Behind Jesse's legacy stands the man who tried to save his life. All but forgotten now, Tom Hudner showed such fierce loyalty to a friend and comrade that he risked his life in the attempt to rescue him. His loyalty transcended color, and that, perhaps, is the greatest legacy of all.

Part 2 | From Strangle to Stalemate

7 : Carlson's Tigers

Lieutenant Commander Harold ("Swede") Carlson, skipper of Attack Squadron 195 (VA-195), gazed at the scene unfolding below and realized he was in a very different war from his last one. Beyond the wing of his Douglas AD-4 Skyraider, he could see the frantic evacuation efforts under way at Hagaru-ri's tiny landing strip. Here and there, a C-47 sat near the runway, its cargo area being loaded with stretchers of wounded Marines and GIs. Although the strip was narrow, uneven, and way too short for regulations, the pilots of FEAF's Combat Cargo Command were throwing caution to the wind in an effort to get the wounded out of Hagaru-ri. The operation was frenzied, but it was proving to be effective. Since December 1, not a single man had been lost in the course of the air evacuation.

Carlson, a 1940 Naval Academy graduate, had seen much combat in the course of his ten-year naval career, but he had never seen anything like this. His first combat cruise back in 1942 had been on board the light cruiser USS *Nashville*. He took part in America's first offensive in the Pacific—the Doolittle raid on Japan. Later, in 1944 and 1945, he served as a torpedo bomber pilot with VT-20 and VC-11.

Swede Carlson, like many of his brethren, had never seen defeat. He had always been on the offensive, from the raid on Tokyo in 1942 through the Battles of the Philippine Sea and Leyte Gulf. But here below him on that day in December 1950, he came face to face with the realities of military disaster.

Not that the Marines had come apart like the Second Infantry Division had a few days before at Kunu-ri. Indeed, the Marines were still full of fight, well disciplined, and exceptionally well organized. But, mixed in with their numbers were the broken survivors of Task Force Drysdale, the three shattered battalions of the 7th Infantry Division, and a smattering of ROK troops caught in the midst of the Chinese offensive.

U.S. Navy AD-4 Skyraiders

Now, with only the small airstrip as its tie to the outside world, Hagaru-ri was a UN island surrounded by an ocean of Chinese troops. Worse, it was an island running out of supplies. Although the C-47s were bringing in about a hundred tons of cargo a day, that figure could not support even a regimental combat team in the field for a day, let alone twenty-five thousand cold and hungry men.

Time was of the essence. The longer the Marines waited to make their run to safety, the less chance they would have of breaking through the cordon of communist troops blocking their path. Hungnam was the Marines' ultimate objective. To get there, they would jump south first to Koto-ri, then to Chin-hung, and finally to the coast and Hungnam's critical harbor. The first step was to get everyone from Hagaru-ri to Koto-ri. That operation would begin on December 6.

Carlson and his fresh squadron realized this at once and knew they had to do everything possible to help the Marines get to the coast. For the next week, they would be occupied with nothing else save the protection of the road-bound convoys pushing south against intense Chinese opposition.

In the midst of disaster, with the threat of an even greater calamity on the horizon, VA-195 endured its baptism by fire. Not only would they emerge from the ordeal as blooded veterans, the pilots of VA-195 would use their hard-won lessons to strike two major blows against the communist cause in Korea before their tour ended in May 1951.

Lieutenant Don van Slooten learned one of those valuable lessons two days after the Marines began their breakout to the coast. Fortunately, the lesson resulted from an accident of fate that allows pilots to learn from their mistakes rather than to die from them.

Don was up that day, along with the rest of VA-195, providing close air support to the UN columns streaming southward. A FAC team gave him a target over the radio, and he dove his AD right down among the treetops during his attack. He dropped his bombs, which had VT proximity fuses, and tried to pull up. As it turned out, he released his load while too low. Before he could get away, his bombs exploded. The blast caught the fleeing Skyraider and tossed it wildly about.

Getting the AD under control, Don realized his plane had been badly damaged. Indeed, he later discovered that the underside was torn and punctured by debris and shrapnel. He barely made it to Yongpo, a friendly airstrip near the coast, where he managed to make an emergency landing. Don spent the night at Yongpo then was picked up and returned to the carrier USS *Princeton* by Swede Carlson. A few days later, his crippled Skyraider was blown up by retreating UN troops so that it would not fall into Chinese or North Korean hands.

It had been a close call, but the lesson sank in. In the future, VA-195's pilots would be very careful not to get too low during low-level bombing and rocket runs. Getting caught in his own bomb blast was not a mistake anyone else wanted to make.

As December wore on, the pilots of VA-195 came to put complete faith in their AD-4 Skyraiders' ability to bring them safely home. Time and again, Skyraiders returned to their carriers looking more like flying sieves than airplanes. They came home with pieces of their tails and rudders blown off by flak hits, portions of their wings shot away by cannon fire, and great gashes—sometimes two to three feet across—torn into their fuselages. No more rugged piston-engined aircraft prowled the skies over Korea during the war.

Designed in 1944, the first Skyraider took flight on March 18, 1945. Initially designated the XBT2D-1, the new aircraft could carry 4,000 pounds of bombs, climb at 3,680 feet per minute (faster than a P-38 or P-51), and achieve 375 mph in level flight. The first production model, redesignated the AD-1, reached fleet squadrons in late 1946.

The AD-4, first produced in 1949, became the standard ground-attack version and the most produced variant of the Skyraider. Equipped with an enormous Wright R-3350 18-cylinder radial engine, the AD-4 could haul aloft 8,000 pounds of bombs, torpedoes, and rockets. With its impressive payload, it became the king of close air support missions during the Korean War. No other CAS-capable aircraft could even come close to carrying what the AD-4 could carry. Weighing in at 24,221 pounds fully loaded, the AD-4 was 7,000 pounds heavier than the initial prototype. As a result, the AD-4's climb rate dropped to 2,800 feet per minute and its top speed fell to 320 mph. Despite the drop in performance, the AD-4 stayed in service for years and was adapted to fill multiple roles, including those of an airborne early-warning aircraft (AD-4W) and a night-attack bomber (AD-4N). A total of 1,051 AD-4s were built. The later versions of the Skyraider remained in production until 1957. So versatile was the Skyraider that it saw service a decade later in Vietnam.

-◆◆◆-

The Marines left Hagaru-ri only after all the wounded had been evacuated by the C-47s of FEAF's Combat Cargo Command. Between December 1 and December 6, they had successfully evacuated 4,312 men under an umbrella of constant air attacks launched from Task Force 77's aircraft carriers and from the Marine squadrons operating from escort carriers offshore and landing strips to the south.

On the morning of December 6, the Marines began the breakout south. Their first job was to clear Hellfire Valley and reach Marine Colonel Lewis B. ("Chesty") Puller's defensive perimeter around Koto-ri.

The 7th Marines led the way, their flanks secured by dozens of Navy and Marine aircraft. FAC teams, scattered throughout the columns, used radio-equipped Jeeps to keep in constant contact with the Airedales buzzing overhead.

Above the Marines, Swede Carlson could see the misery endured by his fellow Americans. At every opportunity, the Chinese attacked, lashing the roadbound Marines with mortars and machine guns. Carlson and his men made repeated strafing attacks to clear the way for the column and to break Chinese resistance with napalm and rocket attacks.

Even with the planes to pave the way and secure the flanks, the column took heavy losses. Fortunately, when the troops met heavy opposition, the FAC teams quickly called in the Airedales, who almost always were able to destroy the enemy with well-coordinated attacks.

By nightfall, the Marines had advanced only five thousand yards south of Hagaru-ri. But with darkness came added danger, for once the sun went down the protective umbrella of blue planes returned home. Only a few squadrons were capable of flying night CAS, an extremely difficult type of mission. Now free from the deadly Corsairs and Skyraiders, the Chinese assaulted the Marine column. Despite the attacks, the Marines pushed on. If they stopped, they would be cut to pieces. Only the hope of reaching Koto-ri and its well-defended perimeter offered any chance of escape.

By 10:00 P.M., the forward elements of the 7th Marines reached Hellfire Valley. A single, well-placed Chinese machine gun suddenly opened fire and sprayed the column with bullets. This forced the Marines to halt their march southward. For two hours, the lone machine gun held up the column until it was finally destroyed.

The push south continued shortly after midnight, but sporadic Chinese attacks slowed progress and cost many lives. Just before dawn, the Chinese assaulted behind the 7th Marines, hitting the divisional headquarters company. Hard-pressed, the Marines called for night-fighters, who came to the rescue. Down on the deck, Marine Grumman F7F Tigercats blasted apart the Chinese assault with napalm and cannon runs that came within thirty yards of the Marines on the road. As daylight broke, a division of Corsairs turned the area into a flaming holocaust when they saturated the attackers with four tons of bombs and napalm. When the Corsairs pulled off target, the pilots could see the Chinese troops scrambling for cover away from the road.

The push to Koto-ri continued. By December 7, the entire force at Hagaru-ri had pulled out. Even the rear guard had taken to the road. If all went well, the last Marines would reach Koto-ri by midnight.

VA-195 flew again on the 7th, scouring the mountains that flanked Hellfire Valley in search of Chinese troops. The Marines were close to Koto-ri now, leaving burned and smoldering vehicles scattered on the roadside in their wake—evidence of Chinese mortar and machine-gun attacks.

At one point, a FAC called in Carlson and his division to a target just a few yards from the road. Arriving on the scene, the pilots could see Chinese troops swarming over the snow. Although the enemy were mere yards from the Marines, Carlson's men flayed their ranks with cannon fire and 250 pound fragmentation bombs. "The Marines were most appreciative of our work," Carlson later recalled.

It was bloody, dirty work, but it helped to save the 1st Marine Division from the fate that had befallen the UN forces at Kunu-ri a few weeks before. With FAC teams still in place and their communication with the aircraft secured, airpower could be brought to bear anywhere the Chinese lurked within a matter of minutes. At times, sixty or more aircraft circled the retreating Marines. Always during the day, at least twenty-four planes remained over the column on call as they waited for a FAC to give them targets. The close coordination between the FACs and the pilots proved vital to the success of the breakout.

By midnight on December 7, the last Marines reached the Koto-ri perimeter. With them came the surviving members of the 7th Infantry Division's units that had been caught on the east bank of the Chosin Reservoir. The next big jump south would start at Koto-ri and move down the single road as it wound through steep mountains to Chinhung. From there, the road to Hungnam was open.

To get to Chinhung, the Americans would have to cross a bridge that traversed a series of huge pipes, located three and a half miles south of Koto-ri, that had been built by the Japanese as part of a hydroelectric dam system in the valley below the road. The Chinese recognized the importance of this chokepoint. If they could blow the bridge, the Americans at Koto-ri would be trapped. Twice they had managed to blow apart sections of the bridge. Both times, American engineers from Chinhung pushed north and repaired the breaks. Finally, the Chinese blew out a sixteen-foot section just before the Marines reached Koto-ri.

Time was short now. The trapped Americans did not have the supplies to stay at Koto-ri for long. They had to get moving if they were to stay alive. But until the bridge was repaired, they would have to stay at Koto-ri. Without the time to build a wooden trestle bridge to span the break, the engineers knew they needed a radical solution. They considered building a bypass, but the terrain made that impossible. With a steep rock wall on one side of the road and a precipitous drop into the valley on the other, there was no way around the bridge.

The engineers decided to use prefabricated bridge sections. A quick check turned up the fact that Puller's men at Koto-ri had two Brockway bridging trucks within the perimeter; however, both were empty at the moment. The bridging sections that the trucks could carry were at Yongpo on the other side of the Chinese roadblocks.

An airdrop proved to be the only answer. The question was whether such a novel idea would work. Since each bridge section weighed close to twenty-five hundred pounds, it would be very difficult to parachute them into the rugged terrain around Koto-ri without damaging them. A test drop at Yonpo confirmed this, as the section was badly crumpled on impact. Larger, stronger parachutes were flown in from Japan, and they turned out to be the solution.

At 9:30 A.M. on December 7, three Marine transport planes overflew Kotori and discharged their unusual loads. All of the bridge sections landed intact thanks to the larger chutes. During another drop at lunchtime, one section was damaged and another fell into enemy hands. Later, three more sections were recovered by the Marines—enough to get them across the damaged bridge.

When the Marines moved out and retook the bridge area on December 9, they encountered little Chinese resistance. In fact, the air attacks combined with the freezing temperatures and Marine firepower had taken a hideous toll on the Chinese troops. The few prisoners taken that day were suffering from frostbite and malnutrition. Chinese sources later revealed that, from the end of November until the end of December, the units attacking X Corps lost 33 percent of their troops as the result of the weather alone. The IX Chinese Army Corps, one of the best formations in the Third Field Army, had attacked the Marines during their southern breakout. Although IX Corps was seasoned during the civil war, it had fought in Eastern China and never experienced freezing temperatures. Thrust against the Marines in December 1950, its troops faced minus 30° weather while still clad in their summer uniforms. Hundreds froze to death.

That mistake helped the Marines to reach Chinhung on December 11. From there, it was a relatively easy march to the Hungnam area, their ultimate destination. By 11:00 P.M. that night, the last of the Marine and UN columns reached Hungnam.

During the breakout, the UN troops lost about one thousand men. The Chinese, however, suffered tremendous losses; almost a dozen divisions were sacrificed in the effort to stop the Marines.

At last at the coast, the remaining units of X Corps formed a perimeter around Hungnam and prepared for evacuation. Covered by TF-77's ubiquitous fighter-bombers and attack planes, a fleet of 193 ships assembled at the port to facilitate the evacuation. Between December 11 and December 24, the ships pulled out no fewer than 105,000 troops of X Corps, 98,000 refugees, 350,000 tons of cargo, and 17,500 vehicles—an incredible feat.

For Carlson and his men, the retreat from the Chosin Reservoir served as their indoctrination into the Korean War. Though many of their Skyraiders had been damaged during the first month of combat, the squadron had not lost a single man. Now, with the Marines and the rest of X Corps safely evacuated, VA-195 would experience their most difficult challenges yet of the Korean War.

8 | The Bridge Busters

Hap Harris was one of those guys that everyone in the squadron liked. Affable and full of good humor, Hap's friends thought of him as a free spirit, a man who blazed his way through life with passion and charisma. As often the case with such jovial types, Hap's friends made him a frequent target of good-natured teasing. Soon after he joined the squadron, Hap's landings became a running joke among them.

To land a heavy combat aircraft on a carrier's pitching flight deck, a pilot was trained to throttle back until his plane was just above stall speed. Then the Landing Signal Officer (LSO) guided the pilot down onto the deck. If the pilot made any mistakes in his approach, he could stall out and crash. Learning how to land without actually stalling took patience, tremendous skill, and stout nerves.

After Hap was married, his pals noticed that his landings were a bit "hotter" than before he made his vows. They needled him and said that his marriage added five knots to his landing speed. A short time later, when Hap announced that his wife was pregnant, the men kidded him that he'd probably add another five knots just to be extra safe—which he did.

Hot landings or not, Hap's peers recognized real talent. Not only did his personality and charm win over his comrades, but his flying impressed everyone. Although Hap had joined the squadron fresh out of flight training at Corpus Christi, Hap had a raw, natural talent behind the controls of his AD. As one pilot recalled, "I also observed that he was a top-notch Navy pilot. We regarded him as one of the best."

On a cold Sunday morning six months later, Hap Harris proved just how good an attack pilot he had become.

—◆◆◆—

Dawn broke over the USS *Princeton* on January 25, 1951, to reveal a scene of bustling activity. Arrayed on the flight deck were CAG-19's Corsairs and Skyraiders, loaded and ready to pioneer a new phase of the air campaign.

Below decks, VA-195 gathered in its ready room to attend the morning's briefing. The pilots soon discovered that this was no ordinary mission. Since arriving in the theater the month before, the squadron had devoted almost all of its efforts to CAS and armed reconnaissance strikes. Today, they would be going after two important bridges west of Sinpo on the east coast of North Korea. This would be the first strike in a massive campaign against North Korea's communication lines—a campaign that evolved into Operation Strangle a few months later.

The idea was conceived on December 15, 1950, when FEAF issued a plan of operation against the Chinese and North Korean logistics and communications centers titled, "FEAF Interdiction Campaign No. 4."[1] The plan identified 172 new targets—45 rail bridges, 12 highway bridges, 13 tunnels, 39 marshaling yards and 63 supply centers.

When it became clear the next month that the Chinese New Year's offensive had failed (mainly due to the communists' lack of staying power on the battlefield), FEAF's General Stratemeyer ordered his air units to begin hitting these new targets.

The weak link in the Chinese army was its logistical support. Without adequate food, ammunition, clothing, and fuel, the Chinese offensives tended to burn out quickly. If their precarious supply situation could be dealt severe blows, FEAF hoped that the Chinese would have major problems undertaking any new offensive.

To help with the new interdiction campaign, FEAF asked the Navy to send Task Force 77's aircraft against rail and bridge targets along the eastern coast of North Korea. Meanwhile, the USAF squadrons would hit targets elsewhere in North Korea. When Stratemeyer issued his request on January 15, the carrier planes were fully committed to CAS and armed reconnaissance missions in support of the hard-pressed ROK army in the east. Consequently, the Navy responded that only when its ground support responsibilities eased would the carrier planes be sent against targets at the enemy's rear.

With the collapse of the New Year's offensive by January 20, Task Force 77 was able to shift some of its operations against the rail line between Hamhung, North Korea, and Susong, China.

The morning briefing on January 25 stressed the importance of the day's target. Two bridges west of Sinpo were key bottlenecks on the eastern rail and highway routes used by the communists to supply their troops in the field. If either or both bridges could be destroyed, a severe blow would be dealt to the Chinese efforts to resupply their battle-ravaged troops to the south.

Swede Carlson's Tigers listened intently to the briefing officer as he described how these two targets had been hit before by FEAF's bombers. Although the B-29s could carry an impressive load, including 12,000-pound Tarzon guided bombs, they had failed to destroy either target. Now, the task had been given to VA-195's Skyraiders.

Each AD would carry three 2,000-pound bombs tucked under the wings and fuselage. Two divisions would be used in the attack, one for each bridge. Swede Carlson's division would include Don van Slooten, Darryl Skalla, and Hap Harris. They would hit the rail bridge while the other division went after the highway bridge.

The briefing ended and the pilots made their way to their assigned planes on the flight deck. The weather was still bitingly cold, and the *Princeton* heaved and bucked in the huge swells that made flight operations in the Sea of Japan so difficult. One by one, the ADs were spotted for takeoff and given clearance to launch. Once airborne, the divisions formed up and proceeded to the target area about thirty minutes away.

Carlson's division reached its target, and Swede put his planes into a race-track pattern over it. To ensure that none of his men were caught in the bomb blast of the plane ahead, he spaced out the ADs so that each began its run about twenty seconds behind the previous one. Swede popped open his dive brakes, rolled over his AD, and screamed down on the bridge in a near-vertical dive. At 1,000 feet, he pickled off one of his bombs, then pulled up sharply to position himself for another run. Overhead, the rest of the division watched their skipper's bomb impact a few yards from the bridge. Though it landed close by, no damage was observed.

Next came Don Van Slooten, followed by Darryl Skalla, both of whom missed as well. Hap rolled in on the bridge and put his bomb close to one of the spans but not close enough to damage it.

For the next several minutes, the four pilots made repeated bombing runs on the bridge, despite harassing anti-aircraft fire. Each time they came up empty. Finally, everyone but Hap had released his last remaining bomb. Hap had one left, and he set up his run recalling the importance of the bridge to the North Koreans and Chinese. He pushed over, diving down on it while hanging in his seat straps. He held the dive as he dove through two thousand feet, then fifteen hundred. At a thousand feet, the bridge practically filled his entire windscreen. He dumped his last bomb, closed his dive brakes, and pulled back hard on the stick. Going down that low was dangerous because the AD could be caught in the bomb's blast, or his excessive speed could prevent him from pulling out of the dive.

Hap's two-thousand pounder howled down onto the bridge and struck it squarely. Bits of debris blew upward in a swirl of dirt, smoke, and flame. When it had cleared, somebody called out, "The bridge is gone! He got it with a direct hit!"

Indeed, the twisted remains of it lay sprawled around the concrete abutments. The target had been totally destroyed with a single 2,000-pound bomb.

Jubilant over Hap's success, the four pilots turned to find their secondary target before going home. During the briefing, the men had been given an alternate target of a series of sheds and warehouses up the coast where the Chinese and North Koreans probably stored military supplies. They found the buildings without much trouble, and Swede ordered the men down on independent strafing runs from the sea toward the town. For fifteen minutes, the Skyraiders raked the warehouses with cannon fire.

With his ammunition low, Swede ordered the rest of the division to form up on his wing so they could return to the *Princeton* together. Just then, Hap keyed his mike and announced, "I've located another target, can I make another run on it?"

Swede considered Hap's request. Usually, he would have sent down two planes to investigate the target. If anti-aircraft fire erupted in the area, the trailing AD could hose down the flak guns and protect the lead plane. In this instance, however, he gave Hap permission to go down alone. Hap's comrades watched him dive down on whatever he had seen.

Suddenly, as Don wrote years later, "We heard the electrifying distress call on the radio, 'Mayday! Mayday! Mayday!' And then, all was silent."

Carlson called out each pilot's name to determine who had been hit. It had been Hap.

Hap's Skyraider never pulled up from that last run. Torn and battered by flak, it hurtled straight into the bay. By the time Swede and the others reached Hap's point of impact, only a huge splash mark remained.

Don and the Skipper made a low pass over the site and saw that a dye marker had been released near the crash site. Each pilot carried a dye marker in his life vest, and it gave them fleeting hope that Hap had survived.

They circled overhead for a few minutes as they intently watched the water below for any signs that Hap had made it out of the plane. They saw no sign of him. In reality, his AD had struck the water with such force that the impact had probably killed him instantly. How the dye marker was released remains a mystery.

Carlson called to the *Princeton* and reported the location of Hap's crash. In hopes that his body could be recovered, another flight from Task Force 77 covered the area while it waited for an air rescue team to arrive. In the meantime, Swede led his dejected and stunned pilots home. Later, they learned that two more pilots patrolling the area had been shot down and killed by North Korean flak. It turned out that they had stumbled across a heavily fortified "hot spot"—probably a major supply center.

Back on board the *Princeton*, Swede's men sagged into their chairs in the ready room and prepared for the debriefing. Don sat down despondently, so grief stricken that he was hardly able to speak. Finally, he broke down and sobbed unashamedly. Hap had been one of his best friends. Years later, he would write, "It was tremendously hard to come to grips with the sudden death and departure of this good friend and flying comrade. And, it is still hard to come to grips with events such as this. One asks, 'Why? What was accomplished? Wasn't the price too high to pay?'"[2]

The question lingered in the minds of all who fought in this new interdiction campaign. Was a bridge or a warehouse worth an American life? One thing for sure, it was a brutal lesson to learn. Nobody blamed the skipper, of course, but Swede took the incident to heart. Never again would he let one of his men roll in on a target without a second plane to back him up.

-◆◆◆-

In February of 1951, Task Force 77 gained the job of interdicting North Korea's eastern rail network. Once assigned, the intelligence and reconnaissance team on board the carriers went to work photographing and documenting the rail system in its zone of responsibility.

Three main rail lines ran south out of Manchuria into northeastern Korea. All three lines merged at the strategic city of Kilchu on the coast. From there, a single track ran south to Kowon, where it split. One branch ran west to Pyongyang, while the other continued south to Wonsan, where it split again. One line cut across the peninsula toward Seoul, and the second line ran south along the coast.

Altogether, Task Force 77 was responsible for interdicting 1,140 miles of track. The lines included 956 bridges and 231 tunnels, or about one bridge for every 1.2 miles of track and one tunnel every 5 miles.[3]

Starting early in February, the task force undertook a systematic photographic reconnaissance of its assigned rail network. The photos were brought back aboard TF-77's carriers and analyzed to determine the bridges and tunnels that could damage the communist's logistical system the most if they were destroyed. In March, TF-77 would devote most of its efforts against these targets.

With this new interdiction campaign came a host of new and difficult targets. Tunnels, the pilots of VA-195 discovered, were scary targets. The reason wasn't so much that they were well-defended—in fact, many times there was almost no anti-aircraft fire—but to hit one required steel nerves and expert flying. Diving down on a tunnel, the Skyraider pilots had to get right on the deck a few feet off the railroad lines. At the last possible instant, they pickled their bombs and then had to pull up sharply to avoid crashing into the mountain. They sweated out their escape as they barely missed trees or the mountain itself, while their bombs skipped along the ground and into the tunnel.

Whatever or whoever was inside—the communists used tunnels to conceal locomotives, rolling stock, and even troops—was in for a nasty shock.

Tex Atkinson, one of the VA-195 pilots, had an interesting experience during one tunnel attack when he was using delayed-fused bombs. After locating his target, he swung down his AD and made a run on a railroad tunnel that passed through a low hill then opened out onto a bridge that spanned a narrow valley. He released his bomb, then pulled his nose up until his AD shot skyward. Overhead, his comrades could see his bomb bounce off the railroad tracks, spin high into the air, and arch right over the hill. It tumbled over the other side and blew up on the bridge. The explosion blasted the bridge apart, scattering debris across the valley below. Later, when interviewed about the freak incident by a *Star and Stripes* reporter, Tex quipped, "I only do this on Sundays."

The air groups had already discovered that their AD Skyraiders were the best attack aircraft available for the job. Naturally, it fell to the few squadrons that had them to execute the most important of these strikes. Rugged, powerful, and able to carry a heavier bomb load than a World War II B-17, the Skyraider was aptly suited for these interdiction missions. The fact that they were hard to shoot down would prove especially important as the campaign wore on. In January, Hap Harris's AD was the only Skyraider lost during the month. In contrast, the Navy and Marine Corsair units were hit hard. Six were lost during January alone. During the first five months of 1951, the Corsair units lost 69 planes. The AD squadrons lost eight. Although these figures partly reflect the larger number of Corsair squadrons, the truth was that the old World War II F4Us could not withstand heavy ground fire. The oil coolers in the wing roots and the unarmored lower cowling made them especially vulnerable. The AD had no such weak spots and could stay in the air despite remarkably heavy damage.

In March, the Skyraider squadrons on board the carriers of Task Force 77 spearheaded the all-out thrust against North Korea's eastern rail system. In the midst of these operations, Swede Carlson and his Tigers earned a place in history for their roles in what author James A. Michener would later refer to as "The Bridges at Toko-ri."

9 | The Battle of Carlson's Canyon

Lieutenant Commander Clement L. Craig spotted the bridge first. It was a beautiful target, sitting a hundred feet off the ground and spanning a canyon six hundred feet deep. On either end of the bridge, steep mountains had forced the railroad's construction crews to build tunnels, which made the area a huge bottleneck along the primary rail connection between Manchuria and the front lines. The canyon itself stretched away to the west, then curved back 180 degrees and snaked eastward again. A few miles to the north of the bridge that Craig had seen, another long bridge stretched across the canyon.

The importance of the area immediately struck Craig. With two large vulnerable bridges and two tunnels, the rail line could be totally severed with a couple of good strikes. A closer look revealed that the North Koreans were already building another rail line parallel to the existing one, and had started construction on a new bridge over the canyon. Later reconnaissance missions discovered two new tunnels already burrowed through the mountains on either side of the canyon. In a matter of weeks, the communists might be able to increase their rail traffic significantly at this point in the line if their construction was unhindered.

Craig returned to the *Princeton* and reported his discovery to Rear Admiral Ralph Ofstie. The most important bridge, the southernmost one that Craig had seen first, gained the identification of "EA1622." It would be the focus of much of CAG-19's efforts in the coming weeks.

The first strike against EA1622 was laid on that afternoon. Air Group 19 went in as a combined force, the Corsairs striking flak emplacements scattered on the two mountains on either side of the canyon as the ADs made their runs on the bridge. The strike proved to be a disappointment. Little damage was done, and the bridge continued to handle rail traffic.

The next day, March 3, 1951, Commander Carlson led seven Skyraiders on a second strike against EA1622. This time, the results were more satisfying. Under the cover of CAG-19's Corsairs, the Skyraiders scored several hits on the bridge, dropping one span into the canyon below and damaging three others. The Americans had cut the eastern rail link between Manchuria and the front lines.

Naval intelligence had estimated that the line provided the communist troops with five thousand tons of supplies a day. This amount was more than adequate for their men who, it was determined, needed about three thousand tons a day to operate.[1] With one well-executed air strike, the Navy had severed the line south of Kilchu and had choked off a vital supply source.

Jubilant, CAG-19 returned to the *Princeton* to report the news. In honor of VA-195's success, the carrier pilots christened the area Carlson's Canyon. In reality, though they had hit the bridge hard, the target had not been totally destroyed. Also, unbeknownst to VA-195 at the time, not long after their attack North Korean engineers and laborers swarmed over EA1622, working frantically to repair the bridge and get food and ammo flowing south again.

It took a few days before TF-77's reconnaissance planes noticed the activity, setting the stage for a month-long struggle of wills between the carrier air groups and thousands of North Korean repair workers. As the battle took shape throughout March and into April, Carlson's Canyon came to symbolize the overall interdiction campaign and its accompanying problems for UN airpower.

On March 7, the carrier planes returned to the bridge a third time. Hitting it again with 2,000-pound bombs, they dropped a second span into Carlson's Canyon. The communist repair crews, however, set to work almost immediately to repair the damage. Working mainly at night, they constructed several temporary piers to support the damaged spans and the make-shift trusses used to replace the two downed spans. The piers, made with interlocking wooden beams called "cribbing," were noticed in later TF-77 photo reconnaissance runs on March 14, 1951.

Analysis of the repair project indicated that the North Koreans were only a few days away from putting the bridge back into operation. Again, a full air group strike was planned against EA1622. This time, though, the bridge would be hit by both heavy bombs and napalm.

Task Force 77 launched the strike on March 15. Again, VA-195's AD-4s led the way. Carlson and his men were able to burn off all the cribbing with well-placed napalm runs. Moreover, the attack planes knocked down another span. Of the six original spans that composed EA1622, only two remained undamaged.

Meanwhile, other naval air groups were keeping pressure on the North Koreans up and down the eastern rail system by hitting bridges, tunnels, and key junctions. As the raids continued, it became obvious that the North Koreans excelled in repairing the heavy damage caused by these raids. Tunnels were rebuilt within hours and temporary bridges thrown up in a matter of days. Tactically, however, the naval strikes were unmitigated successes. As Swede Carlson recalled, "Successful bridge strikes were the rule, and missed or just-damaged bridges were the exception."[2]

Strategically, the raids were not nearly as effective. Since the North Koreans could rebuild a damaged stretch of rail line so quickly, TF-77 was forced to attack the same targets repeatedly to keep the line cut. Destroying the tracks proved, at best, to be only a fleeting success. Along each line, the North Koreans stationed repair crews who could fill a damaged rail bed with gravel and lay new track in just a few hours, making the expense of a raid not really worth the effort. Worse, when the Americans hit heavily defended targets, planes and pilots were frequently lost—at far more cost to the United States than the damage they inflicted on the communists.

It wasn't the fault of the aviators that the interdiction campaign proved so frustrating. They did their jobs, taking down bridges, skipping bombs into tunnels, and cutting the rail lines at vulnerable places. The North Koreans, however, were able to repair the damage at a rate that made the attacks of only limited value.

At EA1622, work on the bridge progressed at an amazing pace. To slow down the repair efforts, FEAF laid on several new type of raids. Since most of the repair work took place at night, the Fifth Air Force sent night hecklers into Carlson's Canyon to disrupt the work and cause casualties among the laborers. Subsequent raids dropped delayed-fused bombs that exploded throughout the night to hamper nighttime repair efforts.

Task Force 77 also began flying night raids against EA1622. Mirroring the Fifth Air Force strikes, Skyraiders from VC-35 and Corsairs from other night detachments rained down death on the repair crews with lightning-quick bomb and napalm runs. Still, with all the effort expended, the North Koreans accepted their losses and continued to work on the bridges.

By the end of March, the North Koreans had managed a minor miracle. Despite the nearly constant raids, they had repaired much of the damage. Task Force 77's intelligence staff examined the latest reconnaissance photos and concluded that EA1622 soon would be operational.

Admiral Ofstie suggested that the bridge be hit by B-29s carrying delayed-fused bombs. Perhaps if Carlson's Canyon could be inundated with these bombs, the Air Force could strike a major blow against the repair crews. Accordingly, FEAF launched a B-29 raid on March 27, but the results proved disappointing. Although the bombs detonated throughout that night and the next day, the North Koreans simply replaced their dead and injured with other workers. The repair effort continued, seemingly unabated.

With the bridge only days from operational status, Task Force 77 again turned to Swede Carlson and his squadron. On April 1, VA-195 returned to Carlson's Canyon and pounded the bridge with heavy ordnance. Poststrike analysis showed that the Skyraiders had knocked down the final two original spans. A full air group strike the following day totally destroyed the bridge. When the Navy bombers pulled off target, all that remained in their wake were the sixty-foot-high concrete pilings that had anchored each of the six original spans. The rest of the bridge lay broken and scattered across the floor of the canyon like so much useless wreckage.

After the April 2 strike, the North Koreans conceded defeat. Repair work ceased, and the communist crews were pulled out of Carlson's Canyon and sent elsewhere. When TF-77's photo planes picked this up, it looked like the naval aviators had scored a tremendous victory in the ongoing interdiction campaign. As it turned out, whatever victory was scored proved to be fleeting at best.

Later in April, reconnaissance overflights discovered why the North Koreans had given up at Carlson's Canyon. The constant raids had made it obvious to the North Koreans that EA1662 was simply too vulnerable to attack. Although it could be repaired after each strike, the size and length of the bridge made it both a time-consuming and manpower-intensive project. After all of the original spans had been destroyed, they chose to build a four-mile bypass line around Carlson's Canyon. The new line required the construction of eight new bridges, but they were all smaller and shorter than EA1622. As a result, they made less inviting targets.

Nevertheless, TF-77 laid on several strikes against the new bridges just before the North Koreans laid rails across them. A short time later, however, the air groups were sent south in search of better, more vulnerable choke-points.[3]

Later in April, when the communists launched their spring offensive, Task Force-77 abandoned the interdiction effort entirely and moved south to support the hard-pressed UN ground troops with CAS missions. The air groups later returned to their interdiction efforts in May, but, during the interim, North Korean repair crews had enough time to get the eastern rail line back in service.

Clearly, the fact that the communists were able even to launch an offensive in April signaled the failure of the UN interdiction campaign. For two full months, FEAF's combat wings had bombed countless bridges, tunnels, rail intersections, and marshaling yards. At night, light bombers had stalked North Korean truck convoys to hamper further the southward flow of supplies. Despite this maximum effort, enough supplies had reached the communists' front lines to facilitate a full-scale offensive.

After the war, General James A. Van Fleet, who had taken command of the Eighth Army in the spring of 1951, commented on the one bridge that symbolized the entire campaign—EA1622: "We won the battle to knock out the bridge, but we lost the objective, which was to knock out the traffic."[4]

The interdiction campaign continued throughout the war. Although it took different forms, it always had the same objective of denying supplies to the frontline communist troops. By late 1951, however, the Navy began to realize that such operations were not only hazardous but produced only limited results. The campaign proved to be a frustrating, bitter experience for the Navy in the years that followed the first raids against Carlson's Canyon.

When war correspondent and author James A. Michener later learned of Carlson's Canyon, he decided that the struggle against the bridge could form the core of a novel about the war. After spending time on board the *Essex*, he merged the events at Carlson's Canyon with CAG-5's experiences. The resulting novel, *The Bridges at Toko-ri*, was an instant commercial success. Perhaps better than any actual account to emerge from the Korean War, Michener's work of fiction expressed the Navy's frustration with its role in the air war.

10 · The Dam Busters

While VA-195 and the rest of Air Group 19 struggled with the new interdiction campaign through February, March and April, major events were unfolding at the front that would determine the nature and outcome of the war.

On New Year's Eve 1950 the Chinese had renewed their offensive southward. The most powerful attacks came on the western side of Korea, where the Chinese were intent on reaching Seoul. On January 3, 1951, the U.S. Eighth Army's new commander, Lieutenant General Matthew B. Ridgway, ordered that Seoul be evacuated. Kimpo Airfield was also abandoned, and the retreating UN forces detonated five hundred thousand gallons of aviation fuel and twenty-three thousand gallons of napalm as they left.

By mid-January, the Chinese offensive had lost steam. The Eighth Army had broken contact with the communists and had set up defensive positions along the Thirty-Seventh Parallel. On January 21, 1951, UN patrols began moving north in search of the Chinese. They found only scattered resistance, as the Chinese had pulled back northward to regroup, resupply, and reinforce their frontline units. Encouraged by the lack of Chinese response to the patrols, Ridgway initiated Operation Thunderbolt. Each corps within the Eighth Army launched a series of reconnaissance-in-force missions that moved forward slowly and aligned its flanks on neighboring units so that any troops of the Chinese Communist Forces (CCF) in the area could not attack its rear.

Thunderbolt was concluded by the first week in February. Its success prompted Ridgway to begin another limited offensive. This one, dubbed Operation Roundup, encountered much heavier opposition than did Thunderbolt. Still, both Inchon and Kimpo were retaken by February 10.

The following night, the Chinese countered the UN advance with an attack of their own. They struck at three ROK divisions, all of which were pushed back or shattered by the onslaught. On February 13, the Chinese hit the U.S. 23d Infantry Regiment and the French Battalion at Chipyong-ni. In one of the most important battles of the war, the two UN formations held off no fewer than six Chinese divisions—eighteen thousand men. For two days, the battle raged as the Chinese attacked from all sides. Ensconced in a series of hills surrounding Chipyong-ni, the UN forces mowed down the attackers with the help of heavy artillery and air support.

Had the Chinese taken Chipyong-ni, a corridor to X Corp's rear areas would have been forced open. Knowing the stakes, the UN forces held firm, despite another massive attack on February 15. Later that day, a relief column opened up Chipyong-ni and lifted the siege. In two days of brutal fighting, the Chinese had lost at least five thousand men. UN losses totaled 23 killed, 259 wounded, and 42 missing. It was the most lopsided victory of the Korean War.

Following the Chinese disaster at Chipyong-ni, the communist troops began to retreat northward. Again, weather and the precarious supply situation caused much loss of life among the Chinese and North Korean frontline soldiers. UN air attacks had destroyed most of the usable housing to their immediate rear, so they had no sanctuary from the weather. Hundreds died of exposure.

On February 18, IX Corps, U.S. Eighth Army, discovered that the Chinese had abandoned their positions. Patrols pushing north found no sign of them. Indeed, all along the central sector of the front, the communists had disappeared.

Ridgway decided to put the pressure on the Chinese and North Koreans again. On February 18, after receiving news about the withdrawal, he ordered IX Corps to advance to the Han River. As it moved forward, X Corps was to hit two North Korean corps at Chechon, where they formed a salient in the UN lines.

Thus was born Operation Killer. Realizing that the Chinese had withdrawn to resupply and reinforce their shattered units, Ridgway determined that the Eighth Army should push north in a slow, grinding offensive designed to inflict maximum loss on the communists.

Operation Killer, officially opened on February 21, 1951, encountered little resistance at first. In fact, weather became the primary problem facing the advancing UN troops. Toward the end of February, the temperature rose above freezing and the new warm spell turned the roads into muddy quagmires that disrupted vehicular traffic all across Korea.

Nevertheless, Operation Killer continued. By March 1, the UN line had advanced midway between the Thirty-Seventh and Thirty-Eighth Parallels.

More important, morale in the Eighth Army had been restored by the offensive, as well as by five-day rest leaves to Japan that had been implemented shortly before Killer began. No longer did the Eighth Army have the smell of defeat about it. Ridgway and his staff had injected both confidence and hope into the command and, in the process, ensured the survival of South Korea. Despite the presence of some seven hundred thousand Chinese troops in Korea by this time, the Eighth Army never would be seriously defeated again.

Following the success of Operation Killer, Ridgway launched his next offensive, Operation Ripper, on March 7. Ripper's main object was the central Korean town of Chunchon. As the biggest road junction in the central sector, the town had great strategic importance. If the UN could take it, the Chinese and North Korean troops in the central sector would have to retreat overland through the mountains to escape encirclement. What's more, Seoul would be outflanked, so any UN thrust at Chunchon threatened the huge Chinese and North Korean troop concentrations in the capital area.

The UN push north proved so successful that, by March 13, the communists recognized that if they didn't withdraw from Seoul, they would be outflanked and cut off. During the next two days, they evacuated Seoul. A parachute assault at Munsan-ni by the 187th Regimental Combat Team failed to block their retreat, but UN troops moving up from the south took Seoul on March 15. It was the fourth and last time the capital changed hands during the war.

On March 23, Chunchon fell to the advancing troops of IX Corps. In the process, however, American intelligence picked up information that pointed to a massive Chinese troop buildup on the central front at a place called the Iron Triangle. By the end of the month, the Iron Triangle, an area defined by Pyonggang at its north, Chorwon at its west, and Kumhwa at its east, contained at least nine armies and twenty-seven divisions, according to UN intelligence estimates.

Despite this concentration of troops to the north, Ridgway continued his offensive operations in the hope that the UN attacks would disrupt Chinese plans for a new thrust of their own. On April 5, the Eighth Army launched Operation Rugged, the follow-up to Ripper. Designed to take Line Kansas — a series of commanding positions just north of the Thirty-Eighth Parallel — Rugged encountered its first major obstacle on April 9.

On that day, the troops of X Corps and III ROK Corps had pushed across the Pukhan River and were heading northward downstream from the Hwachon Reservoir. That reservoir and its dam served as a major water and hydroelectric source for Seoul. In North Korean hands now, it was used as a weapon against the two UN Corps. The communists opened the Hwachon Dam's sluice gates. A torrent of water poured out of the reservoir and flooded the Pukhan River valley. Behind X Corps, the water level rose several feet in just a few hours, destroying one pontoon bridge and forcing the dismantling of another. The North Koreans had probably intended to cut off X Corps with the flooding of the Pukhan, or at least damage its supply lines. Within a short time, however, the UN troops had repaired the damage and continued to move forward. Had the communists released the water earlier, before the UN troops crossed the Pukhan, it might have made more of a difference in the fighting. At least it would have slowed the advance a little longer.

As it was, the Hwachon Dam remained a threat to Eighth Army's security. Not only could it be used defensively to slow a UN advance, but it could also support the expected Chinese spring offensive. By closing the sluice gates, the Pukhan River would slow to a trickle, making it easier to cross. Additionally, since the Pukhan flows into the Han, the Han River would be affected by such a move.

The day the communists flooded the Pukhan, General Ridgway climbed into a light observation plane and flew over the dam for a personal inspection. Despite receiving small-arms fire, he had the pilot circle the area. Later, he returned in a helicopter to inspect the dam again. He concluded that the flood was not as dangerous as first calculated because either the communists had not opened the sluice gates all the way or the Eighth Army's intelligence estimate on the water pressure behind the dam had been wrong.

Whatever the case, Ridgway wanted the Hwachon dam neutralized. Shortly after the flood, he ordered the U.S. 7th Cavalry Regiment to capture the dam and destroy the machinery that operated the sluice gates so as to prevent the communists from flooding the Eighth Army's rear areas again. On April 10, the troopers began their advance. While moving up a mountain road, they encountered two CCF companies that put up fierce resistance. It took some time to push through the Chinese defenders, but the 7th Cavalry was only a half mile from the dam by nightfall.

There the advance came to a halt. The enemy was well dug in, and the 7th Cavalry did not have the manpower to break through. Instead, the regiment's commander, Lieutenant Colonel William Harris, conceived a plan that would take his objective by amphibious assault, thus outflanking the heavy defenses in the mountains to his front. Using nine assault boats hauled to the south shore of the reservoir by Jeeps, a company of troopers and the 4th Ranger Company attacked the dam the next morning. As this operation developed, the rest of the 7th Cavalry launched other attacks to keep the enemy off guard.

It didn't work. The amphibious assault was caught on the reservoir and suffered heavy loses before being compelled to withdraw. The 7th's other attacks were also blunted and took moderate casualties. Following this failed assault, the 7th Cavalry was pulled out of the lines and went into reserve.

Meanwhile, signs of an impending Chinese offensive were seen all across the Korean peninsula. On April 14, UN troops reached the base of the Iron Triangle. Five days later, the Eighth Army reached positions along what had been dubbed Line Utah.

While these last objectives were reached, the Chinese along IX Corps's front began setting scores of brush fires. Some infiltrators even started blazes behind UN lines. At first, this behavior seemed to make no sense. Gradually, though, the many fires created a belt of smoke over the Chinese front lines that extended six to ten miles north. Since the wind was blowing from the south, the Chinese had to send men behind UN lines to keep setting blazes, otherwise, the wind would have quickly blown the smoke clear.

With their positions shrouded in smoke, the Chinese had no fear of UN air attack or aerial reconnaissance as they executed the final preparations for their spring offensive. It was a novel idea that worked well.

To hamper air coordination further, the Chinese began shooting at all light planes flying low over the front. "Mosquito pilots" in their venerable AT-6 trainers became frequent targets. The Chinese made it clear that they did not want aircraft over their lines.

Sunday, April 22, 1951 saw the final UN advances completed before the oncoming Chinese and North Korean offensive. That morning, an ROK Marine outfit managed to push one of its battalions across the Pukhan and take the Hwachon dam. A U.S. Marine engineer unit came forward to destroy the sluice gate machinery. After inspecting the dam, they concluded the job would be far more difficult than they had envisioned. That night, before the engineers could take any further action, the communists unleashed their offensive. The initial attacks forced the ROK and U.S. Marines away from the dam, which would remain a strategic thorn in the side of the Eighth Army.

Along the rest of the front, the communists scored a number of impressive early successes. Several ROK divisions collapsed under fierce assaults, and some UN units were cut off and surrounded. On the west side of the front, a massive battle raged around the Imjin River, where several British units in the 29th Brigade had been trapped. Elsewhere, major frontal attacks struck at the U.S. 24th and 25th Infantry Divisions and forced both divisions to retreat toward Seoul as units on either flank gave ground or disintegrated.

On IX Corps's front, the ROK 6th Division broke under extreme communist pressure. That unit's collapse ripped a large gap in the Eighth Army's lines, which forced IX Corps to retreat southeasterly behind the Hongchon River.

On April 29, UN aircraft caught the North Koreans and Chinese as they launched an assault across the Han River in an attempt to secure a bridgehead on the Kimpo Peninsula. Massive air strikes hit the communists as they crossed and killed most of the six thousand troops involved in the operation.

The few survivors that made it to the peninsula were quickly contained by a regiment of ROK Marines.

East of Seoul, at the junction of the Han and Pukhan Rivers, the communists tried to establish a bridgehead with the intent of outflanking Seoul. Two U.S. Infantry Divisions, the 24th and 25th, met the attack and stopped it cold. For the moment, the Chinese offensive had failed; however, only about two hundred fifty thousand of the seven hundred thousand troops available to the Chinese had been employed in this attack. The second phase of the offensive was only a few days off.

In some places, the Eighth Army was now less than four miles from Seoul. The capital had to be held against the next Chinese assault. U.S. intelligence tracked Chinese and North Korean troop movements and predicted that the communists would again try to cross at the junction of the Han and Pukhan Rivers. It appeared as if the Chinese were going to assault straight down the Pukhan River valley and try to take Seoul from the east.

The Hwachon dam could play an important role in this operation. If the communists closed the sluice gates, they could lower the level of the two rivers, thus making their assaults much easier. General Ridgway decided that it was time to destroy the dam. Since another ground operation against the dam was now impractical, the task was turned over to FEAF and its bombers.

The Hwachon dam proved to be a most difficult target. The Air Force launched several B-29 raids, including one that used the recently deployed radio-guided bombs. The strikes failed to do more than chip the dam's concrete. Standing 250 feet tall, the concrete wall rose out of the Pukhan River valley like a gigantic monolith. As FEAF discovered, it was so thick that bombs and rockets could not possibly destroy it. Even the steel sluice gates, ostensibly the most vulnerable part of the dam, were so well constructed as to be all but impervious to normal air attack. They were 40 feet wide, 20 feet high, and 2½ feet thick.[1]

By the end of April, the Eighth Army was getting increasingly worried that the dam had not been destroyed. Since FEAF had had no luck against it, the Navy would now be given a chance. Perhaps a pinpoint dive-bombing raid could hit the sluice gates. At 2:40 P.M. on April 30, Admiral Ofstie received a priority transmission from Headquarters Eighth Army. The message was an urgent request to destroy at least two of the Hwachon dam's sluice gates. If the dam itself could not be destroyed, perhaps the destruction of the sluice gates would ruin its strategic value. That way at least, the communists would not be able to control the Pukhan and Han River levels to support their operations.

Just three hours after receipt of this message, Carlson's Tigers were airborne and heading for the Hwachon dam. With Swede Carlson on this first dam-busting raid in the squadron's history were five other AD Skyraiders. Each AD carried a pair of 2,000-pound bombs and twelve 11.75-inch Tiny Tim rockets. Five Corsairs went along to provide flak suppression.

The Skyraiders arrived over the reservoir and discovered that the area was not well defended with anti-aircraft guns. Almost unmolested, they dive-bombed the dam and blasted away at it with their rockets and 2,000-pounders. When they pulled off the target, they saw that their ordnance had barely scarred the dam's surface. The rockets proved next to useless. They bounced or skidded off the concrete structure and did no damage at all. The 2,000-pound bombs were fine for knocking down bridge spans, but they could do no serious damage to thick steel-reinforced concrete. Further, it proved almost impossible to hit the sluice gates with bombs.

Frustrated, the pilots returned to the *Princeton* to figure out a better way to attack the dam. Carlson, Admiral Ofstie and the *Princeton*'s skipper, Captain William Gallery, met on the bridge to discuss the problem. They quickly ruled out another bomb or rocket attack. At that point, Captain Gallery suggested using Mark XIII torpedoes. The *Princeton*'s forward magazine housed a small number of these World War II relics, and they had recently been serviced, ensuring that they were ready in case any need should develop.

Using torpedoes was an idea that had merit. However, aside from Swede Carlson, the old torpedo bomber pilot, none of the attack pilots in VA-195 had ever dropped one of the slender "fish." In fact, not a single pilot in the outfit had even undergone torpedo training. Lack of experience aside, the sluice gates were perfect targets for a torpedo attack since the Mark XIII had been designed to blow holes in thickly armored warship hulls. Two and a half feet of steel armor could be penetrated by one good torpedo hit.

Carlson agreed that the idea made sense. Ofstie did as well, and he ordered Carlson to undertake the attack, despite the experience level of the crews who would carry out the mission.

That night, VC-35 and VA-195 met to iron out the details of the attack and to learn how best to make a torpedo drop. Commander Dick Merrick, CAG-19's commander, elected to lead the attack. He and three pilots from VC-35 would form the lead division. A few hundred yards to the right and behind the first division would be VA-195's four pilots led by Carlson.

The next morning, the Hwachon dam strike was ready for action and spotted for takeoff on the *Princeton*'s flight deck. Eight Skyraiders would form the torpedo force. A dozen Corsairs from VF-192 would pave the way and suppress any flak encountered over the target area. Slung under each AD's fuselage rested a single Mark XIII torpedo. Additionally, the Skyraiders also carried a pair of napalm bombs to use against North Korean troops inside a tunnel, located a few miles from the dam, that had been designated the secondary target.

Harold "Swede" Carlson (*left*) before the Hwachon Dam Raid.

Each of the heavily laden Skyraiders rumbled off the *Princeton's* deck without incident. The two divisions formed up, joined with the Corsairs, and winged their way toward the Hwachon reservoir.

Just short of the target area, the Corsairs forged ahead of the Skyraiders and prepared to make their flak suppression runs. Merrick led the ADs down low. They hugged the ridge tops just south of the reservoir until they came to the shoreline. The dam lay across from them to the northeast. It was obscured by a series of hills that jutted out into the water and created a bend in the reservoir.

Merrick took the first division down the last southern hillside. Crossing the shoreline, he leveled out mere feet off the reservoir's frigid water. Carlson did the same. Speeding northward, each division eased out into attack position.

They came to the bend and each pilot banked his plane slightly to maneuver around it. Still, they remained right on the wave tops. Overhead, the North Koreans had strung several metal cables from ridge to ridge across the water at about 800 feet. These were designed to snare and destroy any low-flying attack planes. However, the North Koreans had not expected a zero-altitude torpedo attack, or they would have lowered the cables or stretched anti-torpedo netting across the reservoir in front of the dam.

The Corsairs made their runs as the Skyraiders thundered around the bend in the reservoir. Flak was light and irregular. With the Corsairs keeping the

U.S. Navy, Courtesy of Harold Carlson

A VA–195 AD-4 with a torpedo, ready for the Hwachon Dam strike.

anti-aircraft gunners busy, the Skyraiders could concentrate on setting up their runs. The Corsairs completed their anti-flak runs on both sides of the dam and pulled up to watch the ADs make the final run to the target. The Skyraiders were pointed northeast now, the dam in sight. Individually, each pilot picked out a sluice gate and held it in his sights. This was the most dangerous part of the mission. To release their torpedoes correctly, the pilots had to fly steady and slow. If the pilots flew too high, the torpedo might run straight down and detonate against the reservoir's bottom. To fly too fast risked causing the torpedo to break up or porpoise out of the water. Dodging flak would throw off the pilot's aim and probably send the torpedo careening off target.

Holding steady and true, Merrick and his division dropped their torpedoes at four hundred yards. Seconds later, Carlson's pilots reached the drop point and let their fish go. As the planes pulled up and over the dam, seven of the eight torpedoes were running straight at the dam. One impacted against a sluice gate but failed to explode. One missed, though it exploded. The remaining five blasted apart one of the sluice gates and tore a huge hole in another.

They had breached the dam. As Carlson pulled over it, he looked back to see millions of gallons of water boiling through the two gates. Two thick columns of water spilled out of the ruptures and into the Pukhan River below. Overhead, a VC-61 photo reconnaissance Panther circled the dam as the pilot captured the raid's effects on film.

A torpedo hit on the Hwachon Dam.

The Hwachon dam would never be a threat to Eighth Army again. Those few, well-placed torpedoes had just knocked out one of the most strategically important targets in central Korea.

But the day was far from over. The Skyraiders still had their napalm tanks, so they formed up with the Corsairs and went hunting for their secondary target. They found the rail tunnel and skipped napalm into each end, then turned for home, confident that they had certainly earned their flight pay on this strike. Later, intelligence passed along to VA-195 the fact that the tunnel had housed a battalion of communist infantry. Their napalm attack had inflicted 610 casualties.

The Hwachon dam raid remains one of the most unique attacks of the Korean War. It was the only torpedo attack of the conflict—in fact it was the last use of these weapons ever by American aircraft in combat. It had crippled the dam and removed it as a strategic threat to IX Corps's defense of the critical junction of the Han and Pukhan Rivers.

On May 16, the Chinese launched their sixth offensive of the war. Instead of coming down the Pukhan, however, it started against the ROK corps defending the eastern side of the peninsula. The attacks shattered the ROK III Corps but soon ran into a wall of steel thrown up by well-emplaced UN troops supported by light bombers and fighters.

The next day, the attack down the Pukhan began. Fighting fiercely, the 25th Division threw the attackers back with heavy losses. The communists

National Archives

Readying for a full air group strike.

refused to give up. Between May 17 and May 20, the Reds flung masses of troops against the 25th Infantry Division and the ROK's 6th Division ensconced in well-defended positions. Every Chinese assault was met by fierce artillery missions, close air support strikes, and withering machine-gun fire. By May 20, the Red assaults had been broken on the wheel of UN fire-power. The Chinese never got across the river to establish a bridgehead. Their offensive failed, in part, because of the UN stand at the Pukhan and Han Rivers.

By the end of the month all ground lost to the communists during the latest fighting had been retaken. On June 1, the Eighth Army launched its final major offensive of the war, Operation Piledriver. The advance halted at the end of June when the UN divisions ran into deeply entrenched communist strongpoints. The UN troops dug in opposite the Chinese and North Koreans, and both sides settled down for what would become two years of grueling positional warfare that resembled World War I's western front.

Swede Carlson and his Tigers flew combat missions over Korea for another three weeks following the Hwachon dam raid. On their last mission of their tour, Dick Merrick was killed when his aircraft took several flak hits. As the *Princeton* pulled off station, the pilots of VA-195 were filled with sadness at the loss of their beloved CAG.

It was a bitter end to one of the most successful and unusual tours of any naval squadron during the Korean War. In six months of operations, each of VA-195's pilots had flown about 60 missions. The squadron took part in three major operations of the Korean War. First, it had supported the Marine breakout from Hagaru-ri to Hungnam in the biting winter weather of North Korea. Second, the squadron had played the key role in one of the biggest battles of the entire interdiction campaign at Carlson's Canyon and knocked out its target despite every communist effort to repair EA1622. Third, it had destroyed the Hwachon dam after both B-29s and infantry raiding parties had failed; its success exceeded all expectations and had materially helped to defeat one prong of the second Chinese offensive during the spring of 1951.

Despite their impressive combat record, Carlson's Tigers have been all but lost to history, their achievements obscured by the more glamorous battles between MiGs and Sabrejets that took place far to the north around Sinuiju. Today, however, one small legacy remains. Attack Squadron 195 still exists today after having flown during World War II, Korea, Vietnam, and the Gulf War. Today, VFA-195 flies F-18 Hornets and proudly carry the nickname, "The Dam Busters."

11 | Night Intruders

The Douglas B-26 Invader darted down the valley, its aluminum skin catching the moonlight as it raced along. Below, a narrow, crushed-rock road wound its way around the valley's low foothills. The B-26 continued along, following the road until it opened into a flat, wooded area part way up the valley.

At the Invader's controls, Captain Dick Heyman peered out of the canopy to look for movement on the road below. He banked the wing slightly, moving off his current course. As he did, he caught sight of a pair of lights on the road beyond his wing. He fixed the lights' position relative to a couple of local landmarks. That way, should they go out, he would still have an idea of where he had seen them.

He flew beyond the lights and saw that they came from one of two trucks moving slowly out of the wooded area. As he flew past them, he noticed many more trucks behind the one with the headlights. In fact, the wooded area below seemed to be some sort of bivouac. Trucks were parked tightly together under the trees. Obviously, he had just caught them forming up for the trip south.

Extending beyond his target area, Dick opened the throttles. A few miles later, he banked sharply and the B-26 nimbly responded to his control inputs. Now, as he roared back, the bomber's two Pratt & Whitney R-2800 engines echoed off the hills surrounding the valley. Surely, the sentries on the ground could hear him coming.

He followed the road south back to the wooded area, opening his bomb bay doors as he approached. There were no lights below now, but he had pinpointed the area well. He thundered over it, laying a string of bombs behind him. Their shrill whistles spelled doom for scores of men below, trapped in their encampment with no escape from the aerial attack.

Dick pulled up. He'd been under 500 feet when he made his run, and his B-26 was picking up light flak from the alerted enemy below. Behind him, his bombs began to explode, lighting the night with their reddish-orange glow. He could see the carnage his pass had caused. Dozens of trucks had been caught by his bombs. Shrapnel had gashed their sides, splitting open fuel tanks and loads of ammunition stored in their beds. Gasoline fires erupted as fuel tanks brewed up. Ammunition began to cook off, adding a sort of Fourth of July atmosphere to the scene as tracers zipped in random directions.

Dick made another run up the valley as he held the B-26 steady despite the 23-mm anti-aircraft fire dotting the night sky around him. When he reached the wooded area, he unleashed his eight fixed 50-caliber machine guns while his gunner swept the area with the turret guns. Trucks, men, and equipment alike simply dissolved under the withering strafing attack. Dick walked the rudder back and forth, hosing down the wooded area, the 50s tearing apart everything in their path.

Just a few feet off the deck, the Invader streaked over the burning North Korean bivouac at more than 300 mph. In its wake, it left a scene of utter devastation swathed in smoke and flame. Later, a reconnaissance RB-26 photographed the area and gave Dick Heyman credit for one hundred vehicles destroyed or damaged.

Dick climbed above the valley floor and leveled out at about 1,500 feet. With his ordnance expended, he turned for home. Not a bad night for an old fighter jock who'd spent the last war tangling with the Luftwaffe's finest.

Perhaps the best piston-engined light bomber ever built, the Douglas B-26 proved itself to be durable, fast, and versatile. Carrying a crew of three — usually a pilot, navigator, and gunner — the B-26 became one of the primary weapons employed by the U.S. Air Force against the communist supply lines in North Korea. With its engines cranking out 2,000 horsepower each, it could reach 355 mph in level flight. First used in combat in 1944, the Invader remained in service throughout the Korean War and was even used a decade later in Vietnam. Some variants could carry up to eighteen .50-caliber machine guns, making it the ultimate strafing platform employed by the USAF.

Dick Heyman had joined the 3d Bomb Wing just in time to participate in Operation Strangle — the latest FEAF interdiction effort that spring of 1951. Flying glass-nosed and gunship versions of the B-26 Invader, the 3d Bomb Wing was charged with night interdiction. Targets for their nocturnal missions included road crossings, rail lines, truck and vehicle convoys, and troop concentrations. Occasionally, airfields were also attacked.

National Archives

A B-26 Invader.

As FEAF's daylight aircraft—F-51s, F-80s, and B-29s—raged over North Korea's rail and road systems throughout the first five months of 1951, the North Koreans found it almost suicidal to move large vehicle convoys by day. When they did attempt it, marauding fighter-bombers chopped the convoys to pieces. Moving large convoys made sense only at night, so the North Koreans began hauling their supplies under the cover of darkness. Rail traffic also took to moving at night, speeding from one tunnel to another until dawn.

When FEAF's night intruders conceived and executed increasingly aggressive tactics, darkness gradually offered less and less protection to the communists. By late summer, FEAF's two B-26 wings were knocking out or damaging more than two thousand vehicles a month. They achieved this figure at a time when each wing averaged fewer than forty sorties a night.

Early in 1951, when the first interdiction effort of the year began, the 3d Bomb Wing pioneered night intruder tactics through painful experimentation. It tried all sort of "wild" ideas as tactics were worked out and optimal ordnance loads and types were determined.

Although the 3d Bomb Wing had a long history of treetop-level attacks—during World War II, it had flown strafer versions of the Douglas A-20 Havoc and North American B-25 Mitchell—it had little experience with nighttime attacks on truck convoys. In February 1951, the wing began to experiment with various ways to halt road traffic. One idea was to drop nails at key crossroads in the hopes that passing trucks would suffer tire punctures. The damaged trucks probably would be immobile for several hours, making them vulnerable to fighter-bomber attacks after dawn. That same month, the wing launched Operation Tack.

Using six C-47s, the wing dropped no fewer than eight tons of roofing nails along four main roads south of Pyongyang. To make their drops as accurate as possible, the C-47 pilots dropped down to less than twenty feet off the roads. Major Robert V. Spencer, one of the C-47 pilots, nearly collided with three North Korean tanks driving down his assigned road. He pulled up sharply, narrowly avoiding the ponderous machines. Once clear, he called in a nearby B-26. Despite anti-aircraft fire, Spencer actually made three passes in his lumbering transport to drop flares over the tanks in an effort to illuminate the area for the B-26 crew.

Luckily, the other five C-47s did not have such adventures while dumping their nails and they returned home safely. By the next morning, the nails had trapped twenty-eight vehicles, all of which were destroyed in short order by fighter-bombers.

Eight tons of nails for twenty-eight trucks was not a good trade-off, and the 3d Bomb Wing began searching for another means to harass North Korean road traffic. Someone within the wing came up with the idea of using small metal devices, dubbed *tetrahedrons*, that resemble a child's jack. The idea was to sow them in large quantities over roads and intersections.

FEAF Materiel Command quickly fabricated a batch of these new weapons. Initially, each point on the tetrahedron was made of solid metal, like a nail, but tests revealed that this design did not work. If a truck ran over a solid tetrahedron, its tire punctured but little air would escape since the point of the tetrahedron actually acted as a seal. By hollowing out the tetrahedrons, however, the problem was solved. Each point had a hole that allowed air to escape within a few seconds after a puncture.

Beginning March 14, 1951, the 3d Bomb Wing began to drop the tetrahedrons on North Korean roads. Dick Heyman arrived just in time to fly several of these missions during the first week of his combat tour.

The results were disappointing. The North Koreans switched to solid tires for their trucks, which usually rendered a puncture ineffective. Convoys also equipped their lead trucks with brooms and scoops mounted on the front bumpers to sweep the tetrahedrons out of the way. Clearly, another way to knock out trucks had to be found.

A much better weapon turned out to be the 500-pound butterfly bomb.

Dick Heyman described the butterfly bomb: "After you dropped one, it would open up and these bomblets would come out. They had little wings that unfolded, allowing them to flutter down and land. That's why we called them butterfly bombs. They armed as soon as they hit the ground."

The bomblets lay on a roadbed until a passing vehicle's vibrations detonated them. When one exploded, frequently others went off in sympathetic blasts, carpeting the area with flying shrapnel. The bomblets proved to be an excellent way to kill troops and disable vehicles.

The 3d Bomb Wing also discovered that 260-pound M-81 fragmentation bombs made excellent antitruck weapons. Sometimes, the B-26s would go into action with these bombs double hung on their external racks so they could carry twice as many as a standard load out.

Less effective were the 100-pound M-47 firebombs that the B-26s sometimes carried. As Dick put it, "They weren't worth a damn against our targets." They packed too little wallop against moving truck convoys to do much damage. They were much better suited for fixed targets, such as wood buildings, or for troop concentrations. Regular 500-pound iron bombs were occasionally used, but they also proved to be poor antitruck weapons. They were much better for cratering road junctions and making railroad cuts.

After the 3d Bomb Wing figured out which bombs worked and which didn't, its next problem was to find the enemy convoys. On moonlit nights, North Korean truck convoys sometimes didn't even turn on their headlights, making them very difficult to see from the air. On moonless nights, the lead truck in a convoy usually had its headlights on, but the trucks behind it were blacked out as they followed the leader. Trains never bothered with any sort of illumination. Their engineers preferred the risk of hitting a rail cut and derailing over the risk of attracting UN night intruders.

Once in a while, FEAF night raiders encountered truck convoys that were totally lit up. On July 14, 1951, Captain William L. Ford of the 452d Bomb Wing discovered one such convoy north of Sinanju. He and his crew had just finished shooting up one convoy, destroying 13 trucks and damaging another 15, when a second convoy came into sight. About one hundred trucks were heading south with all of their headlights on. The scene looked more like a peacetime American highway than a wartime supply convoy traversing a dangerous area.

Ford promptly went to work, methodically destroying 25 more trucks and damaging 15 more with strafing and bombing runs. The North Koreans paid a heavy price for that mistake, and it would not be repeated often during the war.

Large and brightly lit convoys were the extreme exception, not the rule. Usually, the trucks would gather in groups of 15 to 20 to make their runs south. Once the North Koreans discovered that a plane was lurking overhead, they would invariably stop moving, shut off all their lights, and deploy whatever weapons they had on hand. This made attacking them rather difficult without some means to illuminate the convoy.

To solve the problem of finding blacked-out convoys, the 3d Bomb Wing employed its six C-47s as flare droppers. Dubbed "Fireflies," the venerable Gooney Birds lumbered over roads and rail areas, ready to drop flares on any convoys they spotted. The C-47s proved effective at first, but since they were so vulnerable to ground fire, they were eventually replaced after U.S. Navy Mark VI flares were adapted for use on B-26s.

Mounted on the S1 rail on one wing, the flares were usually launched by B-26s at about 3,500 feet. Singing slowly earthward under a parachute, they illuminated the ground long enough for the pilot to make two or three quick passes at a target. The trick was to make the runs under the flare so that the crew could see everything on the ground without being blinded by their own light source.

As the spring and summer wore on, the 3d and 452d Bomb Wings developed different flare tactics. The 3d BW liked to fly individual missions, with each B-26 responsible for its own illumination. That way, there would be no threat of a collision with a friendly aircraft. The 452d, however, began operating in teams of two. One plane illuminated the target while the other attacked it. Dubbed "Hunter-Killer" tactics, the 452d used them so effectively that the wing soon exceeded the 3d Bomb Wing's monthly vehicle totals.

Both wings also developed dedicated flare-dropping B-26s. By modifying the bomb bay, just over fifty flares could be carried by a single Invader. A crew member crawled into the bomb bay and tossed out flares on request. The flare-dropping B-26 often operated with up to three other Invaders, providing each night intruder with illumination.

In the late summer of 1951, the 3d Bomb Wing began to experiment with carrying searchlights aloft. Using a navy carbon-arc light, a B-26 could send out a six-foot-wide beam of more than seven million candlepower for almost a half mile. Dick Heyman flew several missions with a searchlight under his wing. Whenever he did, he carried a master sergeant in the right seat who used mechanical controls to move the light around. The master sergeant replaced the navigator in the right seat of the cockpit.

One night, while patrolling a mountainous area just north of the bomb line, Dick thought he saw something moving on a hillside. He banked around and had his master sergeant flip on the light and make a quick sweep. Below, caught in their beam, a tank was creeping along. Marking the tank's location, Dick rolled down on it as his sergeant cut the light. Within a few hundred yards, he fired a salvo of rockets at the tank, saturating the area with explosions. Later, Dick recalled, in an interview with the author, "I don't know if I destroyed it, but I sure gave them one heck of a headache!"

Dick's close friend, John Walmsley, also used a searchlight-equipped B-26 for his intruder missions. On September 12, he pioneered its use in combat when he encountered a convoy north of Hwangju. Dropping 500-pound bombs on the lead truck stopped the convoy cold and gave Walmsley the chance to make repeated strafing and bombing runs on it. On each pass, his right-seat operator illuminated the North Koreans as they frantically tried to escape. Bill Mulkins was in the nose of the B-26C, and he later reported that the searchlight completely panicked the North Koreans. Desperate to escape, they drove their trucks off the road into ditches, crashed into trees, and piled into one another.[1]

Two nights later, Walmsley discovered a train and used his searchlight to make his bombing runs. He managed to halt and disable the train but ran out of ordnance before it could be totally destroyed. Not wanting to let such a juicy target get away, he called in another 3d Bomb Wing Invader. When it arrived a few minutes later, John began flying illumination passes right down the railroad tracks. Using his searchlight on each run, he held his B-26 steady so the other plane could see the target. Each pass he put his bomber right on the deck, flying through a narrow valley. Twice he made such passes, both times attracting heavy anti-aircraft fire.

He came around for a third pass, again on the deck, with his light blazing away. The North Korean gunners found the range, and flak bursts rocked the Invader. Walmsley refused to take evasive action. Instead, he held the plane steady so the other Invader could complete its pass. More flak tore holes in John's plane, ripping through its vital systems. Suddenly, flames erupted and began fanning out along both wings. The light operator, a master sergeant, looked over to his left and saw John fighting the yoke as he tried to keep the plane level.

"Get out!" John yelled at the crew.

The master sergeant reached up, popped the canopy open, and leaped out, aiming for the top of the right wing. He reached the wing just as the B-26 slammed into the side of a hill at the end of the valley. The explosion blew him hundreds of feet into the air and somehow caused his chute to open. He came down in the rugged countryside. His face was horribly burned. Disoriented and in tremendous pain, he wandered around for days before North Koreans captured him. The North Koreans took him to a POW camp, where the guards threw him into a dank cell.

The sergeant received no treatment at all for his ghastly wounds. Gradually, the burned flesh on his face began to rot and attracted maggots. They turned out to be a blessing in disguise. The repellent creatures actually debrided his wounds by eating the decaying flesh. Years later, Dick Heyman listened in horror as the sergeant related how those maggots had probably saved his life. The maggots frequently crawled into his nose, however, and his hands had been so badly burned that he could not use his fingers to dig them out. Instead, he was forced to endure them wiggling around inside his nostrils. Despite this horror, Walmsley's gunner survived the war. Later he recounted his ordeal to Dick Heyman.

John Walmsley died on impact when the B-26 struck the hillside. He was awarded the Medal of Honor posthumously for his actions that night, one of only five given to aviators during the Korean War. In part, the citation reads, "His heroic initiative and daring aggressiveness in completing this important mission in the face of overwhelming opposition and at the risk of his life, reflects the highest credit upon himself and the U.S. Air Force."[2]

-◆◆◆-

Dick Heyman watched the flak burst around him and rock his B-26 violently with each blast. He hung tough, completed his run, and pulled up and over the hills below. Once out of range, he checked the plane and discovered that a piece of shrapnel had torn a hole in one of the engine cowlings. He checked his oil pressure gauge, then his fuel pressure gauge. Neither showed a loss of pressure, which meant the lines hadn't been clipped by the shrapnel. The engine seemed to be running fine, but he continued to watch the gauges until he was satisfied that no substantial damage had been done. Dick decided to continue his mission as long as the engine continued to run without problems.

Anti-aircraft fire had plagued the night intruders by the summer of 1951. The North Koreans, knowing that they had to protect their truck convoys, placed flak batteries on hills and mountaintops that overlooked crucial road routes. At times, the gunners actually had to fire down into the valleys to hit the attacking B-26s. These flak traps could be deadly, and their plunging fire claimed many B-26 crews.

At the same time, some convoys began carrying their own organic light anti-aircraft weapons, machine guns being the most common. The North Koreans stationed observers every few hundred yards along their supply routes to warn passing trucks of danger. When a lookout sounded the alarm, the convoy halted and deployed its air defense systems. The B-26s usually had time to make only one pass before the guns were ready for action. After that, the Invader would be facing an alerted and frequently well-armed enemy.

As a result of these tactics, night intruder missions became increasingly hazardous. Even stopping a convoy, which most B-26s tried to do by knocking out the lead truck to block the road, became increasingly dangerous. As Heyman remembered, "We wanted to make as few passes as possible after we got the convoy stopped. Troops would pour out, and we'd start taking machine-gun and rifle fire. So we always tried to make that first pass really count."

Attacking "down the string"—parallel along the convoy's length—was the most effective way to knock out road traffic, but it also became one of the most dangerous—as Walmsley's crew had discovered that disastrous September.

Light anti-aircraft guns posted with the convoys could get a near zero deflection shot on Invaders attacking down the string, which made them easy to hit. Because of the terrain, sometimes the only way to hit a truck convoy was to attack down the string. Heyman encountered this situation several times when mountains on either side of the road precluded a curving side approach. In these cases, he sometimes picked up battle damage.

He said, "In Europe, when I was hit in my P-38, I always knew it. In Korea, a couple of times, I came back with holes in the airplane and I had no idea I'd even been hit. I may have been rocked by flak. The airplane would shake and jump around. I'd sometimes see the bursts. But, a couple of times I didn't realize I'd been hit. After the mission, my crew chief would come get me when I got finished with the debriefing and say, 'Hey, I found some holes in the airplane!'"

As though flak and small arms weren't enough, the North Koreans stretched thick cables across some valleys. Unable to see them in the dark, marauding FEAF aircraft sometimes collided with the cables and were destroyed or heavily damaged. Heyman never hit one, but several of his friends did. They returned home with their planes missing large chunks of their wings and sometimes even their tails.

Flak, cables, and hazardous terrain combined to make these night missions some of the most difficult operations of the war. Compounding the difficulties, the 3d Bomber Wing operated out of Iwakuni Air Force Base, Japan, until late in the summer of 1951, which forced the crews to fly long, arduous missions that sometimes lasted more than six hours. When the Chinese had attacked that spring, FEAF requested that the light bomber wings increase their nightly sortie rate. The only way to do this was to double up some of the missions. For several months, the crews flew from Iwakuni to their patrol sectors in North Korea, completed their mission, and then flew to K-2 Airfield at Taegu, South Korea. Landing a B-26 at night at Taegu was no easy feat because the pierced-steel planking on the runway had begun to deteriorate. The B-26s landing there tore up dozens of tires, and more than a few accidents resulted. Also, the tires were in short supply, so each one lost at K-2 was hard to replace.

If the B-26 crews got down at Taegu without incident, they could find a place to grab a quick catnap as their planes were readied for the next mission. About an hour later, they were airborne and heading north to their next target area. Four hours later, utterly exhausted, they were back in Japan, after up to ten hours of flight and combat.

In addition to the stress of these missions, the B-26 crews knew that their fates would be grim if they went down in North Korean territory. Like most American POWs, B-26 crews captured by the communists endured torture, trauma, disease, and malnutrition. Harry Hedlund was shot down and captured while his squadron was attached to the 3d Bomber Wing. Of his imprisonment, he later wrote:

> They took me out into the field with a .45 cal behind my ear, kneeling, with my hands down and all that good stuff, just like in the movies. But they didn't shoot me, they just shot alongside me. And they said, "We give you one more chance," and it was back to the interrogation room for more questions. . . .
> One time . . . they tied up this Army Major with his hands and feet together behind his back and left him like that for about a week. He got

little to eat and of course he fouled himself, not being able to go to the bathroom. When he was untied, he found that his wrists were useless and they remained in that condition for about one year. In the meantime, his hands flopped about uselessly.[3]

For light bomber crews captured by the communists, an especially insidious campaign of torture was undertaken. In May 1951, the communists began to claim that Americans had initiated a bacteriological warfare campaign in North Korea and China. The following year, in February 1952, even more accusations followed. Moscow Radio echoed the North Korean claims. One broadcast reported:

> [T]he American interventionists are sending spies and disruptive elements into North Korea for the purpose of obtaining military secrets, poisoning wells, and spreading smallpox and typhus bacteria in various places. One of the more villainous methods practiced by the American interventionists is the sending of lepers secretly into North Korea.[4]

On May 4, 1952, Radio Pyongyang announced that two American aviators from the 3d Bomber Wing had confessed to dropping bacteriological weapons on North Korea in January 1952. Lieutenant Kenneth Enoch and Lieutenant John Quinn had been shot down on January 13, 1952, during an attack on Anju. Shortly after their B-26 went down, the North Koreans had them in custody and began to grill both airmen with relays of interrogators who demanded that they confess to dropping germ bombs.

Held in solitary confinement, Enoch and Quinn endured weeks of interrogation along with psychological and physical torture. The communists berated them and denounced them as war criminals who would never be returned to the United States. If they confessed, however, they would each be declared a "People's Hero" and receive lenient treatment.

For almost two months, the communists kept the pressure on the two men, as well as several other airmen. Finally, in May, Enoch broke under the strain. As he put it later, when faced with a Hobson's Choice of insanity, death, or a ridiculous confession, he finally chose the third option. Quinn also eventually broke down and confessed. The men were filmed as they read their confessions. The film was distributed all over the world by the communists through various propaganda organizations and peace committees.

In his confession, Quinn said:

> I was forced to be a tool of these warmongers, made to drop germ bombs and do this awful crime against the people of Korea and the Chinese Volunteers. . . . At last after much patience on the part of the Volunteers, I realized my crime. My own conscience bothered me a great deal and it is very good to be rid of this burden and to confess and repent. I have realized my terrible crime against the people.[5]

Through Quinn's and Enoch's confessions, the communists were able to convince much of the world that there was a germ warfare campaign being waged in Korea. Later, other American pilots were forced to confess, including World War II ace Colonel Walker ("Bud") Mahurin, USAF. Those who confessed found their military careers ruined when they finally returned to the United States.

Recent revelations by historians working in the archives of former Eastern Bloc countries reveal conclusively that the accusations against the USAF were a construct of communist propaganda.[6] In fact, North Korea's secret police actually infected at least two North Korean prisoners with cholera to further give evidence of America's germ warfare campaign.

As the accusations grew increasingly shrill, the communists staged riots throughout the world in protest against the United States. Although epidemics ravaged North Korea during the war, no hard evidence was ever found that linked the United States to them. In fact, the charges had no merit; the epidemics were a result of the devastation resulting from the war. Despite the lack of evidence, the belief that America used bacteriological weapons still persists today in parts of the world.

12 | A Fighter Pilot's Heart

On the night of June 14, 1951, radar operators of the 606th Aircraft Control and Warning Squadron peered at their screens and watched two dots appear a few miles north of Seoul. Heading south at about 80 mph, one of the blips made straight for Suwon Airfield, while the other turned for Inchon and later dropped a pair of bombs into a motor pool.

At Suwon, a squad of aviation engineers working on the runway heard a tinny, sewing-machine-like engine pass overhead. Seconds later, two small bombs exploded nearby. Nobody was hurt, but the attack shook up everyone.

The two bombs signaled a new development in the air war, one that would profoundly affect the daylight campaign against North Korea. Flying from battered Sariwon Airfield, these two North Korean night intruders represented the communists' first campaign of night harassment against UN installations around Seoul. Without a doubt, the North Korean air crews who engaged in this campaign had to be some of the most courageous men in the history of modern air warfare. Each night, with the most primitive of weapons, they flew into the teeth of the world's most modern air force and air defense system.

Equipped with fabric-covered Polikarpov Po-2 biplanes, the North Koreans relied on the sheer crudeness of their aircraft to get them to Seoul. With an engine that put out less than 90 horsepower—far less than most compact cars have today—the Po-2 could not even manage 100 mph in level flight.

Each Po-2 carried a pilot and a gunner. The gunner had only a handheld Soviet-made submachine gun to use against attacking UN night fighters and ground targets. Usually, the Po-2s carried a pair of light bombs, but some North Korean crews also used grenades. Over the target area, they lobbed them down on whatever installations they could find in the hope that, at the very least, the explosions would deprive the UN personnel of sleep. Once they started to

National Archives

A North Korean Polikarpov Po-2 biplane.

appear with regularity that summer, the Americans began calling them "Piss-call Charlies." The press later cleaned that up to "Bedcheck Charlies."

The Po-2s stayed low and hugged the ground for protection as they sputtered southward on their missions of mischief. Their slow speed and ability to fly right off the treetops combined to make them hard to track on radar and even more difficult to intercept.

La Woon Yung carried out one of the most successful night heckling raids of the war. Just two days after the start of the campaign, he pushed his little Po-2 to Suwon, which was well lit and easy to find. Cruising over the huge American airfield, he lobbed a bomb right into the 802d Engineer Battalion's motor pool, showering the equipment parked there with shrapnel. Moments later, he dropped his other bomb squarely onto a F-86 Sabrejet sitting on the parking ramp. The F-86 exploded, sending debris knifing through the air and into other F-86s parked nearby. When the smoke cleared, one Sabrejet was completely destroyed, four severely damaged, and an additional four less seriously damaged.

La Woon Yung's daring attack had just taken out more F-86s than all the MiG pilots had destroyed since December 1950. Later, Yung recorded the raid in his diary: "I saw with my own eyes that many of the enemy aircraft had been destroyed by my bombing."[1]

This type of attack could not be tolerated by the UN, especially because F-86s were in such short supply. Accordingly, FEAF decided that the best way to deal with them was to initiate a ferocious bombing campaign against all North Korean airfields. This was not a particularly novel idea. Superfortresses had hit the North Korean airfields regularly all year, but a spate of bad weather had forced suspension of these attacks at the beginning of June. Given the breathing space they needed, the North Koreans quickly put Sariwon Airfield into operational condition and busied themselves in repairing other airfields as well.

After La Woon Yung's raid, FEAF put even more muscle behind the renewed airfield attacks. Along with the B-29s, several fighter-bomber groups joined the campaign, and the two B-26 wings were ordered to harass the North Korean repair crews at night with low-level air attacks. Stu Kalmus, a former World War II P-38 pilot, was assigned to one of these night harassment missions that the 452d Bomb Wing drew at the end of June. On the night of June 26, he and his crew saddled up their B-26C, a glass-nose version that lacked a Norden bombsight. Sariwon Airfield was Stu's target. He was supposed to dump his butterfly bombs on the runway from about 1,500 feet altitude.

The night before, another 452d Wing crew led by Wally McDannel had tried to hit Sariwon, their B-26 flying so low that it practically cut the weeds around the airfield. The plan had been to stay on the deck during their approach, then pop up to 1,500 feet at the last second to release the butterfly bombs. This type of ordnance had to be dropped from at least that altitude because of the time it took for the bomb canister to open and release the bombs. When the B-26 had swept over Sariwon, however, North Korean flak filled the skies, and tracers crisscrossed over the plane. Later, the crew learned that they had flown so low across the airstrip that the barrels of the guns defending the target could not be lowered enough to hit them. McDannel had pulled off the target, come around at a higher altitude, and completed his attack. After they landed, however, he and his crew had discovered their butterfly bombs hanging on the racks of the bomb bay.

Now, on June 26, Stu Kalmus and his crew would undertake the same mission. Instead of flying on the deck then popping up to release altitude, Kalmus decided to pass over the target on a westerly heading, extend beyond it for ten to fifteen miles, then split-ess, and come right down on it. Two miles out from Sariwon, the B-26 took flak and small-arms fire. A direct hit in the nose slammed the bomber around and knocked navigator Jack Broadway into the passageway. The nose section was completely destroyed.

Although Broadway had suffered a head wound, he managed to wedge himself forward into the wreckage of the nose so he could give course corrections to Kalmus. As he did, the B-26 rocked repeatedly as the North Koreans found the range. Two feet of the left wingtip disappeared in a burst of flak and flying metal, which peppered the left engine cowling. Another hit damaged the electrical system, and another punctured the Invader's auxiliary fuel tanks.

Stu held his course and made it to the Sariwon runway in spite of the damage. Right over the target, Broadway opened the bomb bay doors from the wrecked nose, and, on his command, Kalmus released the bombs. The Invader raced along the runway and then left the target behind as Kalmus followed an egress route that was determined to be free of anti-aircraft weapons.

They were in the clear, but the plane had been shredded by flak. Some distance out from Sariwon, Stu climbed to 4,000 feet. Suddenly, the left engine's propeller malfunctioned. He scrambled at the controls and managed to feather the engine before the propeller could destroy it or cause it to burst into flames. Now, they were on one fan and the nearest UN field was still far away.

With their one working R-2800 at full military power, Kalmus's B-26 staggered along at 165 mph. Kalmus nursed the plane southward, but even with the one engine at maximum power and the prop turning at 2700 rpm, the Invader was still slowly losing altitude. When Kalmus checked the plane, he discovered that half of the left engine nacelle (enclosure) had been blown away by another flak burst, probably while they were over the runway. With the damaged nacelle, the drag caused by the damaged nose, and the missing two feet of wing, they were lucky to be in the air at all.

North of Haeju, they encountered mountains that rose more than 3,000 feet. They had no way to get over such obstacles, so Kalmus had to weave his way around the peaks. While Kalmus concentrated on flying, Broadway came up out of the nose and squatted next to the pilot's seat. With the electrical system damaged, the instrument lights had failed. Jack stayed next to his pilot, flashlight in hand, shining the beam on the pilot's instrument panel.

Somehow, they made it to Kimpo, circled the field once, then came in for a belly landing. The Invader skidded along on its fuselage before coming to a complete stop near the end of the runway. Stu cut the switches to minimize the chance of a fire, then he jettisoned the canopy. Stu, Jack and their gunner, Tom King, all piled out and hit the tarmac running, afraid their plane would explode at any minute.

They got off the runway and ducked behind a large boulder. Kalmus was surprised to see that the Invader still had a 260-pound fragmentation bomb slung under the left wing, even though he had hit the bomb release and later the jettison switch. Somehow, the bomb had remained stuck on its rack. What luck that it hadn't detonated during the crash landing!

As they crouched behind the boulder and counted their blessings, the B-26 suddenly exploded. When the fire finally subsided, only the tail, part of the cockpit, and their one good R-2800 remained discernible within the wreckage.

For their actions on this mission, Kalmus earned a Silver Star and Broadway received the Distinguished Flying Cross. Jack's head wound was so serious that he was sent to a hospital ship at Pusan harbor.

Summing up his experience, Kalmus later said, "Thank God for Pratt & Whitney!"[2]

If the night missions proved rough, the daylight raids were no picnic either. Earlier in the spring, the Soviets had deployed a new MiG-15 division into Manchuria, this one full of hand-picked pilots who knew their craft well. In June, they would make their presence felt.

The first week of FEAF's airfield campaign had triggered no aerial challenge from the communists. But, on June 22, an F-80 strike against Sinuiju Airfield had drawn a MiG attack that was intercepted by F-86s providing top cover. The MiGs destroyed an F-86, and the Americans claimed two of the Russian planes. That was the third F-86 lost by the 4th Fighter Interceptor Wing in four days of battle between June 18 and 22. Although the Sabrejet pilots had claimed seven MiGs in return, the F-86 losses were the highest of the war to date.

Two days later, the F-80s of the 51st Wing were jumped by MiGs while making a low-level attack on Sinanju Airfield. The F-80s were able to get away and had damaged four MiGs in the process.

At the end of the month, the MiGs hit a formation of B-29s over Yongyu Airfield and also bounced several formations of F-51s. One MiG was claimed during the attacks, and no UN losses were reported. Still, the communists were showing a willingness to mix it up with UN aircraft that had not been previously seen over North Korea.

The Po-2 raids had triggered a massive response by FEAF. In again unleashing the fighter-bombers and medium bombers on North Korea's airfields, FEAF, in turn, had triggered the MiG regiments in Manchuria. What followed was the most intense flare-up of air fighting seen to this point of the war.

The airfield attacks continued into July, with the communists responding aggressively. Despite the infusion of crack Soviet pilots, the MiGs continued to suffer heavy losses. By July 12, UN aircraft, mainly the F-86s, had claimed twelve more MiG-15s without a loss.

After July 12, the communists abandoned their reconstruction efforts on North Korea's runways. The UN daylight campaign against them wound down, but it would be renewed later in the fall when the North Koreans again tried to repair the runways. The June–July 1951 airfield campaign remains one of the most successful air operations of the war. To be sure, it was a hard-won victory that presaged the bloodletting to come during the fall.

If the night missions proved

Unconcerned with the daylight war, Dick Heyman and his crew went about their nighttime raiding missions that June with their regular tenacity and professionalism. On the night of June 23, Dick had just finished a bomb-ing mission and was heading southward when he heard "Dentist" control—the radar operator in Seoul—broadcast a request asking that any aircraft with ammunition left give him a call.

Dick remembered, "I still had all my ammo, but no bombs. I was low on fuel, but I could always recover at an airfield in South Korea if it came to that."

Not sure what Dentist wanted, he called out that he had plenty of ammu-nition.

"What is your ordnance?" Dentist asked.

"Four fifties, three hundred rounds each," Dick replied.

Dentist acknowledged and said, "OK, we've got an aircraft that's strafing in the Kimpo area."

Dentist gave Dick a heading to maintain, then told him to drop low and slow down. He lowered his flaps and opened the cowl flaps, which managed to get him down to about 150 mph. After he completed his turn onto Dentist's heading the controller asked, "Can you get any lower?"

He dropped below 500 feet, and his B-26 soon disappeared off Dentist's radar scope.

It was a clear, moonlit night, and Dick had already been airborne for about four hours. His eyes were well adjusted to the darkness. Below him, the ter-rain was fairly flat with a river through the area and low hills scattered about. A flash of movement caught Dick's eye. Just up ahead and to the right, he caught a fleeting glimpse of the black-green silhouette of a Po-2 buzzing along in the opposite direction. It was so close that it stayed in sight for barely an instant. Then it was gone, running away behind Dick's B-26.

He swung his bomber around, dropping his gear so he could slow down even further. As he circled, he and his crew scanned the night sky, but could see no sign of the little Polikarpov. He kept circling and watching, hoping to catch just a fleeting glimpse of the North Korean. It has been six years since his last dogfight, but his old fighter pilot instincts flooded back with sudden ferocity. He charged onward, intent on scoring a kill.

He found the Po-2 running for home right down in the river channel. "Bam, there he was," Dick later reported. "So I laid the '26 over on a wingtip and gave chase."

He pulled in behind the fleeing biplane, dropping down onto the treetops. In fact, Dick was so focused on the chase that he collided with several trees. Ground crews would later pull numerous branches from the plane.

Dick had a glass-nosed B-26 without any internal guns. Slung under each wing, however, were a pair of .50 caliber package guns that had been sighted in before his flight. Dick didn't think they would be terribly accurate, so he modified his approach. Instead of sticking his gunsight pipper right on the Po-2, he decided to spray the area around the biplane. He started high and off to the right when he opened fire. Gradually, as he held the trigger down, he swept the nose down and across the Po-2's flight path. Once past the biplane, he brought the nose up, and scribed another arc back to the left.

Dick's navigator, observing the whole scene, kept exclaiming, "Get him, Dick! Get him! Get him! Get him!"

With Dick's tracers pouring out around him, the Po-2 pilot tried to get even closer to the water. As he did, the gunner in the rear seat pointed his submachine gun and desperately fired at the B-26 coming up behind them, but he didn't stand a chance. Dick's gunfire scythed into the Po-2 and blasted it apart. In the blink of an eye, flames boiled out along the Po-2's decimated fuselage. It fell out of the air and splashed into the river.

Dick remarked later, "Boom. He went just like that. There was an immediate flash, then he was done burning before he even hit the river."

From the time that Dentist first called him to the destruction of the Po-2 was not more than ten or twelve minutes. The first North Korean night raider of the war had just been shot down.

A few days later, on June 30, Captain E. B. Long, USMC, caught another Po-2 near Seoul and destroyed it with fire from his Grumman F7F Tigercat for the second Po-2 kill. On July 12, another Marine pilot shot down a third one. Following that final kill, the North Koreans quit running nighttime heckling missions for the rest of the summer. With their disappearance from the night skies, the pilots and crews of the B-26 wings again owned the hours of darkness south of MiG Alley.

Later, as the night war heated up, the Soviets employed several night fighter regiments in North Korea. These were defensive interceptors, not offensive aircraft. They prowled over North Korea in search of B-29s but stayed well clear of the front lines. The Po-2s remained the only real air threat to UN bases during the war.

-♦♦♦-

Dick Heyman, old fighter pilot that he was, really wanted to make ace. He had nailed that Po-2, plus he had two kills from World War II. With a couple more slow biplanes, he might become an ace after all. Unfortunately for Dick, he never saw another Po-2 during his tour.

Shortly after John Walmsley's death in September, Dick ran into enemy aircraft one more time. On this mission, he had been given an island off the east coast of Korea as his patrol zone. Going north, though, he encountered thick clouds that forced him to climb to about 8,000 feet. Below him, the ground was totally shrouded by the scud layer, which prevented him from keeping an accurate eye on his location. It was not quite dark yet; he was supposed to begin his patrol just before sunset. He checked in with the local U.S.

Navy radar operator who was stationed somewhere off the North Korean coast. Continuing north, he kept looking for a break in the clouds but no luck, so he flew on.

Finally, he saw something glowing on the horizon. At first, he wasn't sure what it was, but as he drew closer, he realized that it was a city full of blazing house and street lights. All of North Korea had been blacked out for more than a year. This discovery proved a bit disconcerting. Where was he? Could that be Vladivostok? If so, he was way off course.

Below him, several dots suddenly popped out of the undercast and began zipping along on top of the clouds. Dick studied the dots for a moment as his B-26 closed on them from behind and above.

"I called the Navy and asked if they had some prop jobs in the area," Dick explained later, "and the Navy radar controller said no."

Dick asked the operator if he was showing on the screen, and again the controller replied, "Negative." He then added, "You went off my scope fifteen minutes ago."

Now convinced that the dots were communist aircraft, Dick shadowed them for a few minutes until he identified them as Yak-9 fighters. They were clearly unaware of his presence—he was in a perfect bounce position. Once again, the barely suppressed fighter pilot in Dick rose to the surface. He turned to his navigator and said, "What do you say we try to get the tail-end Charlie?"

The navigator looked at him for a moment. They were flying a fully loaded B-26, they weren't sure where they were, and below were 9 Yaks cruising along in a tight vee. It didn't seem like a fair fight.

"Well," the navigator responded slowly, "OK."

Dick considered the situation, then briefed his crew on what they were going to do. He'd firewall the throttle, dive down and make a pass at the tail-end Charlie, then duck into the clouds and make a quick getaway. Dick told his gunner to be ready and spray the other planes with his twin fifties. He pushed the throttle forward, and the heavy Invader began to accelerate. Easing the yoke forward, they began to pick up more speed as they hurtled down on the unsuspecting Yaks. Soon, they were going flat-out, doing over 300 mph in the diving pass.

Dick lined up on the last Yak, watching the fighter begin to fill his gunsight. He was just about ready to open fire when suddenly, like a school of fish, the whole formation broke hard left. As a group, they were turning into him.

The odds stank, and Dick was not going to risk his crew in such a lopsided dogfight. So, he put the nose down and dropped into the undercast. He circled around for a few minutes, then climbed back out of the cloud to have a look. Off in the distance, much closer now, he could see whatever city that was, its lights blazing away as if in peacetime. The Yaks were nowhere to be seen.

Disappointed, he turned south for home, unable even to find his patrol area. They turned out to be so far north that it took almost 45 minutes before they appeared on the Navy's radar scope. Perhaps missing those Yaks had been a blessing in disguise. Given how far north he was, Dick might have created an international incident had he flamed that tail-end Charlie over Chinese or Soviet territory.

Dick wrapped up his tour with the 3d Bomb Wing around Thanksgiving of 1951. In eight and a half months of combat, he had flown 56 missions to add to the 70 or so that he flew in Europe during World War II. When he returned home, he chose to stay in the Air Force instead of returning to his civilian business. During the 1960s, he called in a few favors and finagled a transfer to a fighter-bomber outfit in Thailand. He served as a squadron commander and flew Republic F-105 Thunderchiefs as a Wild Weasel pilot, completing 280 missions before heading for home. He retired as a full colonel after flying twelve hundred combat hours in P-38s, P-51s, B-26s and F-105s in a remarkable career that stretched across four decades and three wars.

During his stint with the 3d Bomb Wing, Dick turned out to be in the right place at the right time that night of June 23, 1951. He carved out a small chunk of history for himself that night, downing the first night heckler of the war in what had to be one of the oddest air battles in American aviation history. In it, this daring Invader pilot from Oklahoma proved he had, and always would have, a fighter pilot's heart.

Part 3 | Mission to Namsi

13 | Prelude to Black Tuesday

Although North Korea's effort to renovate its airfields had failed by July 12, 1951, the communist effort against UN control of the air in MiG Alley was far from being defeated. Indeed, throughout the summer, FEAF received startling signs that indicated a massive air buildup in Manchuria.

In June, FEAF had counted about 690 enemy aircraft based in Manchuria. These included ground attack, fighter, and light bomber types. In July, FEAF estimated that there were at least 445 MiG-15s stationed along the north bank of the Yalu River. That number continued to rise throughout the summer until in September, 525 MiGs were counted.

To combat the MiG-15s, FEAF possessed only eighty-nine North American F-86A and E Sabrejets. Of those, only forty-four were initially deployed in Korea at any one time. The other squadron stayed in Japan until later in 1951, when it finally received clearance to head for Korea.

Lieutenant General Otto P. Weyland, USAF, who took command of FEAF on June 10, 1951, had examined the situation and realized that UN control of the air had become tenuous at best. On the day that he took command, Weyland requested that Washington send him two more jet fighter wings to use in the defense of Japan. Although the Air Force brass in the capital considered the Manchurian buildup primarily defensive in nature, they did concede that an increased threat existed and decided to send FEAF one more wing. This was the 116th Fighter-Bomber Wing, a recently activated National Guard unit that had been slated for duty in Europe. On July 24, the wing and its seventy-five Republic F-84 Thunderjets arrived in Japan. Unfortunately, almost half of the F-84s suffered serious damage during transit across the Pacific. It took several weeks to sort out the problems and get the outfit operational.

Weyland was glad to have the 116th, but he really wanted to augment his F-86 force. In July, he asked Washington for two more jet fighter wings for use in Korea. His request was turned down. The Air Force was spread thin all over the world, and no more F-86 outfits were available to send. The 4th FIW would have to continue to fight alone.

By September, Weyland became increasingly concerned for the safety of his fighter-bombers. Communist air activity was on the rise once again, and his F-80s, F-51s, and F-84s were being attacked by aggressive MiG pilots. To maintain the interdiction attacks above Pyongyang, he would need at least one more F-86 outfit.

If Washington didn't have another wing to send, perhaps they had the aircraft. Weyland asked General Hoyt Vandenberg, USAF chief of staff, for permission to convert one of his existing F-80 wings over to F-86s. Vandenberg turned the matter over to his operations officer, who reported that the Air Force could not support two F-86 wings in Korea and even the capacity to keep one there was questionable.[1] Again, Weyland's request was denied.

Meanwhile, the F-86 pilots in Korea had their hands full. During the month of September, the 4th FIW alone spotted 1,177 MiG sorties. The F-86s intercepted 911 of these and claimed 14 MiGs destroyed for the loss of 3 Sabrejets. The MiGs, however, had caused some damage of their own. Throughout the month, MiG pilots had concentrated on intercepting the fighter-bombers running interdiction missions north of Pyongyang. During the course of several fights, the communists also knocked down an F-51, and F-80, and an F-84. FEAF lost a total of 6 planes in return for the 14 MiGs, for a kill ratio of 2.4:1.0.

On September 20, when FEAF learned that its request to convert an existing wing to F-86s had been turned down, Weyland realized that its fighter-bombers would be too exposed in MiG Alley for continued operations. As a result, he pulled the fighter-bombers out of MiG Alley altogether. The MiGs had scored a significant victory. They would soon score another.

On September 27, 1951, a 67th Tactical Reconnaissance Wing pilot discovered a brand new North Korean airfield at Saamcham while on a photo flight. Quickly, he brought his news back home and FEAF HQ soon had the information. The reconnaissance pilot had uncovered a field overlooked on previous missions. His photos showed that the strip at Saamcham had been under construction for at least a month. Already, revetments and anti-aircraft guns studded the field's perimeter. The runway itself was seven thousand feet long and looked like it was about to be paved. The length and the indications that it would have a hard surface meant only one thing: the communists were planning to send MiGs south of the Yalu River.

Intensive air reconnaissance followed up this initial sighting. Two more fields, all within a twenty-mile radius of one another, were found to the west of Saamcham at Taechon and Namsi. The communists had planned this latest move well. All three fields lay in the heart of MiG Alley and were designed to be jet-capable. To FEAF, the threat was clear. If communist jets began using these bases, MiG Alley could be extended down to Pyongyang and maybe even beyond. Interdiction missions in some of the most vital areas of North Korea would be endangered—indeed, the increasingly tenuous control of the air that FEAF had enjoyed to date would be threatened even more.

How real was the actual threat? Certainly, the mere presence of MiGs in northwestern Korea represented a serious threat to UN air operations. Postwar research, however, indicates that the MiG units deployed south of the Yalu consisted of poorly trained and motivated North Koreans. These MiG pilots were no match for the veteran American fighter pilots. They alone, or even with massive Chinese assistance, could not have contested the skies south of the Chongchon River with any hope of success.

The real punch of the communist air forces lay in the two air divisions that the Soviets had deployed to the Antung area. Both outfits were tough, disciplined, and professional. Many of the Soviet pilots had flown in World War II and several of them were aces. Like the 4th FIW, the Soviet air units operated under strict, politically motivated rules of engagement. They were forbidden to fly south of a line stretching from Pyongyang to Wonsan. They could not fly over the Yellow Sea, and, except on specific occasions, they did not operate above northeastern Korea. The mission was defensive, not offensive. The units had been sent to Manchuria to defend North Korea against B-29 raids and fighter-bomber attacks.

More important, the Soviets did everything they could to mask their presence in the war. Their planes flew with Chinese or North Korean markings, and the pilots at least made attempts to speak Chinese over their radios (although this did not last long). Both their mission and their desire to hide it made it unlikely that they would ever be redeployed south of the Yalu. Instead, they provided air cover for the new fields so that the recently formed North Korean MiG units could move south. The Soviets performed the task with bloody resolution that would soon cost FEAF heavily and change the entire nature of the bombing campaign against North Korea.

—◆◆◆—

General Weyland realized the new North Korean airfields had to be destroyed. The earlier campaign had succeeded in part because many of the North Korean strips lay outside MiG Alley and attacking aircraft did not have to worry about the sudden appearance of communist interceptors.

Now, however, three major airfields within MiG Alley were about to become operational.

The three wings of B-29 Superfortress bombers represented the best weapons to use against the airfields. Each B-29 could carry dozens of 100-pound bombs that could crater runways, aprons, and taxi areas. For this reason, a few B-29 missions should be able to accomplish the same destruction as scores of F-84 or F-80 sorties since the Superfortresses could haul aloft so many more bombs than the jets. Yet, the B-29s had proved to be terribly vulnerable to MiG attacks during the previous spring. To protect the B-29s from interception, Lieutenant General Joseph Kelly, FEAF Bomber Command's new leader, elected to send them against the airfields at night when the MiGs would not be up and about.

The attacks began on the night of October 13 when a pair of 307th Bomb Wing B-29s hit Saamcham Airfield. The Superforts released 278 bombs on their target, but only 24 hit the runway. Even then, all of the bombs that fell accurately struck the extreme northeast end of the field instead of the center, where they would have more effectively choked off air traffic.

For the next few nights, lone B-29s raided the three new airfields. The results were disappointing. None of the fields was heavily damaged, and time was running out. They would soon be operational, and their revetments would harbor MiG-15s.

Kelly had no choice but to lay on daylight B-29 strikes. If the bombers did well, they could knock out the airfields with a couple of raids on each target. The threat always remained, however, that the North Koreans would use their amazing engineering skills to repair the damaged strips quickly, which would result in another long and drawn-out campaign pitting aircraft against repair crews. But, the last major effort against existing airfields in North Korea had prompted the communists to abandon reconstruction efforts, so perhaps the upcoming B-29s strikes would have the same effect. One way or another, FEAF could not afford to see these strips reach operational status.

Each of FEAF's three B-29 wings would be assigned one airfield to attack. The 19th Wing, whose history dated back to the Philippines campaign of 1941–42, received Saamcham as its target. The 98th Wing drew Taechon, and the 307th Wing got Namsi. Each raid would be made by nine B-29s flying in three flights of three each. All raids would be made under the heaviest possible fighter escort.

The fighter escort situation dictated the times that these attacks could take place. FEAF would lay on two bombing missions a day—one in the early morning before 10:00 A.M. and the other in the afternoon after 3:00 P.M. That way, the 4th Fighter Wing's F-86s could cover both strikes. The F-86s were scheduled to fly in the morning, land and refuel, then be up again in the afternoon.

U.S. Air Force

Pre-strike briefing, October 1951.

The F-86s would provide a screening force between the target area and the Yalu River. They would be in position to intercept any MiGs coming down from Manchuria. To provide close escort, the B-29s would rely on the straight-winged F-84 Thunderjets of the 49th and 136th Fighter-Bomber Wings. They would stay close by the bombers to fend off any MiGs that penetrated the Sabrejet screen up north.

Though the F-84s were in use elsewhere as "strategic fighters," in Korea they were used as fighter-bombers. Cutting rail lines, hitting frontline targets, and interdicting rail traffic were the F-84 pilots' specialties. Escorting slow World War II-vintage bombers was not one of them. As a result, coordination and planning between the bombers and the F-84s suffered, causing problems in the air.

The first daylight raid took place on October 18. The 19th Wing hit Saamcham with 306 bombs that effectively cratered the runway. No MiGs rose to intercept, a fact that certainly relieved General Kelly and his staff.

The second raid that day proved less successful. The 98th Bomb Wing struck out for Taechon but missed its rendezvous with the F-84s—the first of many snafus with the heavy Republic fighters. Without fighter escort, the 98th turned away from Taechon and bombed a secondary target away from MiG Alley.

On October 21, 1951, the 98th again went after Taechon. As on the first raid, the B-29s and F-84s failed to join up. Understandably unwilling to venture into MiG Alley alone, the B-29s diverted to their secondary target.

The following afternoon, the 19th Bomb Wing picked up an escort of twenty-four F-84s en route to the target as scheduled. The target this time was Taechon again. The 19th's nine bombers released their bombs over the target just as forty MiG-15s appeared in the area. The F-84s broke into the MiGs and desperately attacked them in an effort to keep them away from the Superforts. The straight-wing jets were so inferior to the MiG-15s that the communist pilots were able to engage and disengage at will, usually by climbing steeply out of the fight, then coming back down in slashing, diving runs.

Flak over Taechon had already severely damaged one B-29 when three MiG-15s suddenly dropped out of a cloud above the bomber formation. They arrowed right onto the crippled Superfort and pounded it with cannon fire before the stunned B-29 gunners could even return fire. Battered and torn by 23-mm cannot hits, the Superfort limped westward to the coast, where the crew bailed out. Fortunately, the entire crew was rescued.

It almost seemed like the communists had analyzed the previous daylight raid on Saamcham and prepared countermeasures against any further attacks. The next few days would all but confirm this supposition.

As for the F-84 escort on the Taechon raid, they had done their best in a bitter situation. Flying an aircraft so inferior to the MiG-15 meant that they could only react to communist moves, not dictate the course of the air battle. This meant the escorting fighter group could not adequately protect their charges. The MiGs could have ignored the F-84s altogether and hit the bomber formation en masse, and the F84s—slower, less agile, and unable to climb with the MiG-15s—would have been next to useless.

In fact, this is exactly what happened on the next raid, which went down in history as the "Black Day for FEAF's Bombers."

14 | MiG Trap

Capt. Francis J. ("Joe") Conley looked out at the aerial armada spread out before him and could not help to be impressed. On this 23rd day in October, FEAF had sent up nine more B-29s, this time against Namsi Airfield. Surrounding the Superforts as close escort, the 49th and 136th Wings had put aloft no fewer than fifty-five F-84 Thunderjets. Up ahead to the north, the 4th Fighter Wing's thirty-four F-86s were streaking for the Yalu River ready to intercept any MiGs going for the B-29s.

Altogether, ninety-eight American planes were in the air. Conley's outfit, the 8th Fighter-Bomber Squadron, was flying almost at the heart of the armada. Assigned as close cover, the 8th's Thunderjets had stationed themselves behind and level with the B-29s. Their job was to fend off any MiGs that got through the Sabrejet screen and the F-84 high cover.

Overhead, at 29,000–31,000 feet, the Thunderjets of the 136th Fighter-Bomber Wing gracefully essed back and forth. These were the high cover F-84s. If MiGs bounced the bombers, these F-84s were the B-29s' only hope of avoiding a massacre. They could use their height advantage to drop down on any passing MiGs, trading altitude for speed in order to catch up to the faster Russian fighters.

Nestled among the 49th Fighter Wing's F-84s, the B-29s lumbered along at 22,000 feet. Below them, at around 14,000 feet, the entire Korean countryside was shielded from view by a thick layer of undercast. The B-29s would have to use their Shoran guidance systems to hit Namsi Airfield this morning.

-◆◆◆-

Conley had never before flown on such a mission. He'd spent his tour getting down in the weeds on ground-attack strikes. Napalm, iron bombs, and rockets were his stock in trade, not dogfighting MiGs and shepherding the slow silver Superforts spread out in front of him. In this he was not unique. For most of the other F-84 pilots, this was also their first escort mission of the Korean War.

Despite this, Conley had confidence that his Thunderjet would see him through, even if they were bounced by MiGs. He had experienced firsthand the incredible amount of damage that the F-84 could withstand and still keep flying, so he had faith his Thunderjet could get him home.

One mission, in particular, drove home just how much punishment the F-84 could take. A few weeks before, he had been on a ground-attack mission north of the bomb line. The target on this strike was a building located at the bottom of a bowl-shaped ravine. He had seen his flight mates miss the building with their napalm canisters before his turn finally came. He dove down, determined not to make the same mistake. Right on the deck, just a few feet off the weeds, he pickled his bombs. Glancing back, he watched as they both sailed right through one of the building's windows and exploded inside. He turned his head forward again. He was too low. Looming before him was the end of the little ravine.

Frantically, Joe slammed the control stick into his stomach. The F-84's nose shot upward just as he reached the side of one hill. With a grinding crash, the Thunderjet impacted against the ground, but due to its angle of attack, it didn't explode. Instead, the plane bounded and skidded, not quite flying but not quite crashing either.

The tip tanks tore off, a great gash opened along the side of the fuselage, and the underside of the plane was torn and ripped. The Thunderjet's wing chopped through a tree, taking off several feet of both tree and wing. Joe held the stick back, giving it throttle. Miraculously, he eased away from the slope. When he reached the top of the hill, the Thunderjet staggered aloft, trailing fuel behind it from a gouged tank.

His buddies clustered around him to assess the damage. What they saw caused their eyes practically to pop out. Wires, hoses, and twisted hunks of aluminum all hung out of the fuselage and tailpipe. Nobody could figure out how the tail had hung together. Whatever had sliced open the side of the fuselage had also nearly chopped off one of the horizontal stabilizers. The rudder was torn up, and the vertical fin was banged and battered.

Joe limped home to Taegu, where he discovered his landing gear had not been damaged. His Thunderjet staggered onto the runway, and he let it roll along the Pierced Steel Planking (PSP), bleeding off speed. Finally, as he began to taxi toward the dispersal area, the tension he had felt all the way home disappeared, replaced by a wave of relief.

But it was not over yet. Suddenly, the back half of the Thunderjet burst into flames. The fuel leak had touched off a major fire around the damaged engine. Joe glanced back and saw the flames licking up along both sides of the fuselage. He had to get out, or he would be cooked in seconds. His hands became blurs of activity as he threw off the seat straps and opened the canopy hood. He flung himself out onto the wing, then slipped off to the ground and sprinted away, unhurt but thoroughly rattled. It had been a close call.

That night, his flight mates took him out for a night on the town in Taegu to celebrate his survival. At dinner, they decided the service was insufficient, so they bussed their own table by throwing the dishes through the windows as if they were Frisbees. Overall, a good time was had by all, except the waiters, and Joe went to bed that night with new respect for the F-84. After that incident, Conley never had a harsh word to say about the Thunderjet. He knew that a plane that could take that sort of punishment and get him home safely was a rare one indeed.

-◆◆◆-

On October 23, Conley and the rest of the 8th Fighter-Bomber Squadron had rendezvoused with the 307th Bomb Wing's B-29s around 9:25 A.M. The B-29s were heading northwesterly on a course of 300 degrees. The F-84s, spread out by flights behind and to the sides of the B-29 formations, weaved from side to side in long, arching esses. The 8th Fighter-Bomber Squadron and the rest of the 49th Fighter Wing were providing close cover. Their job was to drive away anything that penetrated the other escort screens. They formed the last line of defense.

It was the best, and perhaps only way the F-84s could deal with a MiG interception. Without the speed, climb rate, or agility of a MiG-15, the only advantage an F-84 had over its opponent was diving ability. Being heavier, the F-84 could outdive the MiG-15, especially since the MiG tended to buffet at high speeds in dives.

At 9:35 A.M., George Flight, 136th Fighter-Bomber Wing, spotted silver dots high above and to the east of them, coming on fast.

The MiGs were above them.

At the exact instant George Flight sighted MiGs east of the bombers, the first group of F-86s arrived in the patrol zone up by the Yalu River. Composed of Dignity Able, Baker, Charlie, and Dog Flights, this first group consisted of sixteen Sabrejets. A short distance away, the second group of F-86s arrived on station a minute later with fourteen F-86s divided into Dignity Red, White, and Blue Flights. Blue Flight had an extra element attached, giving it six aircraft.

Dignity Able and its associated flights began their screening mission just after entering their patrol zone. Moving northward at first, the group went into a racetrack pattern as all eyes scanned the skies for any signs of MiG activity. Dignity Red and its flights did the same thing, patrolling along north-ward, before swinging around and heading south again.

At 9:41 A.M., Dignity Red got bounced. From dead astern and below, twenty-four MiGs suddenly appeared and tore into the F-86s. At the last second, some-body saw the MiGs coming and the Sabrejets suddenly scattered, dropping their external tanks as they broke to avoid the attack.

Red Flight was quickly dispersed as two MiGs thundered right through the formation. Red Three and Four lost their leader during the break and, for the moment, found themselves out of the fight. Red One and Two broke hard right and swung down in a tight 180-degree turn to take on several MiGs head to head. As they did, other MiG-15s swept by, going flat out for the Yalu.

Red Leader, the 136th Fighter Squadron's commander Major Dick Creighton, swung right onto the tail of one of the trailing MiGs. At 9:42 A.M., he gave chase as the MiG dove away for the safety of Manchurian airspace.

Creighton stayed with him but could not get close enough to get in a shot. Finally, in frustration, he disengaged. Passing close by, he and his wingman saw two more MiGs heading west toward the coast. Creighton got behind one of these fighters and closed rapidly. As his target came into range, he fired three short, sharp bursts. His bullets stitched across the MiG's right wing and tail, and black smoke boiled back in a long rail. He followed the MiG for another minute until he lost sight of it at 8,200 feet. Last seen, the MiG was falling in flames, totally out of control.

At 9:52, Red Leader and his wingman, low on fuel, headed for home.

Red Three and Four, now totally separated from Creighton's element, eventually headed south, where they came across the B-29s at 10:00 A.M.

-◆◆◆-

At 9:41 when the 136th Squadron was bounced by twenty-four MiGs, Dig-nity White Flight had been close to Creighton's Red Flight. Eight MiGs tar-geted White's formation and blew on through it, cannons spewing out tennis ball-sized flaming tracers.

White Flight, led by Captain Ralph Banks, broke hard left and down, swinging in the opposite direction as Red Flight had during the initial break.

Banks managed to draw down on the last two MiGs in the eight plane for-mation that had just attacked them. He and his wingman chased the MiG on the right, while White Three and Four went after the one on the left. At 1,000 feet, Banks pulled the trigger and watched as his .50-caliber guns scored good strikes along the fuselage and into the cockpit. Pieces flew off the MiG, and smoke began belching from the tailpipe. Both F-86s stayed with their quarry as it dove hard for the undercast. As the three planes went through the clouds and out the bottom, Banks fired short, controlled bursts. Finally, the MiG crashed at 9:45 A.M. Ralph and his wingman climbed up to 15,000 feet in a climbing, 180-degree turn. Along the way, they picked up a stray F-86 from Blue Flight—Blue Four, and together the three Sabres headed for home.

Meanwhile, Banks and his wingman had been busy with the right MiG; White Three and Four had gone after the left one. They chased it down to the undercast, closing the range from 3,000 feet very slowly. Finally, just short of 14,000 feet, White Three fired three long bursts at the MiG from absolute maximum range. A thin line of black smoke emerged from its tailpipe. Encouraged, he held the trigger down again, pouring lead out until his guns fell silent, out of ammunition. Seconds later, the MiG disappeared into the undercast. White Three pulled up, turned south, and departed the patrol area with White Four at 9:55.

--◆◆◆--

Dignity Blue Flight had a hairy ride from the time of the initial bounce through its disengagement and run for home. Just minutes before the 9:41 bounce, Blue Three had been unable to release one of his drop tanks, so he pulled off and turned south with Blue Two. Momentarily, they were out of the fight and missed the opening bounce altogether.

At 9:41, the MiGs attacked. Blue Leader Captain Ken Chandler broke down and to the right. Blue Four followed, but Five and Six became separated when Five made a sharp, level right turn and Six lost him in the sun.

Coming around from south to north, Chandler spotted the same two MiGs that White Flight had attacked. He and Blue Four dove after them and closed quickly in a 20-degree angle of descent. At 15,000-foot altitude, Blue Four caught a MiG and opened fire from a range of fifteen hundred feet.

Seconds later, Chandler heard Blue Four announce that he was disengaging. He had expended all his ammunition and was climbing out of the fight. Chandler had lost sight of him and the MiG he was chasing, so intent was he on the other MiG. By now, Ken was only one thousand feet behind the tiny silver fighter, so he opened up with his guns and saw his tracers spear into the MiG's left wing.

Undeterred, the MiG pilot held his dive and disappeared into the undercast. At that point, White Three and Four gave up the chase, but not Chandler. He bounded into the cloud, tore out the other side, and caught the MiG cold. From dead astern three hundred feet away—practically at point-blank range— he let the MiG have it. The pilot must have been startled when .50-caliber rounds smacked into his tail. He kept his cool, though, as he yanked the stick back and popped into the cloud cover again.

Chandler waited under the scud layer. The MiG had to come out some-time. Sure enough, the silver fighter dropped down into plain sight minutes later. Chandler closed to five hundred feet, swinging dead astern to it. He opened fire, getting good strikes along the fuselage as the MiG dove to 3,000 feet.

Chandler kept closing until he accidentally blundered into the MiG's slipstream. His F-86 buffeted wildly, and he lost control of it. Releasing the stick, the Sabre flipped over on its right wing until it inverted and began to head straight for the ground. Finally, with both hands and a knee, Chandler wrestled control of the airplane, righted it, and looked around. The MiG was nowhere to be seen. Disappointed, he turned for home at 9:51.

While the 336th Fighter Squadron tangled with twenty-four MiGs, the rest of the 4th Fighter-Interceptor Wing clustered around Dignity Able Flight, patrolling its assigned sector. As part of the four-flight formation turned south, MiGs were spotted overhead, far above and out of reach. Thirty-two in all, they squatted over the F-86s and began to orbit.

That's when two more groups of MiGs, twenty-four planes in each, came whistling in from the east. Able and Baker Flights were not initially attacked. Instead, the MiG pilots concentrated on the two trailing flights, Dog and Charlie, both of whom absorbed the brunt of that first pass.

Heading south, Charlie Leader saw the MiGs coming off his left wing and broke hard right, extending westward. Although usually a dangerous move in air combat—turning away from an attack instead of turning into it—it worked this time. The MiGs ignored Charlie Leader and focused on Dog Flight.

Dog Flight was having problems even before the MiGs showed up. Dog Three's engine had begun to act up. Just as the MiGs came roaring down, it stalled out. Worse, Dog Leader tried to dump his drop tanks as the threat materialized, but one of them hung up on its rack. No matter what he did, he could not shake it loose.

Nevertheless, Dog Leader led his flight hard right in a breaking turn into the diving MiGs. Dog Flight had been heading north, so this turn sent it hurtling away from Able Flight at 600 mph. The four F-86s zoomed past the diving MiGs, and both sides traded ineffective fire. Before the Americans could react, though, the MiGs were clawing for altitude and leaving them far behind. The MiG had a far superior climb rate than the F-86, which gave it all the advantages in these sorts of slashing attacks.

Just after this first MiG pass, Dignity Dog Three and Four lit out of the combat area. Dog Three's engine kept stalling, and being underneath an umbrella of MiGs was no place for a crippled Sabre. As the flight's second element streaked southward, Dog Two took the lead from Dog Leader, whose tank still clung to the wing rack. As he tried to shake it loose, two MiGs came back downstairs and barreled down on them from dead astern. Both F-86s winged over and pulled into tight 360-degree turns.

When they came out of the turns, both planes were heading southeast. The pilots had lost sight of the other planes in their group. They saw two more MiGs coming down after them from the west. Banking slightly, the MiGs were poised to drop right onto their 6 o'clock. Again, both Sabres banked into sharp 360-degree turns making four revolutions before the danger had passed.

Continuing south, probably in an effort to get clear of the MiGs since fighting with a drop tank jammed under one wing was a terrible disadvantage, the two Dog Flight pilots stumbled across several F-84s orbiting a crash site. Closing in on the scene, they could see the wreckage of a B-29 scattered on the ground. As they passed overhead, two of the F-84s pulled their noses up and made straight for Dog Leader. Not in the mood for this, Dog Leader got on George channel and chewed out the two F-84 pilots until they abandoned the erroneous attack.

From out of nowhere, another MiG came sweeping up from below and behind. At 15,000 feet, Dog Leader and Dog Two broke into another sharp 360-degree turn, again foiling the attack. Four revolutions later, the MiG gave up pursuit and skittered away, climbing like a sparrow as it turned for the Yalu.

Exhausted and low on fuel, Dog Two and Dog Leader were finally able to call it a day. At 10:05 they slipped south for home, climbing to 31,000 feet along the way.

-◆◆-

Up north, as the pilots of Dog Flight fought for their lives, the rest of the F-86s struggled to stay with Able Flight. The Sabres were all between 28,000 and 30,000 feet, while the 32 MiGs hovered above them at 40,000 — too high to catch.

Able and Baker stayed together with Charlie flight orbiting nearby. Any move they made came under the watchful eyes of their MiG blanket. The F-86s were boxed in, unable to engage or to execute any major maneuvers for fear of exposing themselves to a slashing attack. At some point, it appears that the F-86s actually went into a World War I-style Lufberry Circle as they remained in their patrol zone. A Lufberry was a continuous 360 degree turn done as tightly as possible. If more than one aircraft was in the Lufberry, they could cover each other's tails as they circled. Against MiGs, it proved an effective defensive tactic as the Sabre could turn inside their Russian counterparts. The MiGs could make hit-and-run attacks requiring a high degree of deflection, but they couldn't stay in a Lufberry with a Sabre for long.

At 40,000 feet, 32 Chinese and North Korean MiG-15s stayed right on top of the F-86s. They had been ordered south of the Yalu to keep the American jets busy while the 303d and 324th Soviet Air Divisions struck the B-29s. Though inexperienced and not very effective once they engaged, the Chinese and North Koreans were doing their jobs well by maintaining their altitude advantage. From their perch, they could harass the Americans and sweep down in occasional slashing attacks, trading height for energy. As long as they kept their speed up, they could almost always escape any counterattack by climbing back upstairs where the F-86s could not follow.

Though the communists could not beat the Americans man for man since the average USAF pilot proved far superior to the average Chinese or North Korean pilot, the Reds managed to execute this mission quite well. Without losing a plane, they pinned down the Americans and prevented them from saving the Superfortresses that were getting slaughtered to the south.

-◆◆◆-

At 9:50 A.M. that day, two things happened to change the situation. First, Baker Flight lost contact with Able Flight when a single communist jet came downstairs and lined up on Able Leader. Baker Leader saw the MiG coming and turned to cut him off. He got to the MiG just in time, and his long machine-gun burst scared it away. The MiG sailed upward and climbed back to the rest of the enemy fighters above. The move disrupted the formation when the rest of Baker Flight followed Baker Leader.

Second, just after that attack, Able Flight heard the B-29s desperately call for help somewhere to the south. Able Flight went to the rescue—or tried to. Every time the planes turned southward, the MiGs dropped down on them in violent slashing attacks, forcing the Sabres to maneuver wildly, which threw them off course. Nevertheless, bobbing and weaving through each MiG pass, the four F-86s doggedly kept turning back to the south.

Nearby, Baker Flight underwent similar treatment as it tried to get to the bombers. Charlie Flight had also encountered the same tactics earlier. By 9:45—five minutes before the first B-29 distress call came, it had burned its fuel and been forced to break for home.

Of the sixteen F-86s in the original group, only eight now remained to help out the B-29s. Baker Flight made it to the bombers first, but it had only enough fuel for a couple of minutes. It managed to chase one MiG off an F-84's tail, but then twelve U.S. Thunderjets made a lumbering attack into them. Climbing away from the mistaken assault, Baker Flight turned for home at 10:10 as the fuel situation grew critical.

At 10:15, Able Flight finally showed up, still playing cat and mouse with the MiG blanket. Below, stretched out in every direction, the pilots could see a series of tangled dogfights in progress. Smoke trails marked the final descent of several airplanes, and they saw only a few bombers struggling southward. The scene was chaotic, and one Able Flight could not join. Until they finally broke for home, every attempt to join the sprawling air battle instantly resulted in overhead MiG passes. Thoroughly frustrated and bitterly upset at their inability to engage the MiGs, Able's pilots finally had to dive for home. Their screening effort had been a complete failure.

As the F-86s returned to Suwon, they left behind a battle that would doom FEAF's daylight bombing campaign and change the course of the air war.

15 ¦ Death Ride to Namsi

Lieutenant General Georgy Lobov's 303d Fighter Air Division swept southward. He knew that the MiG-15s were all that stood between the B-29s and the destruction of Namsi's new airfield. Close by, World War II's top Allied ace, Ivan Kozhedub, led his 324th FAD behind Lobov's men. Altogether, the two Soviet outfits had put forty-four MiG-15s in the air only minutes after radar operators had analyzed the situation and concluded that a B-29 raid was inbound for one of the new airfields. Twelve aircraft from the two divisions remained on standby in Manchuria should another raid materialize.

This was the sort of mission these Russians had been brought to Manchuria to stop. Many of the Soviet pilots had toured several North Korean cities destroyed by B-29 raids. Ever since, their overriding mission had been to drive the Superfortresses out of North Korean airspace. It was a job that these veteran aviators took to with a vengeance, determined to prevent the sort of horrors they had witnessed on the ground.

While the North Korean and Chinese pilots boxed in the American Sabre-jet screen just short of Namsi, the Soviets swung around to the east and began to close on the B-29s from their unprotected right flank. Around 9:35 A.M., they sighted the B-29s and the cloud of F-84 Thunderjets around them. Coming in at about 35,000 feet, the Soviets had every advantage—surprise, altitude, and speed. On top of that, they had superior aircraft. They were poised and ready to unleash a massacre on the American planes below.

Just before pushing over and going after the bombers, the Soviets broke formation and spread out in loose elements of two planes. Each element was given total freedom of maneuver and allowed to choose its route of attack. Most of them swung around to the south, diving through the F-84s as if they

MiG-15s take to the air.

weren't even there, then banking northward at over 620 mph to come up behind the B-29s.

The Thunderjets could do nothing to stop them.

The 136th Fighter-Bomber Wing saw the MiGs coming first. George Flight sounded the alarm as it was essing eastward across the B-29 formation. Because its pilots had spotted only a fraction of the attack, they thought that only twelve MiGs were coming down on them. The others, as it turned out, had swung to George Flight's right and were now splitting up into elements and arching down on the vulnerable rear of the American raid.

The pilots of George Flight pulled up their noses and did what they could to stop the onrushing MiGs, but the Soviets were going so fast that their head-on attacks proved ineffectual. The twelve MiGs blew past them as their pilots focused on their high side passes against the bomber vees. The American pilots watched as each MiG made its run, then pulled off to the left in stunningly fast climbing turns. The only bright spot was that it didn't look like any of the MiGs had hit their targets.

Baker Flight, 136th Wing, had been flying high on the starboard side of the B-29 formation when the MiGs made their run. As the Soviets dove down, they made their attacks in pairs. Baker Flight dove after one MiG duo and caught them just as they made their climb-out on the west side of the B-29s.

Baker Leader and his wingman each picked one MiG and began to fire desperately. Both reported good strikes. Although one MiG streamed white smoke from its wing root and fuselage, both Russians escaped, much to the frustration of the American F-84s. Behind Baker Lead and his wingman, the flight's other element picked out a single MiG and dropped behind it after he had pulled out of a firing run on a B-29. Baker Three opened fire at fifteen hundred feet and held the trigger down until he was less than seven hundred feet away from the skidding MiG. His bullets stitched the MiG from nose to tail, causing it to wobble awkwardly. Suddenly, the MiG rolled over and fell into an inverted dive. It disappeared into the undercast apparently out of control.

-◆◆◆-

To the left of Baker Flight, Easy Flight had been flying dead astern of the B-29 formations when a horde of MiGs suddenly dropped down their tailpipes. As they dove down, they began splitting up into elements, each picking out a B-29 to attack.

At 29,000 feet, with an attack coming from above and behind, Easy Flight was in perhaps the worst position of any F-84 formation in the high cover. It could not pull up and Immelmann into the attackers, nor could it split-ess down on them. The only thing the pilots could do was to break hard in one direction, turn as tightly as possible, and hope to get in fleeting deflection shots before the MiGs sped down out of range. This option would bleed off most of their speed and put them totally out of position to help the B-29s again, but it was the only recourse.

Easy Flight's leader took it, knowing that the lives of the bomber crews depended on them. He rolled over and stood his Thunderjet on its left wing and spun down on the MiGs as they closed from astern. Struggling against blacking out, Easy Lead just barely managed to drag his F-84s into the oncoming fighters. From 30 degrees ahead, he opened fire on one of the MiGs and kept firing as the MiG swept on past going north while he swung around from southeast to east. His last burst was a 90-degree deflection shot— a fleeting one at best. Although he thought he had scored some hits, the tough Soviet fighter continued on course.

Easy Leader tightened his turn as he tried, at all costs, to stop the MiG. His airspeed plummeted. Without warning, he stalled out and fell out of the fight. With some satisfaction, he last saw the MiG trailing grayish black smoke from the left side of the fuselage and wing. He claimed it as damaged.

Behind him, Easy Flight's other pilots picked out targets and fired away until the MiGs dove past them. As soon as they blazed by, though, Easy Flight was effectively out of the fight.

-◆◆◆-

The 136th Wing's Able Flight probably had been on the port side of the B-29 formation when the first attacks came from behind and to its right. Total confusion engulfed the pilots almost at once. Ahead and off to the northwest, they caught a glimpse of the U.S. 334th and 335th Fighter Squadrons sparring with their MiG umbrella. Seconds later, they caught sight of what they thought were F-86s diving near the B-29s, but they were almost certainly MiGs. This was one of many instances when the F-84 pilots misidentified the swept-wing fighters. The Sabrejet and the MiG-15 looked remarkably similar. Unless a pilot had plenty of experience, it was extremely difficult for him to tell the two apart from any distance during combat at 600 mph.

Below Able Flight, the bombers dropped their loads on what the F-84s assumed was Namsi. With the bombs away, the B-29s began their run for home. At this point, something went wrong. At first all of the Superforts turned to 250 degrees to move out of the target area on a southwesterly heading. After the MiGs swept through, however, the formations broke up. At least three turned to the left and headed almost due south, while five others began turning to the right, as if heading for the coast.

If the F-84s had not operated under impossible conditions before, they certainly were operating under them now. With the B-29s split into two groups on different headings, the Thunderjets did not know which group to cover. Worse, as the MiGs flailed away at the B-29s and others dispersed the F-84 formations, many of the F-84s weren't in position to cover either flight.

As the bombers separated, Charlie Flight moved to cover the three B-29s moving south. At 27,000 feet, they watched helplessly as two MiGs arrowed right past them and struck the one on the far left. They studded it with cannon fire that blasted great gaping holes in its aluminum skin. The Superfortress staggered, mortally wounded, and began to drop out of formation. Seconds before it fell out of control, the crew began bailing out. The fighter pilots saw seven parachutes open.

Charlie Flight hurled itself at the two escaping MiGs, and the flight's leader managed to pepper one of them with machine-gun fire. Nonetheless, the MiG extended beyond firing range and climbed away, leaving the Americans utterly frustrated.

With the MiGs gone, Charlie Flight turned back to cover the B-29 crew as they parachuted into North Korea. At 10:07 A.M., while circling the crash site, Charlie Flight spotted another B-29 going down. Only five chutes emerged. Most Superfortresses carried crews of eleven to thirteen men on these missions.

Shortly after the second B-29 went down, Charlie Flight's pilots turned for home, carrying the sad knowledge that they had just seen the deaths of at least ten American airmen. The final toll would be far worse.

-♦♦♦-

First Lieutenant Farrie D. Fortner led Dog Flight of the 136th Fighter-Bomber Wing's 154th Fighter-Bomber Squadron into the fray just as the MiGs bore down on the Superfortresses from behind. At 9:49, he saw two MiGs make a run on one of the B-29s as it tried to get out of the target area. He led his flight down on it and managed to get off a quick shot at one of the Soviets as he came off his Superfort target. His gunfire raked the MiG's tail, but complete success again eluded the Thunderjet pilots. Although damaged, the MiG used its superior performance to evade further attack as it escaped.

In reality, the .50-caliber machine gun proved to be an ineffective weapon in the minds of many Soviet pilots. MiGs would frequently come home so full of holes that they looked like cheese graters, yet they had held together and brought their pilots safely home. On occasion, one landed with more than one hundred holes carved out of its wing, tail, and fuselage. Had the U.S. Air Force adopted the 20-mm cannon as its standard aerial weapon, as the Navy had done a few years before, many of those damaged MiGs never would have made it north of the Yalu.

Fortner probably did not know this at the time, and he certainly didn't care. After hitting the first MiG, he went into a flying frenzy while he tried to fend off further attacks on his charges.

Two more MiGs dove by and made sweeping runs on the B-29s. Fortner went after them and saw one slide right onto a Superfort's six o'clock position. The B-29 gunners were pouring out lead at the red-nosed MiG. Fortner saw the counterfire strike home, but it did not knock the MiG down. Like the others, this MiG pilot finished his run and climbed out of the fight.

Minutes later, while covering the three B-29s that had swung southward, Fortner's flight spotted two more inbound MiGs. Dog Flight was moving westward over the B-29s, and the MiG attack was coming from north to south behind the B-29s. Unlike previous attacks, this pair of Russians had decided to come up under the bombers instead of diving down on them. At 20,000 feet, they were actually vulnerable to attack from Dog Flight.

Fortner held his course for a moment, then rolled in on the pair of MiGs. As he dove, his heavy Republic fighter picked up speed and he caught one of the MiGs before it reached its firing position on the Superfort. Fortner opened fire and held the trigger down, determined not to let this one get away.

The Soviet pilot saw his attacker at the last second. He broke right and dove for the undercast, but Fortner kept firing. He closed to three hundred feet before strikes in the MiG's wing root started a fire. When Fortner last saw the MiG, both wings were afire. Dog Two and Three later said they saw it crash.

Fortner just scored the only Thunderjet kill of the day.

–◆◆◆–

Fox Flight's day had started poorly and ended worse. The first element had not even gotten off the ground. A runway accident involving Fox Leader and Fox Two scrubbed their participation in the mission and forced Fox Three to take the lead.

Fox Three led his wingman to the rendezvous point, where they escorted the bombers to the target area. Just as the bomber began making their turns to course 250, both Fox Three and his wingman were struck by MiGs. Fox Four apparently was hit by cannon fire, for his F-84 was seen by many Americans to spin down into the undercast totally out of control. One or two pilots reported seeing it on fire.

–◆◆◆–

As the MiGs made their runs, Mercury Blue and Mercury White Flights, both of the 136th Fighter-Bomber Wing, entered the fray. Initially, they were supposed to provide flak suppression for the B-29s, but Fox Flight's runway mishap delayed them on the ground so long that they could not execute their mission. Instead, they jettisoned their bombs and sped north to provide further escort to the B-29s.

At 9:40 A.M., they saw the MiGs swarm down on the bombers in elements of two. The flights made repeated passes at the attacking fighters but scored no hits with the fleeting shots that the fast jets offered them. As they frantically tried to stave off the MiGs, Mercury Blue's pilots saw a single MiG make a 90-degree deflection pass at one of the B-29s. This Russian was obviously an outstanding marksman, as his shells butchered the Superfortress. It fell out of formation, and the surviving crewmen bailed out.

From 9:40 until 10:20, Mercury Blue tried its best to keep the MiGs off the stricken B-29s. Eventually, it linked up with the three B-29s heading south and followed them home, with Easy Flight also in attendance.

Mercury White was also supposed to provide flak suppression but abandoned that mission in an effort to save the Superforts. At 9:40, one of Mercury White's pilots saw a single MiG shooting up a crippled B-29. He broke formation to go after it and chased it north to Pakchon before the MiG was able to escape.

He turned south and ran into a lone B-29, its engine afire. As it struggled along, one wing broke off at the root and sent the huge bomber spinning violently earthward. He saw three chutes emerge from the dying plane.

A few minutes later, he ran into another B-29. This one also had an engine on fire. He followed it south to Kimpo, where he found the rest of Mercury White Flight. Together, the flight landed at Kimpo.

Underneath the 136th Fighter-Bomber Wing, Joe Conley watched the tremendous air battle unfold above him. He could see MiGs streaking down through the high-cover Thunderjets. He could see the MiGs had evaded most of the attacks. In the confusion swirling over him, he even picked out a few F-86s, probably the Blue Flight pair that had turned south earlier when Blue Three's drop tank refused to release. They had stumbled into the raging fight at 9:41, just in time to witness the destruction of the B-29s.

Down among the Superforts, Conley and his flight braced themselves for the attack. Soon, MiGs were zipping by on every conceivable heading, like moths swarming around a porch light. One of the MiGs somehow ended up below him. Confident that his wingman would follow him down, Conley rolled over and arrowed onto the MiG's tail. He lined up the MiG in his sights and began firing quick bursts, some scoring hits on its wing and fuselage. He had the MiG dead to rights, but a quick check of his own six struck fear in his heart. Behind him, his wingman was nowhere to be seen. Instead, the MiG's own wingman had slid behind him and was just about in firing position. Turning hard to avoid the attack, Conley let his quarry go. When he turned back, both MiGs had streaked out of range.

When he returned to Taegu, his wingman had already landed. Infuriated, Conley learned that the man had broken formation and run away just as the MiGs attacked, leaving him alone and exposed. Within hours, the squadron commander confirmed the story and put the man on the first plane out of Korea.

The Soviet attack had succeeded beyond all expectations. Twenty-two pairs of MiGs had torn through the high and close escort F-84s and slaughtered the B-29s. The Soviets counted twenty-one Superforts in the air that day and claimed twelve as kills. A few, General Lobov later stated, got away as they turned for the coast because the Soviets were not allowed to fly over the Yellow Sea. They also claimed four F-84s.

Since the Russians only made one pass each before climbing away and running northward, it is quite probable that several Chinese and North Korean MiG-15 pilots also attacked the B-29s and F-84s. Possibly, when the 4th Fighter Wing's Dignity Able Flight arrived at 10:15 at the tail end of the Soviet attack, some of the MiGs over them decided to take shots at the B-29s. Both the F-84s and the Superforts reported that the attacks lasted until 10:40, long after the Soviets had left the area.

This had been the biggest air battle of the Korean War. Lobov later commented, "Actually, neither in that air battle nor in any other, absurd as it sounds, did we suffer a single MiG loss from the defensive fire of the B-29s."[1]

In fact, according to Soviet sources, not a single MiG from either the 324th or 303d Air Divisions went down that day. Some of the MiGs returned with heavy damage, but all of the Soviet pilots returned safely to their base. The only kills scored by the Americans that day must have come at the expense of the North Korean and Chinese MiG pilots.

The Soviets estimated that their forty-four MiG-15s had attacked twenty-one B-29s and more than two hundred fighters. Considering these odds they thought they were up against, they were elated at the stunning blow they thought they had landed against the hated B-29s of FEAF Bomber Command. Perhaps once and for all, the people of North Korea would be rid of the mammoth silver Boeings that had wrought so much destruction from Pyongyang to Sinuiju.

16 | Horizontal Flak

Captain Thomas ("Tom") Shields and his bombardier, Captain Emil Goldbeck, had never dreamed they would end up in Korea, let alone as part of the lead crew on this mission to Namsi. A few months before, they had been training for atomic bomb missions against the Soviet Union. Their knowledge of secret Strategic Air Command (SAC) tactics was supposed to keep them out of the Korean War. The threat of captured SAC crewmen being tortured to reveal atomic warfare secrets had prompted a rule banning SAC crews from combat duty.

But Shields and his crew had fallen through the cracks. Assigned to the 509th Bomb Wing in 1950, they were sent to England from Roswell, New Mexico, on a ninety-day rotation. When a B-29 required a crew to fly it to Oklahoma City for modifications, Shields, Goldbeck, and their radio operator volunteered because they all had pregnant wives in New Mexico.

They arrived in Oklahoma City and grabbed a flight to New Mexico where they rejoined their families. The next thing they knew, each member of the crew received orders sending them to Okinawa and the 307th Bomb Wing. Puzzled, they took the orders to their wing commander, Colonel John Ryan, who tried to have them countermanded. SAC Commander Lieutenant General Curtis LeMay even got involved, siding with his men. Nevertheless, FEAF Bomber Command was desperately short of experienced crews and the order stood. Reluctantly, Shields and his men packed up their gear, said farewell to their families, and headed to war.

This was Goldbeck's second war. He had been part of a B-24 bomber crew—the youngest airman in the 15th Air Force—during the later stages of World War II. Shields was also a World War II veteran. He had flown B-29s over Japan with the 20th Air Force in 1944–45.

When the crew arrived on Okinawa in the spring of 1951, Shields discovered that his was one of the most experienced crews in the 307th Bomb Wing.

Refueling a B-29 of the 307th Bomb Wing.

They became instructors, helping the wing's reservists relearn their stock in trade. When they weren't training crews they were part of the normal combat rotation. Through the spring and summer, Shields and Goldbeck completed thirty-two missions over North Korea. Most were long and boring against targets they thought were of little consequence compared to what they had experienced during World War II. Aside from a few MiG sightings in the spring, they had encountered no aerial opposition whatsoever—that was, until October 23, 1951.

Given the importance of the Namsi strike, it was natural that Captain Thomas Shields and his crew would lead the mission since they were among the most experienced in the wing. They would lead three aircraft from each of the wing's squadrons, flying at 22,000 feet in a vee-of-vee formation—three plane flights arranged in an inverted V that were further arranged in an overall inverted V for the squadron formation. Shields's Superfort would be the forward plane of the lead vee, while the 371st and 372d Squadrons would be deployed behind and on either side of Shields.

Goldbeck would be the lead bombardier. Once he dropped his bombs, the entire formation would release theirs. Should clouds cover the target area, Goldbeck would use Shoran guidance. Shields's plane was one of the few in his wing with Shoran capability that day. An extra crewman was wedged into the B-29's fuselage to operate the Shoran equipment.

The nine crews scheduled to fly received this information at their early-morning briefing prior to the flight. Significantly, the briefing contained no urgent warnings about possible MiG interception. Nor did it mention that a

Superfort had been shot down the day before in their target area. This omission helped to set the stage for the disaster that was to follow.

◆◆◆

At 9:25 A.M., eight B-29s linked up with their F-84 escort. One of the bombers had experienced mechanical difficulties and turned for home. Heading north, the crews saw the first signs of North Korean activity over Kunu-ri, where the bombers picked up some flak. Just after 9:30, Goldbeck hunkered over the Norden bombsight and turned the B-29 to 320 degrees. They had reached the initial point and were now heading straight for Namsi.

Peering through the bombsight, Goldbeck realized that he would not be able to make a visual drop. The undercast at 14,000 proved so thick he could not see the ground, and there weren't even any holes to peep through. The Shoran operator would have to give him the word to drop.

Behind him, Thomas Shields and his copilot, Roger Penninger, held the B-29 on course despite occasional flak. Between them squatted the 370th Squadron's new commanding officer, Lieutenant Colonel Julius O'Neal, as he watched the bombing run unfold. This was his first mission over Korea.

Just short of the target, MiGs attacked. Some of the Soviet pilots closed to fifty feet before unleashing withering barrages of 23-mm and 37-mm cannon shells. The tracers that shot out of these huge weapons looked like flaming balls of AA fire—except they streaked across the sky horizontally instead of vertically. Some wag had long ago dubbed MiG fire *horizontal flak*.

B-29 number 151, Shields's plane, was singled out by the MiGs and pounded with cannon fire. The right wing took the brunt of the punishment, and the right inboard engine was pounded into burning ruin by several direct cannon hits. Flames poured out of the cowling as the Superfort staggered from the attack.

Almost at once, the B-29 began to fall out of formation, and Goldbeck thought they would have to bail out immediately. Without waiting for word from Shields, who was fighting the controls to keep the B-29 from falling into a spin, Goldbeck salvoed their bomb load. As he did, the rest of the B-29s in the formation dropped their bombs seconds later. They were still short of Namsi, so the bombs simply churned up the North Korean countryside. Goldbeck and his crewmates didn't care. They were fighting for their lives. With the plane going down, they prepared to bail out. But, before anyone bailed, Shields's reassuring voice came over the intercom system: "Wait a minute! I've got partial control. I can still fly a little bit."

After a pause, he continued, "Navigator, give me a heading to a safe island."

They would try to make it to the Yellow Sea, where they stood a better chance of rescue.

As Shields turned for the coast, in all probability this was the moment when the 307th Wing's formation fell apart. His plane banked to the right and four bombers followed. Three however, stayed on a heading of 250 degrees before swinging to the left.

Captain Robert Krumm's B-29, number 045, stayed with Shields and turned right toward the coast with him. There had been a short lull in the fighter attacks between the time that Shields's plane was hit and the point where the formation split. Now, however, the MiGs descended on the bombers with unique fury.

A MiG closed to point-blank range and savaged Krumm's Superfortress. As something exploded behind the right inboard engine, the plane, mortally wounded, plunged out of formation. When last seen, it was going through the undercast, although observers reported it did not appear to be out of control.

Two of the three B-29s that followed Shields took serious hits within the next few minutes. One managed to limp to Kimpo and crash-land, but it was so damaged that it never flew again. The other bomber, piloted by Lieutenant William Reeter, was singled out by Soviet MiGs and raked with cannon shells from nose to tail. Reeter managed to drag his crippled bomber, with six wounded men on board, to Kimpo. In all probability, this was the B-29 Easy Flight of the 136th Fighter Bomber Wing escorted south at the end of its mission.

Just coming off what he thought was the target, Lieutenant Fred Beissner suddenly heard the other nearby crews call out, "MiGs!" He glanced over at his aircraft commander, Captain James Foulkes, and saw him calmly continue his turn off target. They turned south with two other B-29s and moved away from Shields and his group.

Suddenly, Foulkes and Beissner's aircraft shuddered violently. From his copilot's position, Beissner could not tell at first where they'd been hit. Then a MiG-15 zoomed right past their left wing, level with them. Beissner could see the MiG's vertical stabilizer quite clearly. It looked unnaturally large behind the fighter's short fuselage. The MiG seemed to hang in front of them for an instant, and Beissner felt that he was watching the incident in slow motion. Suddenly, time speeded up again as the MiG bolted for the blue sky, its nose almost vertical as it chandelled away.

On the intercom, the crew began calling out damage to the left wing. Beissner couldn't see it, but apparently the number two engine had been destroyed.

In describing the damage, Beissner said later, "At least one cannon shell got us in the back part of the engine, which means it came through all the fuel lines and fuel controls, plus an oil tank. There's a lot of magnesium back there behind the engine, and the fire extinguishers were back there also."

With all the flammable materials that the shell went through, fire was inevitable. Sure enough, the crew reported flames. Foulkes triggered the fire extinguishers, but they did not put out the fire. Struggling to stay in formation, Foulkes decided to shut down the engine and feather the prop. The prop refused to feather; the control lines to it must have been severed. With the prop windmilling, it caused so much drag that they couldn't stay with the rest of the bombers.

Foulkes turned for the coast, trying to get over water before he lost control of the plane. With fire already burning on board, they would clearly never make South Korea. Heading southwesterly, the crew made ready to bail out.

The fire began to spread. Beissner, on the opposite side of the aircraft, couldn't see it at all, but the reports from the crew began to alarm him. By now, flames had engulfed the wing from tip to root. If they weren't put out soon, the plane surely would be destroyed. Knowing this, Foulkes tried one last desperate measure. Hoping that he could blow out the fire, he eased the bomber into a dive, but it didn't work. When he pulled up just above the undercast, the fire was eating away at the wing's last supports. Foulkes knew they had run out of time. He ordered everyone in the rear half of the plane to bail out. Everyone but the navigator, the pilots, and the flight engineer jumped at this point. Next to Foulkes, Beissner stayed on the radio and called out repeated Maydays. When the seven men behind the flight deck had safely jumped, Foulkes told everyone else to get out.

The bombardier bailed out first through the nose wheel hatch. The navigator followed seconds later. Beissner set the auto-pilot and climbed down off the flight deck and into the nose, while Foulkes remained at the controls. Assuming his aircraft commander was coming down after him, Beissner leapt through the nose wheel door. Seconds later, Foulkes made it through the hatch, the last one to leave B-29 number 940.

Meanwhile, Tom Shields and Roger Penninger were working frantically in the cockpit, trying to coax B-29 number 151 the last few miles to the Yellow Sea. By now, a major fire had broken out in the wing behind the right inboard engine. Seconds before, they had feathered the prop and used the automatic fire extinguishers, but the damage was too extensive. The MiG that hit them had torn mortal wounds in the wing. They staggered westward as the fire continued to spread, eating away at the wing from the area between the nacelles to the junction with the fuselage. Just a few more seconds and they'd be over the water where rescue crews could reach them.

Without warning, the right wing collapsed. It tore free of the fuselage and went fluttering away, flames spinning wildly from it. The B-29 heeled over violently and began to spin.

Goldbeck was trapped in the nose. The centrifugal force generated by the spin pinned him down. He fought wildly to reach the nose wheel hatch. Somehow, he got to it and popped it open. Behind him, Colonel O'Neal came forward and was struggling to reach the hatch as well. Goldbeck grabbed him and pulled him along. By now, debris was flying around in the nose section. Something—possibly a shard of Plexiglas—struck Goldbeck on the head and tore open his scalp.

Bleeding, he still managed to push O'Neal out the nose wheel hatch. Without hesitation, he flung himself out after the colonel.

Shields and Penninger, along with the engineer, remained trapped on the flight deck. None of them got out.

Ted Smith, the navigator, joined up with the radio operator, a panicked sergeant, in the front bomb bay. By now, the plane was falling vertically, so Smith actually stepped out on the bomb bay door and used it as a springboard out into thin air.

The radio operator jumped clear. Because the radio operator's compartment was so cramped, crews assigned to this position usually wore chest parachute packs. These were still cumbersome, so they often took off the chutes and snapped them to their harnesses. Apparently, the radio operator didn't have it snapped to his harness.

He jumped out of the plane without wearing a parachute.[1]

Farther back in the fuselage, Sergeant Cross, the senior gunner, was trying to get both waist gunners out of the plane. One of them wrapped his arms around his gunsight and began screaming, "I'm going down with the plane! I'm not getting out!"

Cross and the other waist gunner pounced on the man and tried to pry him free of the gunsight. With the bomber spinning and the terrified gunner using all of his strength to clutch the gunsight, it was a useless task. Leaving him there, they climbed forward and bailed out from the rear bomb bay.

The tail gunner, a new kid to the crew like most of the other gunners, had sworn to friends before the mission that if he had to bail out, he wouldn't do it from his tail position. Nobody had understood this as the tail gunner had the easiest exit path of all the crew. Instead of going out his own hatch, he had decided to go out through the hatch used by the Shoran operator. The last anyone saw of him, he was crawling forward from the tail, the plane's crazy gyrations throwing him all over the place. He never got out.

-◆◆◆-

Emil Goldbeck pulled his ripcord and saw the silk chute surge out over his head and deploy. He hung there, relief washing over him as the undercast approached below. He floated through the cloud layer and came out the other side to find the wide expanse of the Yellow Sea. He was not safe yet, though. As he came down, a strong wind beat at his chute. Below, the swells of the sea looked ominously large.

He splashed into the water. When he hit the surface, his chute did not collapse. Instead, it caught the wind and began dragging him through the swells. Emil struggled to free himself of the chute harness, but every effort met with failure. He swallowed salt water, and his strength eroded with each try to extricate himself. Describing it later, he said, "I was like a corpse getting dragged along by the chute."

Emil decided to reach for his dinghy, which was attached to his harness and Mae West. He thought he might stand a chance if he could get it open and actually climb on board. The alternative was to be drowned by his chute as it pulled him through the swells. His wet fingers slipped over the snap on the dinghy's cover. Just as he was about to free it, another swell slammed into him. Gagging and coughing, he realized that the end to his endurance was near. Another swell battered him, and the chute continued to drag him along.

He would make one more attempt to pop the dinghy out. With every ounce in his reserves, he grabbed at the snap and managed to free the raft. It inflated immediately, and he threw himself onto it. Reaching back, he grabbed one of the shroud lines and yanked as hard as he could. The chute collapsed and fell into the water.

For the moment, he was safe.

—◆◆◆—

Colonel O'Neal had been the first out of the nose wheel hatch. Goldbeck had seen his chute open; it was one of the new-type parachutes that had alternating panels of white and orange. He saw the colonel fall through the undercast and then lost track of him. According to Goldbeck, he had jumped without his dinghy. In the rough swells, he almost certainly drowned.

The Shoran operator landed in the sea a short distance from Goldbeck. While floating in his dinghy, Goldbeck found him, face down, dead in the water.

Of the seven men who had jumped, only four were alive. And rescue seemed to be a distant hope.

—◆◆◆—

After jumping clear of number 940, Fred Beissner free-fell through the undercast, clutching his D-ring as he tumbled. When he emerged from the cloud cover, he yanked the ring and felt the tug of his chute opening overhead. Why he decided to free-fall as far as he had, he has never quite understood. That decision possibly saved his life. The fierce winds that Emil Goldbeck encountered under the scud layer were also prevalent where number 940 went down. The wind had surely blown the other three men from the flight deck closer toward shore than he. Had he deployed his chute earlier, he probably would have been blown inland, or at least closer to the shore, where communist patrols would have either killed or captured him.

As he floated toward the water, his B-29 came twisting down from the clouds, its left wing missing. They had jumped just in time. The fuselage and right wing plummeted into the sea and exploded in a great geyser of water and debris. Trailing behind it, the left wing, sheathed entirely in flames, fluttered down. It splashed down a short distance from the rest of the Superfort.

Beissner went into the water about twenty miles off the coast. He swallowed some salt water and vomited, but he was able to climb into his raft. He threw out his sea anchor and began to bail out the raft—a futile job since more water slopped inside every time a wave hit him.

The sea was running very rough, with swells of eight to ten feet. As he rode the waves, Beissner saw a Grumman SA-16 Albatross amphibious plane sitting on the water in the distance. It didn't look too far away, so Fred pulled out his signal gun and fired a flare. He expected the SA-16 to taxi over and pick him up, but the Albatross stayed upwind and never got close to him. Frustrated, he fired another flare and even used a smoke flare. Still, the SA-16 did not come to get him.

Off to the east, somebody fired another flare. It must have come from one of the men who had jumped with him. That flare was ignored as well, and he didn't see another flare from that area after that.

Frustrated, he watched as the Albatross trundled away on the water. He soon lost sight of it. They had left him. And now the current was sweeping him straight toward the North Korean coast.

A few miles from Beissner, Goldbeck rode the swells and worried about the current. He had landed only a few miles offshore, and now the current was sweeping him inexorably toward the coast. By 1951, the thought of capture by the North Koreans inspired dread in nearly every airman. The prospects for B-29 crews were particularly grim. Goldbeck realized that if he did reach shore, the North Koreans would probably kill him.

Then there was the matter of his scalp wound. In the chaos surrounding number 151's lasts few seconds of flight, he had been clipped by something that cut open his head. Getting out and down into the water had preoccupied him, so he had barely noticed it. Now, floating in the choppy sea, he lay in his dinghy and kept wiping blood from his eyes. Wet, cold, and shivering to begin with, his scalp began to ache, adding another dimension to his misery.

Sixty minutes after bailing out, he heard engine sounds nearby. Looking around, he spotted a Grumman SA-16 Albatross bounding along in the swells toward him. The amphibian had already picked up Smith, Cross, and the waist gunner; the crew now hauled him aboard.

There was a flight surgeon with the SA-16's crew. He spotted the Shoran operator's body a short distance from where they picked up Goldbeck. Against orders, he jumped into the water and began swimming for the body to retrieve it. Suddenly, an enormous swell struck the surgeon and swept the body out of reach. The flight surgeon gave up and tried to get back to the Albatross, but the swells hampered his every move.

Finally, after tremendous effort, the crew managed to reach him and haul him back into the Albatross. The amphibian's pilot was so angry that he went aft and chewed out the surgeon in front of everyone. Later, the pilot also received a good bawling out by his squadron commander. He had landed in such rough seas that the SA-16 almost didn't get airborne again. The reprimand, however, was tempered by a later commendation for his rescue of four men from B-29 number 151.

The SA-16 returned to Seoul, where Goldbeck spent the night in a hospital. The flight surgeon had stitched up his scalp wound, but he was still suffering from it and his near drowning. The next day, a C-54 picked him up and took him to Japan for an extensive debriefing.

For his efforts to save the crew, Captain Thomas Shields earned a Silver Star. He had stayed at the B-29's controls to give his men a chance to escape. In doing so, he had condemned himself to the very fate from which he had sought to save his crew.

-◆◆◆-

Fred Beissner remained in the water for eight hours. At one point, an F-51 Mustang passed overhead, and Fred tried signaling it with a mirror. Amazingly, where flares had failed, this old technique worked. The Mustang circled around and must have radioed his position, because, a short time later, another plane showed up and dropped him a larger raft. He paddled over to it and climbed in. Fortunately, it was dry and warm. He covered himself up and hunkered down in the raft to await rescue.

It didn't take long after the raft had been dropped. An Australian frigate showed up and pulled him aboard, exhausted but otherwise intact. The ship searched for the rest of number 940's crew but found no sign of any of them.

In those eight hours on the water, the current had taken Beissner sixteen miles eastward toward shore. The frigate picked him up six miles off the coast of North Korea. Had he not free-fallen so far after jumping clear of the B-29, he probably would have ended up on shore at some point. That almost certainly would have been fatal.

The eight men who jumped early were never picked up by search and rescue teams. Almost certainly, they parachuted into North Korea, where they were either captured or killed by the communists. A few made the POW lists, but the majority of the crew perished.

The other three crewmen from the flight deck had landed in the water with Beissner but much closer to shore. Beissner is certain that the current carried them into North Korean hands. They never made the POW lists, so they probably were executed on the beach.

Captain Krumm's aircraft, number 045, crashed on a mudflat near or on the coast. South Korean guerrillas operating in the area later came across the wreck and found three dead crewmen still inside the wreckage. Under the tail, they found two more bodies of the crew. One was so badly mangled that he was unrecognizable. The other body appeared almost unharmed at first until the partisans looked closer. He had three small bullet holes in his head. Apparently, he had bailed out of Krumm's plane and fallen into North Korean hands. They executed him and dumped his body at the crash site.

Krumm's copilot, New Jersey native Lieutenant John J. Horner, remained on the missing-in-action (MIA) list for more than a decade. His body was not at the crash site, nor was he ever seen again by UN forces.

One of Krumm's gunners suffered a similar fate. Airman 3d class Gerald E. Johnson, an eighteen-year-old from Pennsylvania and only a year out of high school, also disappeared. His body was not recovered by the guerrillas, nor did he turn up as a POW during Operation Big Switch after the war. His fate, like the fate of most of the crewmen who were shot down over North Korea that day, remains a mystery.

First Lt. Douglas K. ("Doug") Evans was not happy. Somehow, he had managed to pull a twenty-four-hour shift as aerodrome officer at Kimpo on

October 22d. He was a fighter pilot, not a pencil pusher, and as the night wore on, the myriad of red tape confused and frustrated him. It ended up being quite a busy night, and he found only enough time to take a few quick cat naps.

The next morning, he was ready to fly the counter-air mission with the other Sabrejet pilots of the 336th Fighter Squadron. He wrote later, "As I got no real sleep as night AO, the wheels wouldn't let me go on the next morning's mission—**#&*%!!"[2]

He watched the F-86s from the 4th Fighter Wing take off without him, then turned and walked to his tent as the outfit disappeared to the north. They had not been gone long when somebody tipped off Doug that a huge air battle was in progress. Knowing that any aircraft low on fuel or damaged would head for Kimpo, Doug grabbed his camera and went down to the flight line to take some action shots as they came in.

A few F-86s came in first. They landed without incident, and soon a small crowd had gathered with Doug. Pat Green, one of the Sabrejet pilots on the mission, joined him just in time to see one of the crippled B-29s lumbering in.

The B-29 settled onto the runway. One engine belched fire and smoke, and the left gear's tires were flat. When it touched the runway, the Superfort awkwardly bounced back into the air. The bomber slammed down on the runway and blew another tire. The exhausted pilots lost control at that point. The Superfort slewed to the left and skidded sideways—directly toward Doug and the rest of the observers.

The crowd scurried for cover, running at top speed from the flaming, dying B-29. It plowed off the runway, dragging a huge plume of dust in its wake as it tore through the dirt right where Evans and his friends had been standing. Fortunately, the gear didn't collapse. The Superfort came to a shuddering stop just as the crash crews reached the scene. They swarmed over the bomber, put out the fire and eased the wounded from the shell-torn fuselage.

When the rescue crews departed, a small crowd clustered around the B-29. Doug walked around it, examining the many gaping holes in the wings and body of the plane. He wrote later, "You could crawl through some of those holes—37mms, I guess."[3]

Two more Superforts, both badly shot up, lumbered in and managed to get down on the runway. Later, one would be patched up enough to fly to Japan, but the other was destined for the boneyard, as was the first one.

Following the Superforts, F-84s began straggling in, many flying on the last fumes trapped in their gas tanks. A few came in so hot that they blew tires on the runway in their haste to get down. Others came in with battle damage— evidence to the onlookers that the MiGs most certainly had come out top on that day.

Of the nine B-29s on the mission, three had been shot down short of Namsi. One aborted before the initial point. Of the remaining five Superforts, only one managed to escape the wrath of the Soviet MiGs. Two that did get down at Kimpo would never fly again. Another B-29 made it to Japan, while the final one touched down at Kimpo, then continued on to Japan later.

In effect, only three B-29s returned to their home base in Japan. The loss was devastating to the 307th Wing and a terrible shock to General Kelly and his staff. In fact, the disaster would shake the very core of SAC and prompt General LeMay, SAC's cigar-chomping commander, to visit Korea to find out what had gone wrong.

The B-29s claimed three MiGs during the raid. That number is surely high. The Superfort's World War II–vintage fire control system could not track targets going as fast as the MiGs flew during the engagement. In other words, the turrets could not turn rapidly enough to get the B-29s' guns on target. This flaw had not been corrected despite its discovery early in 1951. Also, if Soviet General Lobov is to be believed, no Soviet MiGs were lost on the mission. Any communist jets shot down by the B-29 gunners were probably stray North Koreans or Chinese who had followed the 4th Fighter Wing south to the scene of the interception.

This air battle, the largest of the war to date, had exposed just how tenuous FEAF's hold on air superiority was over northwestern Korea. Already, the fighter-bombers had been pulled out of MiG Alley—a tacit admission that the communists had gained the upper hand. Now, FEAF discovered that daylight B-29 missions into MiG Alley were going to be exceedingly costly in the future.

Examining the situation, FEAF reached two conclusions. First, the medium bomber wings could not possibly sustain such casualties over the long haul. There weren't enough trained crews or replacement aircraft available. A drawn-out battle of attrition, such as the Eighth Air Force had fought in World War II, was therefore not an option for FEAF. Second, the B-29 represented the pinnacle of World War II–era bomber technology. Five years before, it had been a world-beater, faster than many fighters of the day. In 1951, it was the last of a dying breed, a piece of aviation history that could not hope to survive in the new era of air warfare, in which the jet fighter reigned supreme.

Perhaps more than any other FEAF mission of the war, the Namsi raid came under microscopic scrutiny. The F-84 wing commanders, in writing their reports, stressed that because the egress route had not been adequately explained to them, they did not know how the B-29s were going to come off the target. When they split up and went in different directions, the situation became even worse, and the group that turned toward the coast suffered severely when the F-84s didn't follow at first.

The 4th Fighter Wing's intelligence officer, Art Beckwith, summed up the situation quite well in a report titled "An Analysis of Aerial Engagements over North Korea on October 23, 1951." The report has survived in the wing's unit history. It concludes by stating:

> In summary, three major comments can be made from the engagements on 23 October 1951. First, there was confusion on the part of fighter escort and the B-29s in the rally point and route of return which greatly impaired the mission of the fighter escort aircraft. Secondly, the MiGs were aggressive and in numbers which made possible the temporary supremacy of the enemy in aerial warfare over North Korea. Their tactics seemed to be well-planned, their formation appeared excellent, and their discipline appeared superior to that seen thus far in the Korean War. Thirdly, the enemy aircraft were in sufficient numbers to engage the F-86s in areas away from the bombers. These factors could well presage a new phase of aerial warfare over North Korea.[4]

While in Korea, General LeMay sat down with the 4th Fighter Wing pilots who had flown that day, ostensibly to have a roundtable discussion with them. Instead, he exploded in a fiery tirade and blamed the entire disaster on the 4th's lack of aggressiveness. To say that the Sabrejet pilots resented that accusation would be a monumental understatement.

At the end of the year, the 4th Wing issued a scathing report meant to counter LeMay's criticism and the comments being bandied around in the States about their unit's performance:

> Throughout this war, there has been a lot of speculation as to why the F-86s don't shoot down a lot more MiG-15s. From infrequent reports received here from the United States, it seems that our inability to kill a lot more MiG-15s has been laid to everything from airplane instability to gunsight trouble and lack of pilot ability or aggressiveness. Almost all the experts, except those who actually fought here, looked at everything but the thrust coming out of the tailpipe.
>
> Give us the ability to match the MiG-15 in climb, ceiling and top speed, and we can double and triple our kill rate. Give us an *advantage* in these flight characteristics, and a MiG won't come south of the Yalu River after first contact. When a man goes hunting with a gun, he's got to get close enough to whatever he's after with that gun to kill it.[5]

In the final analysis of the fighter cover, the real problem lay in two areas. First, there simply were not enough F-86s in Korea to handle the air forces of three major communist nations. The thirty-four Sabrejets up that day represented the only planes capable of meeting the MiGs on anything close to even terms. And, on this day, thirty-four F-86s were just not enough to handle 140 MiGs. Second, as an escort fighter, the F-84 Thunderjet was useless. Too slow, too heavy, and too outmatched by the MiG-15 in almost every flight

An F-86 takes to the air.

characteristic, the F-84s were simply unable to keep the Soviets from chewing apart the Superfortress formations. It would not have mattered if there had been thirty or three hundred F-84s protecting the B-29s that day. The MiGs would have gotten through no matter what they did.

FEAF assimilated the reasons for the Namsi disaster and made two major changes that changed the course of the Korean War. First, all daylight B-29 raids were suspended by the end of October. After a few minor missions were flown following the Namsi raid, the medium bombers hit North Korea exclusively at night.

The Soviets had accomplished half of their mission. Their fighter regiments had been brought to Manchuria with the specific mission of driving the B-29s out of North Korean skies. Namsi saw the end of daylight flights. Through 1952 and 1953, the night war over North Korea gradually intensified until the Soviets deployed two dedicated night fighter units and began again to take a heavy toll of B-29s.

After Namsi, no longer would the B-29s have the same effect on the war as they had before. Namsi was their swan song. Afterward, their effectiveness and survivability steadily continued to erode.

Second, to hit strategic targets in North Korea, FEAF increasingly relied on its fighter-bomber wings to get the job done. Even that did not entirely solve the problem because the F-84s and F-80s were so inferior to the MiG-15. A year later, an FEAF raid demonstrated just how costly such missions could be when MiGs intercepted them. On September 9, 1952, 175 MiGs hit an F-84 strike laid on against the North Korean Military Academy at Sakchu. The

Sabrejets providing escort managed to tie up about 100 of the MiGs, flamed 6 of them, and hit 6 more, but about 75 MiGs broke through the F-86 screen and made a quick, devastating pass through the bomb-laden F-84s. As the MiGs attacked, the F-84s were forced to jettison their ordnance. Three Thunderjets went down in flames; others suffered various degrees of damage. Again, the MiGs saved a target from destruction.

The Namsi raid had one positive effect on FEAF. After months of pleading with Washington for more F-86s, the Air Force finally relented and allowed General Weyland to convert the 51st Fighter Wing into a Sabrejet outfit. Late that fall, the 51st Wing turned over its F-80s to another Fifth Air Force wing and began working with F-86As and F-86Es. The 51st Wing flew its first Sabrejet mission of the war on December 1, 1951, and remained in the thick of the fight until the war ended in the summer of 1953. Even with the addition of the 51st Fighter Wing's Sabrejets, FEAF's air superiority squadrons remained heavily outnumbered by the Manchurian MiG units for the rest of the war. Nevertheless, the 51st Wing reduced the odds a little and took some of the burden off the 4th Fighter Wing, whose pilots were frequently stressed to their limits and beyond during those hectic final weeks of 1951.[6]

Although they returned to Manchuria flushed with success that morning of October 23, 1951, the communists failed to learn the lesson that they themselves had inflicted on the Americans. Clearly in the no-mans's-land of MiG Alley, piston-engine bombers of any kind were dead meat for swept-wing jet fighters. At this point in the war, everything but a MiG or an F-86 stood a good chance of getting shot down if it ventured into northwestern Korea. In their haste to exploit their October successes, however, the communists ignored this fact and sent an entire Chinese bomber squadron to its doom. In doing so, they unwittingly set the stage for the meteoric rise to fame of one of America's most courageous and reckless fighter aces, Major George A. Davis, Jr., USAF.

Part 4 | The Fighter Pilot's War

17 | Payback

It took the 4th Fighter Wing almost a month to avenge the disaster of the Namsi mission. On a bitterly cold day in November, the F-86 pilots encountered the rarest of communist aircraft over MiG Alley: bombers.

In early November, the North Koreans began harassing the ROK-held islands off the coast of northwestern Korea with infantry attacks. Taehwa-do was one of the most important of the ROK outposts. Located near the mouth of the Yalu River, it fell under North Korean attack sporadically throughout the month. To support the North Korean raids, the Chinese committed a squadron of Tu-2 bombers. On November 6, they struck for the first time. Sneaking down from Manchuria, they successfully bombed Taehwa-do and escaped north without running into any UN aircraft. About three weeks later, they tried again.

Doug Evans had flown the morning mission on November 30 despite a malfunctioning headset. He had launched long after the rest of the wing was headed north, and was unable to catch up with the wing. Nevertheless, he pressed on after them, speeding into MiG Alley alone. On the way, he passed near Sariwon Airfield and caught sight of what he thought might be aircraft arrayed around the runway.

When he couldn't catch the rest of his squadron, he turned back south, dropped down on the deck, and made a strafing pass at Sariwon, even though the aircraft were gone by the time he came back. That done, he returned to Kimpo, satisfied that he had at least accomplished something.

Later that morning, a call on his field phone ordered him to the afternoon briefing. The call surprised him. Because he had flown that morning, he was

168 • Crimson Sky

National Archives

F-86s of the 4th Fighter Wing.

not on the duty roster for the afternoon hop. Always eager to fly, though, he grabbed his gear and headed to combat ops with his friend, Andy Merrick. They learned that a developing crisis had forced the wing to throw out the flight schedule and assemble its best pilots for the next mission. Looking around, Doug saw the best of the best—Major Winton ("Bones") Marshall, Major George Davis, Dick Creighton, and Colonel Harry Thyng—all soon-to-be aces—were waiting around for the briefing to begin.

The pilots were told that, earlier that day, enemy aircraft had hit Taehwa-do again, and another attack was expected. The 4th Fighter Wing was to fly a CAP mission over the island and intercept any hostile aircraft threatening the ROK units stationed there. The idea of running into a formation of Soviet-built bombers enthralled the F-86 pilots. To date, they had fought exclusively against other fighters. The thought of wading in amongst a flock of prop-driven Tu-2s was too tempting a vision to be true.

Early that afternoon, thirty-one F-86 pilots eagerly lifted from Kimpo and began the flight north. The three squadrons stayed together in tight formation. Instead of climbing for altitude, they flew low along a north-south mountain range to shield their approach from communist radar.

Colonel Ben Preston's Red Flight led the mission. Behind him were six more F-86s from the 336th Fighter Squadron rear. Next came the 334th Fighter Squadron. "Bones" Marshall's 335th Squadron, ready to provide high cover for the other two squadrons, brought up the rear.

At 3:45 P.M., Dignity Special Flight—four F-86s—pulled away from the main formation and turned west just as the rest of the formation began racing for altitude. Dignity Special provided Preston with a reserve should MiGs swamp the rest of the wing and also would cover the wing's egress from the patrol area.

Around 3:50, Red Flight's pilots dumped their external tanks and made a left turn toward the coast. They followed the Yalu River westward but kept it a few miles off their right wings.

Behind Preston's Red Flight, Al Simmons led the other half of the 336th Squadron's F-86s to the left as well. Simmons, a native of Bend, Oregon, had five other Sabrejets with him in his White Flight. The extra element included Doug Evans and Dave Freeland.

As the 336th spread out into its normal combat formation of loose elements and flights behind its commander, George Davis's 334th Squadron reached the Yalu and swung westward. Davis was an ace from the 348th Fighter Group of World War II. During two years of fighting in New Guinea and the Philippines, he shot down seven Japanese planes. He had arrived in Korea only the month before and had taken over the 334th a short time before this mission. Already, he had earned the respect of his fellow pilots for his natural aggressiveness and his quiet, easygoing leadership style.

The 334th put up two flights that day, Dignity Able and Dignity Baker. Flying with Davis were several excellent pilots, including Captain Ray Barton, a southerner who led Able Flight's second element. He would have a wild experience on this day.

Two F-86 squadrons, eighteen jets in all, were now speeding westward toward the mouth of the Yalu and their assigned CAP station over Taehwa-do. Behind them, Marshall's 335th Squadron reached the Yalu several minutes after the other two squadrons and also turned left. Bones had eight F-86s from his outfit, four each assigned as Dignity William and X-Ray Flights. Altogether, the 4th Wing would soon have twenty-six fighters over Taehwa-do, with another flight patrolling to the south in case it was needed.

As the three squadrons moved down the Yalu, the pilots saw large formations of MiGs heading southward high above them. Everyone kept a close eye on them, lest they get boxed in. For some reason, however, none of the MiG-15 formations harried the F-86s as they flew toward their patrol area.

One MiG formation just ahead and above Red Flight consisted entirely of Soviet planes. In that flight was Boris Abakumov, an element leader with the 196th Fighter Air Regiment. A veteran pilot, he had been fighting in Korea since April and eventually claimed fifteen kills, with official credit for five.

Abakumov's regiment had been patrolling for some time and was now on its way home to Manchuria. The Soviet pilot looked down and saw nine Chinese Tu-2 bombers. They looked terribly vulnerable as they headed south, and he later wondered why the ground controllers in Manchuria did not direct his formation to provide extra cover for them. Lacking such orders, Abakumov and the rest of the 196th continued into Manchuria, where they landed and refueled.

-◆◆◆-

Over the coast at 4:07 P.M., Ben Preston sighted the same Tu-2 formation that Abakumov had seen just minutes before. Low on the 336th's starboard beam, the formation was coming straight down at them from Manchuria. The twin-engine bombers were cruising south at about 180 knots as they followed the coastline at 8,000 feet. The F-86 pilots thought there were twelve of them flying in a vee-of-vee formation with four Tu-2s in each flight. Four flights of Lavochkin La-9 piston-engine fighters provided close cover. Instead of weaving over the bombers in order to keep up their speed, the La-9s had taken rigid stations on either side of the Tu-2s and flew at the same altitude and speed as their charges. Above the propeller aircraft, a squadron of sixteen Chinese MiGs provided high cover.

Preston studied the situation for only a split second before ordering the 336th Squadron to attack at once. Calling out, "Tally-ho," he led Red Flight around in a tight, diving right turn. He made the first attack of the day, tearing down on the Tu-2s in an awkward head-on pass from the right quarter while still banking sharply. When he opened fire, the La-9s began scattering in every direction. He missed.

Pulling up, he flashed over the bomber formation and swung around for another pass. Below him, an La-9 crossed in front of him. Preston dipped his nose and let the Lavochkin have it with his six 50-caliber guns. This time, his aim was true. The La-9 burst into flames and crashed at 4:09.

After finishing off the fighter, Preston made another run at the bombers without success. Then, low on fuel, he and the rest of his flight disengaged and moved out over the water before turning south.

White Flight came down on the Tu-2s only seconds after Preston's flight began its run. Simmons made a front quarter attack on the bombers but missed his target. Pulling up in a steep left chandelle, he saw the MiG high cover still moving southward above and in front of the Tu-2s. Apparently, they did not see the F-86s, because they had not changed course or dropped their external tanks.

Simmons found himself in a perfect position to bounce the MiGs. Behind and below them, he knifed upward and picked one out of a flight of four. As he bored in for the kill, he noticed that the enemy jets all had red noses and red stripes above their horizontal stabilizers. He lined up on his MiG and pinned the pipper to its tailpipe. At point-blank range, he pulled the trigger.

His guns barked briefly, sending a shower of tracers cascading around his target. But after two hundred rounds, all his fifties stopped, apparently jammed. Frustrated and low on fuel, he disengaged and headed for Kimpo.

Robert Akin, White Two, followed Simmons down during the initial pass, picking out the last Tu-2 in the right trailing formation of four. He opened fire from the right front quarter and reported good strikes on the plane before he broke off the pass. As Simmons chandelled to the left, Akin lost him and began his own climbing turn to come back after the bombers.

Fifteen hundred feet behind Akin, Buford Hammond led White Flight's second element down on the bombers. As Hammond closed, he saw Akin shred his target with hits on the rear fuselage and tail. Hammond probably selected Akin's Tu-2 as his target. He pelted the Chinese plane with lead, riddling one propeller. As he zoomed past it, he could see the Chinese pilot beginning to feather the engine. Akin would later receive credit for this Tu-2.

Leonard Merook, White Four, followed Hammond down. He picked out the second Tu-2 in the lead Vee but observed no hits during his firing pass. He climbed out behind the bombers and executed a 180-degree turn. Behind the Tu-2s now, he had set himself up for a perfect second pass. As he came down onto the Chinese bombers, an La-9 broke into him. Deftly, he dodged its attack and waded into the Tu-2s. As he closed on them, he saw one falling out of formation. He followed it down and took film of it, which probably resulted in confirmation of Akin's kill. As Merook pulled off the dying bomber, he glanced up in time to see the high-cover MiGs drop their external tanks at 4:09, a full two minutes into the F-86 attack. In jet combat, two minutes was a lifetime. The MiG pilots had awakened too late to save their bomber comrades.

Doug Evans watched the rest of his squadron pounce on the bombers before he and Dave Freeland had their turns. The squadron's initial run had not been nearly as effective as Preston must have hoped, which was due primarily to the awkward angle from which they had attacked. Since the squadron was low on gas—it had reached bingo fuel two or three minutes before sighting the Tu-2s—Preston had no choice but to press his attack without any tactical finesse. Any maneuvering around the bombers would probably have squandered the squadron's fuel reserves.

Consequently, Doug made his pass from the front quarter, as had the rest of the squadron. With his wings still vertical, he pulled his nose over onto a Tu-2 stationed on one side of the trailing vee. He curved down on it, firing a sharp, well-aimed burst. He had only a split second to fire, but that was enough. As he rocketed past the Tu-2, he could see how his fifties had chewed up the bomber's right wing and engine. It appeared to be heavily damaged.

Doug was a real tiger and wanted this Tupolev more than anything. He arched up and back around in a quick chandelle before picking up his bomber quarry again. His second pass, this time from astern, finished it off. A fire erupted in the right-engine nacelle. By the time Doug completed his second run, the flames had spread the length of the right wing. Trailing a long tongue of fire and smoke, the Tu-2 fell into the sea. Evans watched it go down, and then called out over the radio, "White Five's got a flamer!"

Before he could savor his kill, however, an La-9 rolled out in front of him. He turned for it and closed with lightning speed. In an instant, it was in range and Evans fired a burst at it. "The ammo went out like a long arm reaching for the La-9," he wrote in his memoirs, "and almost at the instant of contact he broke left and the bullet stream went right through the spot he vacated. Closest thing I ever saw, and flash—we passed him."[1]

The La-9 pilot must have been frantic to save his bomber comrades. After breaking hard to avoid Doug's pass, he pulled in behind White Six, Dave Freeland. Dave was busy covering Doug's tail. The Red pilot got in a fleeting shot at Dave's F-86 before it sped out of range. Fortunately, the Chinese pilot's marksmanship failed to match his courage, and he missed.

The fight had cut deeply into Doug's fuel reserves, but he was in no mood to leave the battle just yet. He scribed an arc around the bombers again and came down in a tight bank to make a beam attack on a Tu-2. He had turned too soon, however, and found that he could not pull enough lead to hit it. Tucking the stick back to his stomach, he tried to drag his nose over the bomber, succeeding only in nearly blacking out from the G forces.

He fell short of the Tu-2s and passed right behind their tails through their prop wash, with his wings still perpendicular to the ground. Doug looked up. Just beyond his canopy, he could see the Chinese gunners in each Tu-2, their heads following the course of his Sabre. Although he could not see their guns, he was close enough to hear them chattering.

An instant later, he extended out beyond the side of the bomber vee, racing upward in a climbing turn. He came around again only to discover that the other F-86 squadrons had now entered the fight. The sky in front of him came alive with F-86s darting in and out of the lumbering Tu-2s like sharks excited by the scent of blood in the water. MiGs and La-9s flitted about uselessly, unable to stop the unfolding slaughter. Below the fight, he watched a burning Tupolev smack into the sea and explode in a shower of water, smoke, and flames. Above him, an La-9 exploded, disintegrating into thousands of tiny pieces. The engine dropped past him like a safe falling from a skyscraper in a Warner Brothers cartoon. He muttered to himself, "Look at all that stuff raining down."[2]

Doug and Dave Freeland were now deeply into their fuel reserves. If they stayed in the area any longer, they might not get back to Kimpo. Yet, for Doug this was the opportunity of a lifetime and he decided to make one last pass.

Two La-9s stood between him and the bomber Vees. He and Dave piled on them and sent both fighters scurrying out of the way in tight turns. Doug thundered past one and, from less than a hundred feet away, caught sight of the Red pilot staring up at him.

He continued on, having to dodge two parachutes on the way back to the Tu-2s. Sabrejets were everywhere, striking at the Chinese from every direction. As he weaved his way back into firing position, a flight of Sabrejets came down on him, firing at the bombers. They forced him to break off his attack, lest he run right into their bullet streams. That was enough for one day. Gathering up Freeland, he ducked out of the fight after hearing an order to disengage. They sped out to sea and rejoined the rest of the 336th. He made it to Kimpo with fifteen gallons of gas left in his tanks.

-◆◆◆-

Three minutes after the 336th slammed into the communist raid, George Davis tipped his Sabre over and led the 334th squadron into the fight. At the head of Able Flight, Davis arrived just as the bombers banked left and changed course so that they were now heading southeast. The course change, combined with the three-minute delay, meant that Davis and his men were in a much better position to attack.

Continuing west, Davis let the Tu-2s slip under and behind him as they ran for dry land, as if somehow that would save them. When they were a fair distance behind, Davis swung his squadron around in a sharp left turn and descended on the bombers from the rear.

Davis made the squadron's first pass. His F-86 came arching down in a wide, shallow pursuit curve. He fired on a Tu-2 and held his trigger down. His bullets, whipsawed across the Chinese plane and caused it to drop from the formation. Davis passed it going flat out before hauling up his Sabrejet's nose and breaking to the right. His wingman followed, but the second element completed their runs, missing their targets, and broke left, losing Davis in the process.

It was now 4:16 and the F-86s were desperately short of fuel. Davis ignored his own gauge's sagging needle and pulled around for another pass. Again, he executed a classic pursuit curve, the way he had been taught in 1942 as a young aviation cadet.

He waited until the Tu-2 was close before he unleashed his fifties again. He caught the bomber cold. A short burst and its fuel tank detonated. A huge explosion of smoke and flames erupted from the Tu-2 as it tumbled toward the sea. It hit the water at 4:17.

This was Davis's fourth kill of the Korean War.

And he wasn't finished yet. He banked his F-86 over and broke hard. In doing so, he lost his wingman, Able Two. Low on fuel and now without support, Able Two turned for home just before 4:20.

Prudence dictated that Davis do the same. With MiGs in the area, it was no place for a lone F-86. Davis, however, was never prudent during a fight.

He figured that he had just enough fuel for one more pass. This time, instead of a nice, by-the-book pursuit curve, he threw caution to the wind and came up on his target from dead astern. Although this gave him a zero deflection shot, it also gave the Tu-2 gunners the same advantage. He was exposing himself to heavy return fire.

The gunners blasted away at him as Davis bored in for the kill. He ignored the tracers zipping past and waited to fire until the bomber filled his sights. Then, he cut loose with another series of short, disciplined bursts.

An explosion rocked the Tu-2, spreading flames along the bomber's length and breadth. It fell out of formation just as three of its crew hit the silk. Seconds later, at 4:18, the plane plunged into the Yellow Sea. Davis has just scored his second kill of the day, a minute after his first.

He should have turned for home at this point. His fuel situation wasn't getting any better, and his tail was still exposed to attack now that his wingman was Kimpo-bound. Once more, Davis ignored convention. He swung around again and charged into the bomber formation. He drilled another Tu-2 with a sharp burst that sent it into the sea. This time, nobody got out. His third kill smacked into the whitecaps at 4:19 not far from his other two victims.

Davis realized that he had to leave now if he were to make it back to Kimpo. He disengaged and met up with other Sabrejets rallying offshore. He found Colonel Preston, linked up with him, and together they began the flight home. Minutes later, Davis's headset crackled with a desperate cry for help. Able Three was in trouble.

–◆◆◆–

Ray Barton, Able Three, had led John Burke, Able Four, down behind Davis on that first pass at the bombers before breaking left toward the east. In doing so, he lost contact with his squadron commander. It was bound to happen: the scene around the bombers was so chaotic. He checked behind him and saw Burke tacked onto his wing. Safely protected, he brought his F-86 down for another run at the Tu-2s. As he dove on their shredded formations, he picked up the bomber that Davis had damaged on his initial pass. He fired a long burst until the Tu-2 blew apart in a "brilliant explosion" as Ray's fifties probably speared the fuel tanks. Pieces of the bomber rained down, and the fuselage hit the water at 4:18, about the same time that Davis scored his second kill.

Ray chandelled back above the bombers and prepared to make another run. Instinctively, he checked his tail, noting that a jet was following him inside his turn. Confident it was John Burke, he executed another pursuit curve, then pulled up again. He checked his six and relaxed as he saw Burke back there, still turning inside his chandelle.

Once more, he dropped down on the bombers. He missed his target then decided that it was time to head for home. Disengaging, he leveled off and ran west toward Taehwa-do.

Suddenly, a bright orange fireball streaked over his canopy. He twisted in the cockpit to look over his shoulder. That wasn't Burke behind him at all. It was a MiG, and it was pouring cannon shells at him.

He broke as hard as he could and came around in a horizontal 360-degree turn, a sort of one-plane Lufberry circle. The MiG, unable to follow, disengaged. Barton did not waste time pointing his nose southward. Alone now, he was hundreds of miles from safety, and MiGs were on the prowl.

Not a minute later, four MiGs singled him out and bounced him from above. Frantic now, Barton broke into their attacks and continued turning as tightly as he could without blacking out. He scribed two complete circles in the air before the MiGs gave up and sped away.

Critically short of fuel by now, Barton again turned southward. Just as he did, two more MiGs dropped on him. He broke hard to the right and climbed straight into the sun. The MiGs tried to follow him at first, but they lost his F-86 in the sun's glare. It was a shrewd maneuver and it probably saved his life.

At 10,000 feet, he banked around and once more tried to move southward. By now, he was practically over Taehwa-do, which meant that he hadn't made any progress toward Kimpo at all since disengaging from the bomber flights.

Two more MiGs ruined any chance of escape at this point. They came at him like bulldogs, forcing Ray into a tight Lufberry. When he emerged from the maneuver, he saw the MiGs were still on him. Twisting and turning, he dodged their intermittent bursts as best he could, calling for help as he traded altitude for energy. As he threw his Sabre all over the sky, a cannon shell blasted a good-sized hole out of his right wing.

At 1,200 feet, he finally managed to get some breathing space. He looked around and spotted a single F-86 streaking to the rescue. It was George Davis.

Critical fuel situation be damned, George Davis was not about to let one of his own pilots die if he could help it. When he heard Ray's distress call, he had left Colonel Preston and turned back for Taehwa-do with his throttle wide open.

He found Ray running south just off the water. Above him, Davis picked out a single MiG at 3,000 feet. This one was hurrying north without a wingman. In all likelihood, the Chinese pilot had lost his number two while trying to stay on Able Three's tail. Now, it would cost him.

George crept up right behind him before diving down in a high stern attack. His finger touched the trigger, held it down for a brief instant, and watched as his fire cut the MiG to pieces.

Trailing debris, the stricken jet plunged downward and crashed just off Taehwa-do. It was Davis's fourth kill of the day and his sixth since he had arrived in Korea the month before. He became America's fifth jet ace of the war.

Linking up with Ray Barton, he nursed his thirsty bird back to Kimpo.

-◆◆◆-

John Burke, Able Four, had followed Ray Barton down on his second pass picking out a Tu-2 of his own as he went. He lined up on the trailing Tu-2 on the right and observed good strikes on the left wing. The wing tank exploded, and the Tu-2 dropped out of formation and crashed into the water a few seconds later.

As he came off this run, Burke spotted an F-86 breaking left and climbing. Thinking it was Able Three, he followed. He quickly realized his error and called out for Ray to waggle his wings. He received no response.

He began looking around for Ray and then discovered that his radio headset plug had popped out. He stuck it back in the jack just in time to hear Barton calling for help at Taehwa-do. Burke turned for the island, but Davis got there first, flamed the MiG, and announced that the situation was under control. Knowing that Ray was safe, Burke turned for home, happy in the knowledge that he had bagged his second scalp of the war.

-◆◆◆-

Bones Marshall seethed with anticipation. Below him, he could see the 336th and 334th Squadrons beating the heck out of the Tu-2 formations. Here, he was just an onlooker at the moment, along with the rest of his squadron. He had been ordered to stay above the fight and fly high cover for the other two squadrons in case more MiGs should arrive.

Now, the opportunity of a lifetime lay a few thousand feet off his left wing, and he could do nothing but bore holes in the sky. For a tiger like Marshall, it was the very definition of frustration.

Finally, the call came from Ben Preston. "Bones," the colonel called out, "Come on down and get 'em."[3]

Marshall didn't have to be invited twice. He led the 335th Squadron around the Tu-2s and split-essed down into the fight. High and behind, Bones positioned his squadron for a perfect bounce. He led the way, flaying a Tu-2 in the rear formation with gunfire as his F-86 hit Mach 0.9. The bomber steamed flames after only one burst. He kept firing and closed the distance in seconds. Just as he completed his run, the surviving crew bailed out.

He set up for a second stern attack and closed on a Tu-2, spraying out his ammo in a single long burst. He clobbered the bomber hard but did not see it crash. As he pulled up, Marshall ran straight into a pair of La-9s. He nudged the stick over and tacked his nose onto one of the Soviet-built prop jobs. A short squeeze on the trigger and the La-9 completely disintegrated in a massive explosion. Quite possibly, this is the La-9 that Doug Evans saw blow up right over his head.

Sweeping past the ugly smudge of smoke and falling debris, Marshall took a second to look around at the fight raging on all sides of him. Just then, the remaining La-9 turned into him and unleashed a torrent of cannon fire. His wingman, John Honaker, saw the La-9 swing around and called out a warning that probably saved Marshall's life.

When Marshall heard Honaker's call to break, he instantly rolled over and pulled back hard on the stick just as a cannon shell exploded through the canopy and impacted against his headrest. He blacked out, and the F-86 spun out of control, falling toward the coast.

Bones regained consciousness just in time to see the earth spinning toward him. He recovered from the spin as he heard John Honaker's voice on the radio calling out Bones's predicament. John told the other F-86 pilots that he'd spun in and no chute had appeared. When Marshall climbed, Honaker saw him and joined on his wing. They were safely away from the fight now, so both took a few minutes to examine the damage to Marshall's F-86.

The cannon shell that hit the headrest had also split open Marshall's helmet, which damaged his radio headset so that he could only receive transmissions. With his transmitter knocked out, he couldn't talk to anyone. Worse, the shell had peppered his chute pack with holes, making a bail out impossible. Flying shrapnel and Plexiglas had torn up his hands, face, and neck, and he was bleeding. A piece of shrapnel had also clipped his oxygen mask so that to keep it on his face, he had to hold one hand against it. In addition, the F-86 took hits in the left wing and fuselage behind the canopy.

Considering the severity of the damage, Marshall gave some thought to landing the Sabrejet on the beach. He could await a rescue helicopter and be back to Kimpo by late evening if he was lucky. In the end, he chose to stick with the aircraft and try to nurse it home to Kimpo. John stayed on his wing, keeping a vigil over him in case they ran across MiGs.

Somehow, on the last of his fuel, Bones reached Kimpo and began his final approach. Just short of the runway, another F-86—possibly George Davis's plane—cut in front of him. Bones knew that if he tried to land, he and Davis would collide on the ground. Reluctantly, he pulled off and circled around, letting the other F-86 land first. This was a lucky decision as it turned out.

Davis's F-86 had run out of fuel and he was making a dead-stick landing. For him, there was no second chance. Fortunately, he landed without incident.

Marshall came down and landed. His gear had extended and locked, so he didn't have any hydraulic damage, as he had suspected earlier after hearing the fuselage behind him had been hit. As he rolled to a stop, he knew he'd scored two kills, making him the sixth American ace of the Korean War.

-◆◆◆-

While the F-86s threaded their way southward for home, the shattered remains of the Tu-2 strike limped back north. They had failed to hit Taehwa-do because they had to jettison their bombs short of the target, and all of the surviving planes were badly shot up. Despite their escorts of sixteen MiGs and another sixteen La-9s, the Tu-2s had been savaged by the American Sabres.

Boris Abakumov stood by the runway and watched the raid return home. Much like Doug Evans, he witnessed three shattered bombers settle onto the runway where he stood. The three Tu-2s were all that was left of the original group—either twelve or nine total, depending on the source. The three survivors were all laced with bullet holes, testament to the near complete destruction of the squadron.

Abakumov could only shake his head in wonder. Why had the Chinese not asked his regiment for assistance? What a waste.

-◆◆◆-

The parallels to the October 23 mission to Namsi are almost eerie. First, in both cases, the intercepting fighters came in from the west, making contact while still high above the bombers.

Second, the close escort—be it F-84s or La-9s—proved next to useless in the engagements. The high cover of swept-winged jets were not a factor in either fight. Both battles saw the high-cover fighters positioned ahead of and above the bombers, where the swept-winged jets were either pinned down or caught napping, making them unable to help the bombers.

Most important, the results of the two missions proved almost identical. The bomber squadrons had been cut to ribbons, forcing a change in policy by both air forces. As a consequence of the October 23 mission, the American B-29s had abandoned daylight raids, choosing instead to attack under the cover of darkness. After November 30, communist bombers disappeared from the North Korean skies. Although night heckling Po-2s ran missions sporadically throughout the war, the air forces of the communist countries never again made concerted air attacks against UN targets. In fact, not until January 1953 was another Tu-2 ever spotted by the 4th Fighter Wing. Like its brethren, this

Tu-2 stood no chance against the F-86 Sabrejet. Ray Kinsey of the 335th Squadron shot it down. That kill became the last bomber destroyed by the Fifth Air Force.

—◆◆◆—

As dusk fell on Kimpo that November 30, exuberant pilots clustered together at Combat Ops, telling and retelling their roles in the mission. Everyone was laughing and celebrating, and the scene reminded Doug Evans of a locker room after winning the big game. Through it all, the intelligence staff took copious notes. Initially, claims totaled six Tu-2s, a MiG-15, and three La-9s destroyed, with three more Tu-2s damaged. Not a single F-86 had been lost, although Bones Marshall and Ray Barton both had hair-raising close shaves.

Later, after viewing gun camera film from the mission, FEAF awarded two more Tu-2s as destroyed. If there had been nine Tu-2s, as Abakumov asserted, the initial count exactly matched what the Soviet pilot witnessed in Manchuria—six of nine shot down and the other three damaged.

American accounts stress that there were twelve Tu-2s, and eight were shot down. Marshall, in two accounts of the mission, claims that there were at least thirty Tu-2s, of which only six or seven were left when he made his initial pass.

In all likelihood, there were nine Tu-2s flying in three vees of three planes each. Whatever the true number, the results were a complete disaster for the communists, and a tremendous victory for FEAF at a time when such a coup was badly needed, coming as it did on the wake of the Namsi raid.

Major George Davis was the hero of the hour. His incredible display of gunnery resulted in four kills—three Tu-2s and one MiG-15. He had become a jet ace, the fifth of the war, and was one of the first Americans to become an ace in both World War II and the Korean War. From this mission onward, Davis's career began its meteoric rise. To his comrades, he was the best shot in the Fifth Air Force and perhaps the best fighter pilot to take an F-86 in harm's way during the entire Korean War.

Like so many pilots whose reckless abandon in combat earned them glory and fame, Davis's meteoric career burned hot and short. Just eight weeks after his greatest success, he was a victim of his own brashness when his F-86 fell flaming from the skies of MiG Alley.

18 | More Guts than the Law Allows

Born on December 1, 1920, George Andrew Davis Jr. graduated from high school in Morton, Texas, before moving on to Harding College. In March 1942, he joined the Army Air Forces as an aviation cadet. He received his wings in February of the following year, and joined the 348th Fighter Group in New Guinea seven months later. It was the start of a combat career that stretched through two wars and resulted in twenty-one confirmed kills.

He stayed in the Pacific for two years, seeing heavy action in some of the most vicious air battles of the war, using his flying skill, marksmanship, and commitment to teamwork to stay alive. With seven kills, he proved himself to be a solid and effective member of the fighter group.

On December 10, 1944, Davis was chasing a Japanese Kawasaki Ki-61 Hien in his P-47 Thunderbolt when his point-blank gunfire caused it to explode. He was so close when it blew up, he practically rammed the wreckage. Another time, while escorting B-24s to Clark Field in the Philippines, he tangled with a Mitsubishi A6M Zero and shot it down. Seconds later, he picked up two more Zeroes and dove to the attack. From out of nowhere, another Japanese fighter swept down on him from above, lacing his P-47 with machine-gun and cannon fire. One 20-mm round exploded in his left wing, puncturing an oxygen tank, and blowing out the left tire as it lay nestled in the wheel well. Davis disengaged and limped home with film of his final kill of the war.

His flying skill earned him a slot on the Air Force Demonstration Unit after the war. Flying F-80s, the group toured the air show circuit to show off the new jet fighter to the taxpaying public. Following a stint with the 1st Fighter Group, he received orders for Korea, where he joined the 334th Fighter Squadron in October 1951.

Courtesy of Al Dymock

George Davis scored four kills on a single day—twice. He is pictured here, third from left, with other pilots of the 4th Fighter Wing.

Davis actually became more brazen, more aggressive, and more willing to take risks in Korea than he was during World War II. Overzealousness is most often the product of youth and not often seen in a veteran airman with 266 Pacific war missions under his belt. Yet, as he made a name for himself with the 336th, his fellow pilots shook their heads and wondered how a man who took such risks would ever survive his tour.

From the outset, something in Davis pushed him to the edge in Korea. He threw caution to the wind, and flew with a brash abandon that bordered on the fanatical. He became a modern-day Frank Luke as he carried out attacks no matter what the odds and no matter what the tactical situation.

Slight and wiry with hawkish features and a devil-may-care grin, Davis struck Doug Evans as quite mild-mannered on the ground. His slow Texas drawl only enhanced that image and certainly belied the fact that he was a hard-charger in the air.

First Lt. Alfred W. Dymock Jr., who flew with George in the 334th Squadron, remembered him as a quiet man who didn't socialize much with the rest of the squadron. He and Davis sometimes argued tactics. Dymock

Al Dymock.

was in favor of looser formations that would allow more pilots the opportunity to get in shots at passing MiGs. With the system in place in 1951, the 4th Fighter Wing preferred larger formations, which limited the opportunities for clement leaders and wingmen.

Claude ("Charlie") Mitson, an Idaho native, knew Davis before the Korean War when they served together in the 71st Fighter Squadron, 1st Fighter Group. On the ground, like everyone else, Mitson saw Davis as an easygoing, quiet sort. He rarely saw Davis drink, and, as far as he recalled, Davis never smoked. "He was a true gentleman," Mitson said. "He was not stand-offish at all. He was easy to approach and talk with, and he wasn't rowdy like other fighter pilots."[1]

Although quiet and modest on the ground, George was an absolute daredevil in the air. All his easygoing charm vanished when he slipped into a fighter's cockpit. From the moment his engine started, he was pure pilot, pure tiger. Nobody beat George Davis in a fair fight.

Mitson had ample respect for Davis and his flying skills because he would frequently take on the squadron's young lieutenants in mock dogfights. Said Charlie of these long-ago battles, "When George Davis fought you, you knew that he was going to whip you."

In addition to his skill as a pilot, Davis had an uncanny knack for hitting targets in the air. It must have been a natural gift, and Bones Marshall once called him the best deflection shooter in the entire Air Force.

Deflection shooting was a rare talent, one that Davis had honed in the skies of the Southwest Pacific. In fact, he once nailed a Zero with a 90-degree deflection shot—probably the hardest of all to make. Another kill, his second in New Guinea, went spiraling down in smoke and flames after he hit it with a 25-degree deflection shot. In Korea, his ability to hit a target from any position with any amount of deflection inspired awe and respect among his peers.

The MiGs decided to come out and play again on December 5, 1951. Unfortunately for them, they ran smack into the 334th Fighter Squadron with George Davis at its head.

Just northwest of Sinanju, Davis was patrolling with a flight of Sabres when a sliver of silver against the blue sky caught his attention. Two MiG-15s were scurrying along, heading southeast toward Sinanju. Davis didn't hesitate an instant. He broke into the pair of enemy fighters and raced after them in pursuit. He caught the trailing one practically over Sinanju. He fired a long burst at it, and the MiG began to burn. The pilot quickly ejected, and Davis saw his chute open.

Davis continued his patrol and flew westward until he reached the coast. A few minutes later, at the mouth of the Chongchon River, he stumbled across a dogfight in progress. A single MiG had managed to get behind an F-86 and was now poised for the kill. Sweeping down on the MiG, Davis saw it break off the attack and begin clawing for altitude to the northeast, but his F-86 proved too fast for the MiG. Coming down on the dogfight, he had gained enough speed to follow the MiG into a zoom climb and close to gunnery range. He cut loose with his fifties and was gratified to see the MiG suddenly spin out of control. As it fell earthward, the pilot bailed out. In just minutes of combat, Davis had scored two more kills. They were his seventh and eighth victories of the Korean War, all of them scored in eight days of action.

Scoring four kills in a single day was not terribly unusual in World War II, but it was almost unheard of during the Korean War. The fights over MiG Alley in Korea were so quick, intense, and violent that most pilots didn't get a chance even to line up on four separate targets, let alone shoot them down. Three-kill days were recorded by Air Force aces, including Charles Cleveland, Iven Kincheloe, and Joseph McConnell, but Davis was the only pilot to score four in a day for the UN side. What's more, he did it twice.

His first four-kill mission came on the bomber intercept (see chapter 17). Thirteen days later, on December 13, he found his way into two furious dogfights and emerged with four MiG scalps for his collection.

On the morning mission, George led his squadron into a brief fight that scattered a formation of MiGs all over the sky. The F-86s soon spread out, and the squadron ended up totally dispersed.

Dymock flew on the mission and recalled that, during the initial contact, the MiGs proved both "experienced and skittish." As he remembered the fight, none of the 334th Squadron's pilots scored during that first brief clash with the MiGs.

After the squadron gave chase, however, Davis was able to overtake two MiGs and send them both spiraling down into the North Korean countryside. Nearby, Dymock also scored when he and his wingman ran into twenty-eight MiGs coming down from Antung. They climbed into the attack, and the MiGs broke into a defensive turning circle. While his wingman covered him, Dymock selected one and shot it down, despite the presence of another MiG slightly above him who could have come to the rescue.

As the MiG pilot struggled to get out of his crippled plane, Dymock closed to less than thirty yards and could clearly see the markings on the fuselage and wings. It was a North Korean MiG, the first he had seen since arriving in the theater in July 1951.

The morning sweep returned to Kimpo just before noon. The Sabrejets had scored three kills—two by Davis and the one by Dymock. Dymock also got credit for damaging another MiG during the mission.

That afternoon, Dymock was looking forward to flying again when Capt. Theodore S. Coberly of the wing's headquarters Flight, came down and took over Dymock's slot. Disappointed, he watched the 334th Squadron take off and speed north, eager to do battle with the MiGs again. It did not have long to wait. In MiG Alley, the 4th Wing ran into a large formation of MiG-15s. The wing swung behind the MiGs and waded into their midst. A dogfight was soon raging all over the sky as the F-86s gave these MiGs a lesson they would not soon forget.

According to Dymock, the enemy fighters were flown by a raw North Korean air regiment that was totally unable to counter the aggressive and disciplined tactics of the F-86 pilots. As a result, they dropped like flies. It became a turkey shoot. Within a few minutes, more MiGs went down than on any other mission of the war to date.

Mitson flew on that mission with the 336th Squadron. He recalled that, soon after contact, his squadron broke down into elements. In the chaotic fight that followed, he and his wingman were able to catch a MiG from dead astern. Charlie, a former World War II paratrooper, closed the range and let fly with a barrage of .50-caliber bullets. The rounds chewed into the MiG's wings and fuselage. Pieces blown from it began streaming back to strike Mitson's F-86. When he returned to Kimpo, his ground crew found chunks of melted metal in his air intake. For years, he saved them in a little box along with his cuff links.

While Mitson was scoring his second kill, Davis was also having success. He and his flight, which included Ted Coberly as his second element leader, ran into a flight of ten MiGs. Davis chopped down two of the MiGs, as Coberly closed to eight hundred feet on another and sent a long burst into the MiG's wing roots. The MiG exploded just as Coberly swung off target to line up on another. The pilot bailed out of the burning MiG.

On their return to Kimpo, the F-86 pilots were full of adrenaline and excitement. When the debriefing showed that ten MiGs had been shot down, including Davis's third and fourth kills for the day, the 4th Wing's pilots knew that they had inflicted a major defeat on the communists. During that one day, they had encountered an estimated 145 MiGs on two missions and had downed 13 of them.

Davis had secured his place in aviation history. With twelve kills, he was the first American jet pilot to reach the double-digit mark. During about two weeks of fighting, his aerial skill and marksmanship had catapulted him into acehood and fame. He was now the war's leading ace.

This December 13th mission represented the pinnacle of his career, but, in some ways, it helped to secure his downfall. Both Mitson and Dymock recall that, as December wore on, Davis grew increasingly contemptuous of the enemy pilots. In his mind, they were lousy pilots, especially compared with Japanese pilots whom he had fought in World War II. As Dymock said later, "George just didn't respect the MiG pilots."

Mitson also noticed this trait in George. He had known Davis for years. They had served in the 1st Fighter Group together. Davis had been the 71st Fighter Squadron's adjutant, and Mitson had always looked up to his piloting ability and combat skills. Now, however, he saw Davis growing "quite contemptuous of the MiG pilots." This contempt drove him to take bigger and bigger risks, as he "considered himself immortal." According to Mitson, in Davis's mind, no MiG pilot would ever knock him down, no matter what he did in the air.

Throughout the Christmas season of 1951, the pilots of the wing talked about George over beers in the officer's club. "Old George is going to get himself killed one of these days," became a common refrain heard among the tight-knit groups of fighter pilots huddled around their tables.

One day, as the 336th Squadron gathered for a mission, Ben Preston walked into the room with this three squadron leaders in tow. He introduced each man in turn—Dick Creighton, Bones Marshall, and George Davis.

"Take a look at these guys," Preston intoned dramatically. "You'll be reading about them for the rest of your lives."

Both Preston and the media made a big deal out of the wing's aces. For Preston, it was probably a way to encourage and inspire his pilots. The press, on the other hand, gave them plenty of attention since the Sabrejet pilots were the only ones scoring tangible victories over the communists during a period of stalemate in the ground war. They became almost household names in the United States, and each ace's latest successes were duly reported for public consumption.

Davis, ever the modest gentleman on the ground, was becoming obsessed with his own MiG tally. Dymock recalled, "George was out to build his score."

Charlie Mitson remembered Davis "dwelling on his score a lot." He added, "George's main goal in life was to shoot down MiGs."

This statement hit dead center. For Davis, even his own life and safety came second to adding another kill to his score. The pilots called it *MiG Madness*, a rare affliction but one that was almost always deadly. George Davis developed it during the winter of 1951–52.

On February 10, MiG Madness got the best of George Davis and his years of training. Back in his days with the 348th Group during World War II, he had been the consummate team player. Personal glory and individual success came second to staying alive and protecting his buddies. Now, on his final patrol over MiG Alley, he was about to throw it all away.

Leading eighteen F-86s north, Davis and his squadron had orders to screen out any MiGs that attempted to intercept a fighter-bomber attack laid on at Kunu-ri. Apparently bored with the patrol, Davis left his squadron's formation and took his wingman up to the Yalu to look for action. His leaving formation—especially when he was the leader— was highly unorthodox and incredibly dangerous. Two F-86s caught by themselves would be no match for a skilled Soviet MiG regiment. Because MiGs usually flew in large formations, any contacts that Davis ran down would almost certainly outnumber him.

Near the Yalu, Davis and his wingman picked up five MiGs milling around on the north side of the river. This area was off limits, so Davis turned south and moved back toward the 334th Squadron's main formation. He stayed on that course for only a short time before banking to the west. As he and his wingman turned, Davis sighted ten MiGs heading southeasterly at high speed below them at about 32,000 feet.

Davis decided to bounce them. Continuing his right turn, he swung around until his nose was also pointed southeast. Now above and behind, he was in a perfect bounce position. He and his wingman were about to attack ten MiGs—five-to-one odds, and chances were high that more MiGs were in the area.

Over MiG Alley, American pilots usually could pick up MiG formations from great distances since the Soviet-built fighters tended to trail thick white contrails from each wing. Due to some meteorological freak, however, the MiGs were not making their familiar white tracks that day. Quite possibly, another formation of MiGs lurked above the one that Davis was about to attack.

To the south, Doug Evans was patrolling with the rest of the 336th Squadron. He heard over the radio that Davis had left his formation to go hunting with his wingman. Minutes later, he heard Davis's familiar voice call out, "Look now, Baker Two," to his wingman. This was a common expression the pilots used to tell their wingmen to confirm a possible kill. Evans knew Davis had lined up on a target and wanted to make sure if he shot it down, Baker Two would see it fall.

Davis dropped down behind the MiGs and blasted through their formation. Red pilots scattered in every direction, totally panicked by the surprise bounce. One MiG hesitated just long enough to be blown apart by Davis's expert marksmanship.

At this point, many pilots have been content with a single kill and would have used the speed gained in the initial dive to disengage and climb back over the MiGs. Termed a *slashing attack* or an *energy fight*, such a move would have virtually guaranteed that none of the MiGs could get a shot at him or Baker Two: they wouldn't have had the speed to follow or the time to turn around and get behind the F-86s. Safely above the MiGs, Davis and Baker Two could dive on down again and make another quick pass. These were the same tactics that MiG pilots used so frequently and successfully. Of course, by the time they came downstairs, the MiGs would be ready and alerted, but that could be negated by the speed advantage of the F-86s that resulted from the dive.

George Davis ignored this option. Instead, he immediately went for another kill. In doing so, he pressed his attack, and his luck, beyond all limits. Rolling in on a second MiG, he was still in a right bank when he got behind the fleeing fighter. This time, when George squeezed the trigger, his bullets hacked open the MiG's right wing root. His lead had obviously hit something vital. Almost at once, a thick stream of black smoke poured from the holes made by his bullets. The MiG entered a dive and never recovered. It crashed into the mountain range almost six miles below.

That would be George's fourteenth and last kill. For even as he was lining up this last victim, another MiG had singled him out. Exactly where it came from is a mystery. Most believe it was part of the original squadron Davis had bounced. After he and Baker Two had waded into the enemy formation, this particular MiG had possibly swung around for a stern attack. Or, it could have been part of a higher group of MiGs that Davis and Baker Two had failed to see.

No matter where it came from, it bored in on Davis from seven o'clock.

"Look out, Baker Lead!" came Baker Two's frantic call. It came just a fraction too late. Davis had bled away his speed advantage, and now, with the MiG behind him, he was a sitting duck.

The MiG opened fire as Davis slowed down even more while trying to get behind a third MiG. Baker Two saw cannon shells rip into the left side of George's fuselage just below the canopy. Almost certainly, they decimated everything inside the cockpit.

The F-86 suddenly spun out of control and began twisting down from 32,000 feet.

"Oh no," cried Baker Two, his voice thick with dread. He called to George repeatedly but received no answer. The drama over the radio quickly attracted many other voices, all demanding to know what was going on. Baker Two could only say that Davis's plane had taken a hit in the cockpit and was going down out of control.

No chute emerged. It was a long fall from 32,000 feet. The F-86 exploded against the side of a mountain, not far from the death pyres of Davis's final two victims.

—◆◆◆—

According to several 4th FIW pilots, following the mission, Baker Two received the grilling of his life. He was debriefed for hours as various high-ranking officials bombarded him with questions and intimated that Davis's death was Baker Two's fault. Davis was a national hero. A scapegoat had to be found. It was a terrible and totally unfair ordeal.

Davis had bitten off more than he could chew. Being aggressive was part and parcel of a fighter pilot's life in Korea, and doing wild and audacious things sometimes paid huge rewards. The 4th Wing's pilots were fond of saying, "You don't need to be crazy to be a fighter pilot, but it helps."

But there were always limits, and Davis exceeded them on February 10, 1952. His disregard for them cost him his life, as well as Baker Two's emotional well-being for many months. According to several 4th FIW pilots, Davis's wingman was sick at heart and was very nearly shattered by the ordeal that he went through after the mission.

George Davis received the Medal of Honor posthumously for his actions on February 10. In part, the citation read:

> Rather than maintain his superior speed and evade the enemy fire being concentrated against him, he elected to reduce his speed and sought out

still a third MiG-15. During this latest attack his aircraft sustained a direct hit, went out of control, then crashed into a mountain 30 miles south of the Yalu River. Maj. Davis's bold attack completely disrupted the enemy formation, permitting the friendly fighter-bombers to successfully complete their interdiction mission. Maj. Davis, by his indomitable fighting spirit, heroic aggressiveness, and superb courage in engaging the enemy against formidable odds exemplified valor at its highest.

To this day, Doug Evans remembers what Dick Creighton concluded about George Davis. Perhaps it is the great ace's best epitaph: "He had more guts than the law allows."

19 | Stalemate in the Air

Following the wild air battles of the fall and winter of 1951, the communists never again made a serious effort to achieve command of the skies over North Korea. Gradually, as 1952 wore on, UN fighter-bombers, usually guarded by the two F-86 wings now operational (the 4th and 51st), reappeared in MiG Alley. On some strikes, up to eighty-four Sabrejets covered their straight-winged brethren as they went about their bombing runs. The MiGs still showed up over MiG Alley in large numbers. More than thirteen hundred MiG sorties a month were sometimes reported by UN pilots, and 90 percent of those sightings occurred within MiG Alley. The communists seldom operated outside northwestern Korea and conducted no more large-scale campaigns to expand MiG Alley's borders.

At night, the Soviet 351st Air Regiment busied itself against B-29 strikes against bridges and airfields. At first, flying Lavochkin La-11s, the 351st did not achieve much success. The piston-engined aircraft were just too slow to catch the B-29s. In February 1952, however, the regiment converted to MiG-15s. Over time, its effectiveness gradually increased, especially when the Soviets established modern radar sites and ground control centers. MiG-15s did not carry a radar system, so the Soviet night fighter pilots were totally reliant on ground vectors and searchlights to locate their prey at night. As these systems improved, so did the performance of the 351st Regiment.

The Soviet unit scored its biggest success to date on June 10. Twelve of its MiGs intercepted a B-29 raid on a vital rail bridge at Kwaksan and shot down two B-29s. A third B-29 was riddled with cannon fire and barely made it to friendly territory.

As the MiGs continued to operate against the B-29s, FEAF realized that the Superforts needed night escort. Although the 319th Fighter Interceptor Squadron at Suwon possessed the best night fighter in the U.S. Air Force—

the F-94 Starfire—it was prohibited from operating over North Korea for fear that its top secret, state-of-the-art electronics systems would fall into communist hands.

The U.S. Marines had a night fighter unit, VMF-513, in Korea. Operating the twin-engined Grumman F7F Tigercat, the Marine unit was the only one capable of covering the B-29s at night throughout the summer of 1952. Beginning in July, the F7Fs began flying support for the B-29s. They usually patrolled ahead of the Superforts as they swept the sky, from the initial point to the target area, to ensure that no MiGs lurked in their path.

A summer of these escort missions proved that the F7F was no solution to nighttime MiG intercepts. With its two piston engines, the Tigercat lacked the performance needed to engage the MiGs. Fortunately, in November, VMF-513 received twelve new Douglas F3D Skynights. Although slow and awkward for a modern jet fighter—its top speed was only about 480 mph— the Skynight proved to be a better answer to countering the nocturnal MiGs than anything else available.

In January 1953, the Starfire squadron finally received authorization to fly over North Korea and joined the Marines in covering the B-29s at night. Interestingly, by early 1953, FEAF began using almost identical escort tactics at night as they had in 1951 during the final daylight raids. The slow Skynights, providing close cover, flew a few thousand feet directly above the B-29s. When a Superfort was attacked or illuminated by a searchlight, the Skynight pilot dropped down behind it to look for MiGs. Meanwhile, the F-94s provided a screen twenty to thirty miles north of the target area.

FEAF's night fighters scored some successes—the F-94s claimed two MiG-15s and an La-9 (probably an La-11) during the final months of the war—but they were never able to stop the Soviet interceptors entirely from knocking down B-29s. Like the daylight air war, the nighttime air war settled down into a grim battle of attrition with no clear-cut victors.

Although the fighter-bombers returned to MiG Alley in 1952, FEAF could not claim command of the air over northwestern Korea. At times, the F-84s and F-80s were hit hard by sudden MiG attacks, despite every effort on the part of the F-86s. At the same time, the communists were either unable or unwilling to capture control of the air. Rather than initiating another massive campaign to establish total control, the combined communist air forces settled for hit-and-run strikes against UN aircraft and their F-86 protectors.

In the end, nobody won total control over MiG Alley, and the air war gradually came to mirror the action on the ground. MiG Alley turned into a sort

Maj. Frederick "Boots" Blesse, a ten kill ace.

of no-man's-land where no aircraft were safe from attack. Even with two F-86 wings, FEAF could not drive the MiGs from the sky because there were simply too many of them.

To an extent, the communist numerical superiority was countered by the excellent training of the average American fighter pilot. Even the top Soviet ace of the war, Yevgeni Pepelyaev, confessed that even the best-trained Soviet pilots were not as well prepared for combat as their American adversaries. It was this advantage that kept the Sabrejets over MiG Alley as they took a steady toll of MiGs. Nevertheless, training did not offer the decisive advantage needed to gain total control over North Korea. Only more F-86s could have done that, and the United States just didn't have any more to send.

◆◆◆

As the air war grew stagnant and offered no conclusive victory for either side, the American leadership in Washington began using FEAF's bomber assets to put political pressure on the communist's negotiator at the Panmunjom talks. By hitting sensitive targets, Washington hoped that the communists would make concessions at the truce table.

The first of these campaigns began in late June 1952 when FEAF began attacking North Korean hydroelectric power stations. Instead of forcing concessions from the communists, however, the raids actually undermined America's position because world reaction was universally hostile. The raids were seen as attacks on civilian targets, as well as a dangerous expansion of the nature of the war. Even Great Britain, the most stalwart ally of the United States, protested the attacks, fearing that they might trigger World War III.

Undaunted, Washington persisted with this new use of air power. On July 11, 1952, targets in Pyongyang were hit by hundreds of napalm-dropping fighter-bombers. Again, the goal was to break the deadlock at Panmunjom. Despite tremendous damage, no concessions were forthcoming at the truce talks.

The pressure was intensified after this Pyongyang raid. During August, FEAF aircraft systematically attacked eighty North Korean cities and transportation centers, usually with advance notice to civilians in order to minimize casualties.

Even these incredibly destructive raids had no effect at Panmunjom. Finally, out of frustration, FEAF and Task Force 77 launched the single largest strike of the war on August 29. Some 1,403 aircraft struck what was left of Pyongyang and utterly devastated the capital. Nothing worth attaching remained in the city. Again, the communists didn't budge at the truce talks.

Washington persisted with using FEAF's destructive capacity as a bargaining ploy into 1953. Just before Truman left office, a massive series of strikes hit the Sinanju bridges in hopes of breaking the deadlock at Panmunjom and ending the war before President-elect Dwight D. Eisenhower took office. All eleven bridges targeted in the five-day assault were destroyed, but the campaign had no effect on the communist diplomats.

After Eisenhower took office, he continued this strategy. On May 13, 1953, he turned FEAF loose on North Korea's irrigation dams. Although a three-day series of raids caused widespread damage, especially to North Korea's rice crop, it too failed to draw concessions from the communists.

Overall, the strategy had completely failed. Nonetheless, it did not stop future American presidents from adopting the same course of action—with similar results. The seeds of America's flawed air strategy in Vietnam can be found in the last year of the Korean War.

With a bloody stalemate over MiG Alley, the bombers being diverted for political reasons, and the night bombing campaign suffering from well-directed interceptions, 1952 passed into history as one of the most frustrating years ever encountered by U.S. combat aviators.

Amid this difficult and bloody time, one last significant episode played out over the Sea of Japan. For a brief moment, America's leaders held their breath and prayed that Stalin had not just unleashed World War III.

20 ǀ The Edge of Disaster

They could see the MiG-15s pass high overhead, dragging contrails behind their silver tails. To the pair of Navy reservists struggling for altitude below in their Grumman F9F-5 Panthers on October 18, the MiGs were hardly more than dots. Mere dots, perhaps, but their unexpected arrival off Task Force 77 seemed to be an ominous omen. They had come down from the north, straight out of Vladivostok. They were probably flown by Soviets, which later evidence confirmed.

Now they were heading straight for the American carriers. Lieutenants David Rowlands, USNR, and Royce Williams, USNR, passed 20,000 feet as they climbed after the silver Soviet jets. Their squadron, VF-781, had gone off to war with the latest version of the Grumman F9F Panther, the -5. This new and improved Panther had a more powerful engine which was supposed to give its pilots a better chance against the faster MiGs.

The MiGs streaked over the two Navy fighters until the Americans lost sight of them. The contrails suddenly ended, leaving only a series of white track marks in the sky. Rowlands and Williams then had to rely on the radar plotters on board the carrier USS *Oriskany*, who vectored them toward the MiGs. Neither pilot could see them.

Out of nowhere the MiGs whistled down. There were eight of them in two flights of four. The closest flight dropped in front and off to the left of the Americans and closed to make a head-on pass. Williams broke left and turned into them, Dave Rowlands hanging on his wing. The other MiG flight, which Rowlands didn't see, circled behind them in an attempt to launch a hammer-and-anvil style attack.

Rowlands still wasn't sure what these Soviets were up to. The fleet had moved off North Korea and was now barely a hundred miles from Vladivostok.

Then the Soviets started shooting. They made a head-on pass, their noses winking fire as tracer rounds shot past both Panthers.

"I'd never been shot at before by an airplane," Dave later remarked in a 1997 interview, "so it was kind of a new experience. It scared me to death."

The MiGs passed them by, then climbed and turned for a second pass. Williams broke hard left and circled around to latch onto one of the MiGs. Somehow, as he made that tight turn, Dave lost him. "That was really bad form, because you're supposed to stay with your leader. We were all running around by ourselves."

Separated and outnumbered four to one, the Americans screamed into their radios for permission to fire. It took a couple of seconds to get the response from the *Oriskany*, but they were cleared to shoot.

The dogfight was on.

Dave Rowlands's love affair with aviation began at the Orpheum Theater in Madison, Wisconsin. His father was a banker and state senator who frequently received guest passes to the movies. One afternoon in the mid-1930s, he took Dave to see *The Dawn Patrol*. This epic saga of World War I fighter pilots enthralled Dave, who hung onto every word and was delighted by every scene. Two decades later, he would get a dose of real air-to-air combat.

After joining the Navy in 1949, he completed flight training at Pensacola then joined VF-781 just after the outfit returned from its first Korean tour. Nicknamed the "Pacemakers," VF-781 was a reserve unit from LaSalle, Minnesota, led by Lieutenant Commander Stan Holm; its core group of pilots were World War II vets used to carrier ops and combat flying. While stationed at Miramar, the Pacemakers had shown their support for the war effort by volunteering to a man once hostilities broke out.

A year later, the squadron deployed aboard CV-34, the USS *Oriskany*, and was soon off the Korean coast with TF-77, flying close air support and flak suppression missions north of the Thirty-Eighth Parallel.

Although the squadron had trained for air-to-air fighting, it had never seen an enemy MiG before the October 18 mission. Enemy fighters might have been scarce, but North Korean flak was anything but rare. On some missions, they flew through clouds of the stuff. Once, Dave and the squadron attacked a marshaling yard a few miles from the legendary bridges at Toko-Ri. During the attack, Dave dove to strafe a locomotive only to lose his section leader on pullout. While looking for him, Rowlands wandered over one of the bridges, which prompted the flak batteries below to unleash a barrage. His Panther was peppered by shrapnel, and one round blew an enormous hold in the leading edge of his wing. The shock of the blast slammed his head against the canopy, knocking him out cold for a couple of seconds. When he regained consciousness, he leveled out and rejoined the squadron. One of his fellow

National Archives

F9F Panthers over Task Force 77.

pilots, flying alongside his Panther, marveled at the damage, "Geez, Dave, you're all shot up!"

Rowlands managed to drag his crippled Panther home to the *Oriskany*. When the crew examined the plane, they discovered that it was unsalvageable. They stuck it in a dark corner of the hangar deck and stripped it for parts.

Eight against two was not good odds, but there was no way the Americans could escape the Soviet MiGs. Their Panthers couldn't do anything better than the MiGs, so they just had to gut it out until the MiGs were either shot down or ready to disengage.

After the initial pass, Dave received clearance to open fire. He did, blasting away at fleeting targets as the MiGs swarmed around him. From the beginning, he was overwhelmed at this avalanche of Soviet fighters pouncing on his lone Panther. It was impossible for him to rejoin Williams, who had disappeared moments before.

In fact, while Dave was fighting for his life, Royce was busy shooting up a MiG lagging behind the rest of the flight that had made the head-on pass. He hit the MiG with cannon fire and sent it earthward in a smoking spiral. Gun camera film later confirmed this one was destroyed.

Meanwhile, Dave found himself in deep trouble. Making passes at him from all sides, the MiGs were forcing him to evade, juke, and duck their lightning-quick runs. Somehow, in the midst of it all, he managed to swing behind one MiG and give it a long cannon burst. He saw the shells smack home, blowing off hunks of metal from the MiG's fuselage.

"I was shooting the shit out of him," he later commented. "Pieces kept flying off of him and I thought any second now he's gonna blow and I'm going to fly through the debris. The guy never blew. I don't know where the hell he went."

Just as Dave had the MiG dead to rights, another MiG got in behind him and forced him to break off his attack. Now, he was low on ammunition with the MiG still on his tail. He turned hard to avoid it, but the Soviet pilot stayed with him and snapped out bursts as they scribed a circle in the air. They went around again, this time the Panther's speed fell off as Dave turned tighter and tighter.

He couldn't shake the MiG. It hung in right behind him as the pilot waited for the perfect shot. The Panther's nose started to drop off; Rowlands fought the controls to keep it in the turn. He thought, "The minute I drop off, this guy is going to get me. If I descend, he's going to get me. What do you do?"

He stayed in the turn, and pretty soon, the scene was reminiscent of the old World War I-era Lufberry circles as the MiG and Panther went around and around. The Panther, even with its new engine, could not keep this up for long. As Rowlands tucked in the nose tighter, the little Grumman stalled out. Nose down, Dave fell out of the Lufberry circle and knew he was meat on the table for the MiG behind him. "Here it is," he thought as he twisted in the seat to see what the MiG would do.

For some reason, it disengaged. Instead of going after him, it leveled its wings and clawed for altitude. He couldn't believe it. He had stalled out, and the MiG had so much power it actually climbed out of the turn. The superiority of the snub-nosed Soviet fighter was stark and obvious.

Low on energy, Dave's Panther was still an easy target. He kept the nose down to build up some airspeed as the radio crackled in his ears. Royce Williams was calling that he had been hit and was trying to make it to a cumulus cloud drifting below them at about 10,000 feet.

Sheer luck came into play. As Dave gained airspeed, he caught a fleeting glimpse of Williams's Panther. It was the first time he'd seen his section leader since the initial pass. Williams was diving for the cloud, a MiG-15 tacked onto his tail and firing away. "This MiG was firing at him," Rowlands remembered, "and the bullets were going over his head and under his airplane. And I thought, 'One of these seconds they're going to hit him.'"[1]

He turned toward Williams and dove after the MiG. Williams's Panther was bobbing up and down and careening wildly toward the cloud as the MiG shredded its hydraulic system and shot up the controls. Rowlands swung his plane behind the MiG. Its short fuselage swelled in his gunsight. He was walking right up behind it, and the pilot didn't have a clue.

At point-blank range, Dave pulled the trigger. He expected to see the MiG dissolve into torn debris as his four cannon did their work. Nothing happened. The guns with ammunition left had been burned out by his prolonged bursts earlier in the fight. His Panther had been defanged; there was no way he could save Williams now.

Dave overshot the MiG, despite throttling back and dropping his air brakes. He found himself passing close alongside the Soviet fighter. As he blew by, he saw the pilot staring back at him. Rowlands studied the plane and searched for any sort of markings that would be useful to the air intelligence officer. Deep down, he was also a little worried that this fight might be some horrible mix-up and the planes actually might be F-86s. Clearly, though, this was no F-86 he was gawking at from just a few wingspans away. More interesting, as far as he could tell, it didn't have a single marking on it anywhere. No red star adorned the fuselage, no tail code, no stripe or colorful band wrapped around the wings. Nothing. It was truly odd.

As he slipped by the MiG on Royce's tail, another MiG got behind Dave. It climbed right up his six, getting in a perfect position for a killing shot when Lieutenant John Middleton miraculously arrived on the scene. John had been below the fight, covering the original flight leader, Claire Elwood. Claire's engine had malfunctioned just as the MiGs were picked up on radar. As a result, the *Oriskany* had vectored the second section—Williams and Rowlands—to intercept while the other two pilots headed for home.

Once relieved of his escort duty, John had turned back toward the fight and climbed through the cumulus cloud. When he popped out the other side, he saw Royce's Panther trailed by a MiG with Dave's fighter alongside. Behind Dave, another MiG lurked. John, still climbing, made a head-on pass at the trailing MiG and blew it out of the sky. The Soviet pilot ejected, and the Americans could see his chute open as he descended toward the freezing Sea of Japan.

Just as Middleton cleared Rowland's tail, Williams hit the cloud. A split second later, the remaining MiG and Rowlands also plunged into it. The trio soon split up inside the murky whiteness, and Williams was able to slip back toward the fleet.

Rowlands's cockpit was glowing with red warning lights, and he knew it was time for him to go home, too. He had run his engine at full power during the twenty-minute fight, despite training that stressed not to use full power for more than three or four minutes. There was too much risk of burning out the engine and consuming more fuel than he could afford. It held together just fine, despite the abuse air combat necessitated.

With Royce and Dave heading back to the fleet, John Middleton remained in the engagement area. The MiGs had all disappeared by this time, so John decided to stick around and keep an eye on the downed Soviet. His decision, according to Rowlands, was "playing guts ball." Any minute, more MiGs could show up. If Middleton was caught alone in an inferior aircraft, his chances of survival were not good.

He thought it worth the risk. If the pilot could be rescued it would be a great intelligence coup. Nobody had yet been able to capture a MiG pilot, let alone a Soviet pilot. Knowing that the Soviets might return to search for their comrade, Middleton dropped down to 1,000 feet and began orbiting the man in the water. He circled and waited for someone to arrive, all the while transmitting his position to the fleet. For some reason, later described as faulty plotting, the Americans never showed up. John waited for as long as he dared, then slipped back to the *Oriskany* on the dregs of his fuel. The one real chance that the United States had of questioning a Soviet MiG pilot had been lost.

Sometime later, the fleet picked up a slow-moving target on radar. Possibly, the blip represented a Soviet air rescue plane searching for the lost pilot. Chances were the man had long since died of exposure in the icy Sea of Japan.

When Williams returned to the fleet and dropped out of the cumulus cloud at 1,200 feet, the sky around his crippled Panther filled with ugly black AA smudges. Panicky gunners aboard an escorting destroyer had mistaken his straight-winged jet for the enemy. Fortunately, Royce was able to avoid their fire and trap back aboard the *Oriskany* without further incident.

When Dave dropped out of the cloud, he too was greeted with anti-aircraft fire. He called down and told them to stop firing. They did, but it "seemed like it lasted forever" before the last gun fell silent. Finally, unhampered by flak, he took his Panther down and put it on the *Oriskany*'s deck.

The debriefing was tense, as was the entire fleet at that point since nobody knew what game the Soviets were playing. Was this the first attack that would presage a Soviet entry into the war? Did the American pilots just take part in the first battle of World War III? Or was it just a Soviet test of their air defenses that had used live pilots and real bullets? Nobody knew for sure, and that made for some nervous brass hats that day.

Worse, during the debriefing, it became clear to VF-781's intelligence officer, Bob McPhail, that the pilots in the fight couldn't really describe the enemy planes. Try as he might, he couldn't squeeze any useful information out of Royce, John, and Dave. "We were asked to describe the MiGs," Dave said in a 1997 interview, "and we couldn't. So they thought we were assholes! The point was that they weren't marked, and that they wanted to make sure of that."

Waiting for the next Soviet move, the fleet reviewed the few details gleaned from the pilots involved in the fight. During the attack, the Americans had also picked up and recorded all of the Soviet radio transmissions between the MiG pilots and their ground controllers. They heard the order given in Russian by the ground controller to open fire on the Panthers, which put to rest any doubts as to how the fight started.

The Soviets did not come back. The air battle was not the prelude to a general Soviet intervention in Korea nor was it the flash that could have started World War III. But, for a few hours, the American military held its collective breath as it hoped for the best but feared the worst. When the crisis had passed, the fear turned to indignation and outrage.

FEAF had long suspected that Soviet pilots were involved in the fighting over MiG Alley, but it had been unable to obtain any clear-cut evidence to support its suspicions. Aside from the Il-4 that VF-53 had shot down in 1950, no aircraft flying from Soviet territory had been involved in the Korean fighting. On October 18, 1952, however, there was no doubt that the MiGs were flown by Soviet pilots from Soviet territory. They had acted aggressively and had made a determined effort to test Task Force 77's defenses, which could have been construed as an act of war.

When President-elect Dwight Eisenhower learned of the attack, he was incensed. Some months later, when he arrived in Korea on an inspection tour, he asked to meet the pilots who had tangled with the Soviet MiGs. Rowlands, Williams, and Middleton flew to Seoul where staff officers hustled them into a tiny room at the headquarters of General James Van Fleet, Commander in Chief, UN Command. The three junior officers were surrounded by generals, including Van Fleet and Mark Clark, Commander, Eighth Army, as well as an array of admirals. As Eisenhower's son, Major John Eisenhower, mixed highballs for everyone, the pilots enthralled their brass-heavy audience with the details of their engagement.

When the meeting broke up, Admiral Arthur W. Radford talked to the pilots and told them that all details of the mission were classified. They were not to discuss it with anyone, not even their wives. They all vowed not to say a word, and returned to the *Oriskany* to finish up their combat tours.

VF-781 flew combat missions over Korea until May 1, 1953. Being reservists, most of the pilots went back to their civilian pursuits. All but forgotten today, VF-781 holds no reunions, and most of the Pacemakers have long since lost touch with each other.

Dave Rowlands stayed in the Navy for a few more years and worked in Hawaii on new jet-penetration techniques. He left the Navy for a job with Pan American Airways. His lifelong goal of flying for the airline had finally come true. One evening in the summer of 1957, he flew into Paris and stayed at a local hotel. The next morning, when he wandered downstairs for breakfast, a friend called out to him, "Say, are you the same Dave Rowlands who fought those MiGs?"

Shocked, Dave didn't quite know what to say. Then, he saw the headlines in the morning paper. Sprawled across page one was a description of that fight, complete with the names of all the Americans involved. Somebody in Washington decided it was time to declassify the incident, and this was the first Dave learned he could talk about it.

21 | The Soviet Riddle

What about the Russians? For years, Western writers and historians have puzzled over the allegations that the Soviets sent pilots and air regiments into Korea to fight against the United Nations. Circumstantial evidence abounded. Sabrejet pilots spotted MiG-15s flown by red-haired Caucasians. Occasionally, UN listening posts picked up Russian-language transmissions from MiGs around the Yalu River. But Westerners never actually knew how involved the Soviets were until forty years after the war. Not until the collapse of the Soviet Union in the early 1990s did the first authentic accounts of the communist side of the air war become known in the Western world.

Even before the Korean War, the Soviets had maintained an air presence in China. In February 1950, Soviet Premier Joseph Stalin sent a fighter regiment into China as a show of support. Later that year, in August and September, the 29th Fighter Air Regiment was transferred from Kubinka to China. It would be one of the first MiG units to enter the Korean War.

After the near complete destruction of the North Korean Air Force, Stalin made the decision to go to Premier Kim Il Sung's aid. According to recent information emerging from the former Soviet Union, Stalin had encouraged North Korea to attack its southern neighbor. Soviet advisors had helped to plan the invasion, and Stalin sent Kim Il Sung most of the weapons that his army would use against South Korea. Consequently, after the Inchon landing and the Chinese decision to enter the war, Stalin had to come to Kim Il Sung's rescue in some manner. Doing so, however, was a risky proposition. Open aggression against the United States could certainly provoke global war, something that Stalin wanted to avoid. The Soviets had to walk a fine line between supporting an ally and running the risk of starting World War III.

Stalin settled on sending air units into Manchuria to help defend North Korean airspace. He ordered the MiGs to operate under absolute secrecy and two limitations designed to make sure that the presence of Soviet pilots did not become known to the West. First, the Soviet pilots were forbidden to fly south of a line extending from Pyongyang in the west to Wonsan in the east. In practice, the Soviets operated almost exclusively in the northwestern corner of Korea—referred to as MiG Alley. Second, they were not allowed to operate over the Yellow Sea. This limitation gave UN pilots a sanctuary similar to one that the communists had over Manchuria. The Soviets feared that if a pilot went down at sea, American search aircraft might rescue him and discover their involvement. Probably, VF-53's encounter with the Il-4 over the Sea of Japan in September 1950 influenced the decision to restrict the MiGs to overland operations.

Additionally, air men killed in action over Korea were not sent home to their families. Instead, they were buried in an old cemetery at Port Arthur that dated back to the 1904–05 Russo-Japanese War. To cloud the issue further, the Soviets maintained the charade that any of their pilots flying in Korea were simply "volunteers" doing their part to check American aggression.

At first, other precautions were taken, but they were gradually discarded as the war progressed. The initial Soviet regiments in Manchuria wore Chinese quilted uniforms. Before going into combat, the pilots learned important air combat phrases in Chinese so that they could avoid speaking Russian over the radio. The latter restriction was ignored almost from the very start. Once in combat, the Soviet pilots quickly slipped into their native tongue since it wasn't feasible to fight using a foreign language that most had only begun learning a few weeks before.

Initially, the 151st Fighter Air Division deployed to Korea in the fall of 1950. The 151st was not trained to Western standards nor was it even remotely ready for action when circumstances forced its commitment to battle in November 1950. Although the MiG proved superior to everything in FEAF's inventory at the time, the Soviet pilots were unable to exploit that advantage because the UN pilots consistently outfought them.

Those first MiG sorties that shook FEAF so badly were flown entirely by Soviet pilots. Not until later in the war did any Chinese or North Korean MiG squadrons become operational. The Soviet 151st Division battled for control of the sky over North Korea from November 1950 until April 1951. During that period—considered the first phase of Soviet involvement in the war—the 151st took a real beating at the hands of FEAF's more-experienced and better-trained airmen. In December, the Soviets were rudely shocked by the arrival of the 4th Fighter Wing's F-86s. Suddenly, their overwhelming performance advantages evaporated, and they were fighting an aircraft with equal ability in everything but rate of climb. The MiGs took heavy losses in the ensuing months.

The situation changed, however, with the arrival of two new divisions, the 303d and 324th Interceptor Air Divisions, in March 1951. Both divisions had well-trained, handpicked pilots, many of whom were World War II aces. Ivan Kozhedub, the top Allied ace of World War II, commanded the 324th Division, and Georgy Lobov, who later became a lieutenant general, commanded the 303d Division.

Between them, the two air divisions counted about 56 operational MiG-15s among four or five fighter regiments. The 324th had two subunits, the 176th Guard Fighter Air Regiment (FAR) and the 196th FAR. Commanded by top Korean War ace Yevgeni Pepelyaev, the 196th went on to claim 104 UN aircraft through the course of the 1951 campaign for air superiority. In return, it lost ten MiGs and four pilots. The 176th Regiment was not nearly as well prepared as the 196th, and its first battle with F-86s amply exposed its shortcomings. In its first combat mission, three MiGs fell to FEAF's swift fighters. Eventually, however, it too became a successful outfit, claiming 103 UN aircraft while losing seventeen MiGs and five pilots.

These two air divisions remained in Korea until early 1952 when they were rotated out of combat. Many of the Soviet pilots had flown more than one hundred combat missions during the course of their approximately twelve-month tour.

Throughout 1951, according to Soviet sources, the 303d and 324th Divisions downed 510 UN aircraft. UN losses for that period, however, totaled about 40 planes lost in air-to-air combat. During that period, the Soviets lost 52 MiGs and erroneously claimed a 10:1 kill ratio against FEAF's fighters and bombers.

The units that took over for the 303d and 324th Divisions in early 1952 were not nearly as well trained and ready for combat against FEAF's Sabre-jets. In fact, when the 97th Air Division replaced the 324th in February 1952, it performed so poorly that it had to be pulled out of combat. Because of this, the 196th Regiment had to be redeployed into action to cover for the 97th's failure.

After FEAF switched to night bombing with its B-29s, the Soviets deployed the 351st Air Regiment to Manchuria. A night-fighter outfit, it initially went into action with the Lavochkin La-11, a late-model piston-engine aircraft. In February 1952, however, the unit switched to MiGs and began to have more success against the B-29s. One pilot, Anatoli Karelin, became a night-fighter ace, shooting down five Superforts during the course of a tour, and he was proclaimed a "Hero of the Soviet Union." He very nearly didn't complete that tour, however; while stalking his fourth kill, he actually collided with his B-29 target. When the tail gunner began firing at him, he unleashed his cannons on the big bomber and sent it down in flames. Again, while chasing his fifth and final kill in February 1953, the Superfort's gunners riddled Karelin's MiG with 117 holes and severed his fuel lines.

During the final year of the war, the 351st Regiment was joined by another air regiment trained for night missions, the 535th FAR. Between the two units, Soviet pilots claimed eighteen B-29s and three F-94s in nocturnal combat through March 1953.

Soviet pilots serving in Korea were generally highly motivated and very determined. Many had been given tours of North Korean cities burned out by B-29 raids. These raids were barbaric in their eyes and convinced the pilots that they were fighting to save the North Korean populace and to check American aggression. The fear of failure was also a strong motivational factor. Many men were sent home in disgrace after failing in air combat. In a few cases, entire units failed and were sent home. The pilots also knew that Soviet officials would retaliate against their families if they fell into enemy hands, and not a single Soviet pilot was taken prisoner during the war.

From time to time, disagreements over kills broke out among the Soviet pilots. Some were caught blatantly padding their scores, although this activity was more common in the North Korean MiG units. Yevgeni Pepelyaev had such an experience after a hard-fought battle with an F-86. He had shot it down, but, upon returning to Manchuria, he learned that the deputy commander of the 176th Guard Regiment had already claimed it as his victory. The 64th Fighter Air Corps, the umbrella organization for the Soviet air divisions in Manchuria, settled the issue by examining the gun camera footage. A review of the film clearly indicated that the deputy commander had been nowhere near shooting range of the F-86, whereas Pepelyaev was right behind it. The latter received credit for the kill, and the other pilot was disgraced by the incident. Even though he had fourteen planes to his credit, he was not made a Hero of the Soviet Union because of his dishonesty.

Pepelyaev also hinted that a darker fate awaited this pilot when he wrote, "It is dangerous to lead the leadership, especially those in Moscow, into error, and, besides, to be caught red-handed. Such things are not forgiven."[1]

Altogether, the Soviets claimed a total of 1,300 UN aircraft destroyed during the Korean War. According to their figures, their units in Manchuria lost a total of 345 MiG-15s in combat and in operational accidents. The numbers don't match. Initial claims by FEAF came to 792 MiG-15s destroyed in return for 58 Sabres. After the war, the USAF admitted to 103 Sabre losses. Meanwhile, a USAF revision of the MiG kills during the war set the total at 379.

Instead of belittling either side's efforts, the figures belie the true nature of the Korean air war. Far from being an American walkover, as the initial UN kill ratio has been used in the past to demonstrate, the fact was the Russians and the Americans were almost evenly matched in the air. Both sides took their losses, scored successes, and suffered stunning defeats. In the end, neither side was strong enough to impose its will completely on the other. The difficulty and danger that existed over MiG Alley serve only to highlight the efforts of all pilots who fought and died so long ago in that crimson sky.

22 | The Hybrid War

Almost fifty years have passed since the United States fought in what has to be one of the oddest air wars of history. It was a war that pitted old technology against new, jet fighters against piston-engine aircraft, and Soviet pilots against American. It was a hybrid war fought with old tactics and old ideas, but, as the fighting wore on, new tactics evolved that would shape the nature of wars to come, providing many lessons about the future of air combat. In the war's immediate aftermath, some of those lessons were heeded, others were not.

The United States Air Force left Korea flush with the knowledge that its excellent training program had saved the day over MiG Alley. In air combat techniques, its pilots were clearly superior to their Soviet, Chinese, and North Korean counterparts. This edge helped to stave off disaster when the speedy MiG-15 joined the fight in late 1950 and to maintain at least limited air superiority throughout most of the Korean War. It was an advantage that the Air Force trumpeted proudly after the fighting. Yet, it took only a few years before the Air Force had largely squandered that advantage.

As the 1950s wore on, the Air Force became increasingly obsessed with intercepting Soviet strategic bombers. The last generation of fighters from that decade, the F-102, F-106, and F-101, were all conceived to be primarily ultrafast interceptors. To fly these new supersonic aircraft, the Air Force trained a new generation of pilots to scramble in a heartbeat and chase down huge, multiengined bombers. In the process, they neglected fighter-to-fighter combat training. Indeed, in some units, mock dogfighting was specifically prohibited. Getting caught "rat-racing" could get a pilot in a world of trouble. Not until Vietnam and the subsequent establishment of the Red Flag air combat program was this mistake rectified.

National Archives

An HRS-2 helicopter returning a downed pilot.

Korea demonstrated the limitations of a strategic air war in the atomic age. Because most of North Korea's military equipment and supplies came from China and the Soviet Union, a strategic air campaign was bound to have, at best, limited results. The core idea behind that type of operation was to destroy the means of producing these things. The factories and refineries that the North Koreans and Chinese relied on were out of bounds to the Air Force, so little could be accomplished by destroying the few worthwhile targets available. As the war continued, FEAF's bombers were increasingly used as an instrument to force the communists to make concessions at the peace table. This strategy failed completely and served only to engender the wrath of much of the world. Yet, a decade later, the administrations of Lyndon Johnson and Richard Nixon tried the same thing—with similar results.

As a result of the Korean War, however, both the Navy and the Air Force recognized the importance of helicopters in search and rescue (SAR) operations. During the 1950s and 1960s, the two branches experimented with SAR techniques in combat and honed their techniques. In Vietnam, they came of age and the first baby steps taken in Korea helped to save hundreds of downed aviators. The basic elements of Bob Wayne's rescue outside of Pohang are reflected in modern SAR operations.

McDonnell F2H Banshees.

The Navy emerged from the war with a clear understanding that its World War II–vintage carriers would need to be modified if jet aircraft were to operate from them with a comfortable safety margin. With their narrow straight decks, the previous generation of carriers provided dangerous platforms for the operation of heavy jet aircraft. Landing accidents abounded because jets frequently flew into a barrier or hit aircraft parked along the forward half of a flight deck.

The angled deck proved to be the solution. Devised originally by the British, the U.S. Navy quickly adopted the idea and began to modify existing flattops in 1952. Throughout the rest of the 1950s, the Navy reconfigured its *Essex*-class carriers to incorporate angled decks. The angled deck allows aircraft that land hot or miss a wire simply to roll off the left side of the carrier, remain airborne, and come around for another landing attempt. With the straight-deck carriers, that sort of mishap resulted in a crash into the barrier or parked aircraft and possible injuries to the deck crew.

Steam catapults were also introduced to replace older hydraulic models that lacked the power to launch a fully loaded combat jet into the air. The older *Essex*-class carriers could not launch fully laden Panthers and Banshees because their catapults were not strong enough to shoot these heavy aircraft off the deck. Consequently, combat loads had to be lightened. Again, the British devised the solution. Instead of hydraulic catapults, the British turned to a new steam catapult invented by Commander C. C. Mitchell, RNVR. By 1954, the first American carrier equipped with the new catapult, called the C11, became operational. The C11 was so effective that it could launch aircraft successfully even while the carrier was riding at anchor.

During the Korean War, all participating UN air units had expended immense energy interdicting the communist supply and transportation lines. On reflection, the interdiction campaign demonstrated only moderate success. It helped to limit the capabilities of the Chinese and North Korean armies at the front, but in no way did it destroy their ability to fight. Further, America's pilots and planners discovered that the more primitive the transportation network, the more difficult it was to successfully interdict. Trucks could be destroyed and bridges could be knocked down, but the Chinese and North Koreans simply relied on their manpower advantage. Hauling supplies south on A-frames, thousands of peasants made up any shortfall in supplies caused by the American campaign. Short of killing all of the peasants, there was no way to choke off the front completely from its supply centers. This lesson was destined to be learned again during the Vietnam War.

America's treatment of its Korean veterans following the war also offers some lessons. When the airmen, soldiers, sailors, and Marines returned to the United States following their tours, they found a country apathetic to their experiences. They were expected to pick up their lives where they had left them before they went to war. There were no parades or brass bands. Thankfully, they were not accorded the treatment that many Vietnam veterans were to experience but neither were they given the same hero welcome received by their World War II counterparts. The Korean generation fell between the cracks. Once the cease-fire was signed, America quickly forgot about its bloody "police action."

For almost fifty years, most of the pilots and aircrew interviewed for this book have remained silent about their experiences. Most of them had never been contacted by a historian, and many had never even talked to their families about Korea. The reunion associations of World War II squadrons are well organized and host well-attended annual meetings, but many of the Korean units do not have such organizations.

Perhaps another reason for this fifty-year silence can be found in America's own attitude toward the war. There was no "Home Front" during the conflict, as during World War II: no scrap drives, no massive rallies for war bonds, no big Hollywood effort to get the country behind the war, and certainly no nationwide mobilization for the war. Korea was limited and distant, a remote war fought by professionals and reservists while the country went about its business as it does in peacetime. The longer the war continued, the more that interest waned.

Even today, that apathy remains in our society. Rare are the books on the Korean War, particularly its air operations. When looking back on this century, Americans want to learn about World War II and its decisive victory. Korea is seen as one of those "dirty little wars" that brought no clean victory. So, it has been forgotten like other unpopular and puzzling conflicts.

The veterans of Korea are graying warriors now. As their numbers diminish with the passing of the years, their memories will die with them and be lost forever to history. Unlike the World War II generation, the airmen of the Korean War will pass without having their voices echo through history, without having broken that strange apathy displayed by their country toward their experiences.

Therein lies one great lesson of Korea. The next time America sends its sons and daughters into a war as bloody, frustrating, and lengthy as Korea, the nation needs to rise above its former mistakes and honor, or at least acknowledge, the service and sacrifices made in our collective names. To consign them to history's dark corners would be repeating a terrible injustice.

Glossary

Ace: A combat pilot with at least five enemy airplanes to his credit.

AG: Air group. U.S. Navy fleet carriers each carried one air group. An air group usually consisted of two or three fighter squadrons plus an attack squadron. Also, an air group sometimes included a photo detachment and a night detachment.

Bogey: An unidentified aircraft.

Break: A sharp, sudden turn designed to shake off an attacking aircraft.

CAG: Commander, Air Group. This officer was usually a full commander; his squadron leaders were generally lieutenant commanders.

CAP: Combat air patrol. A U.S. Navy term for a patrol of fighters that circled a carrier task force in order to intercept any incoming aircraft. A constant CAP was maintained over Task Force 77 throughout each day of the war when conditions permitted flying operations.

CAS: Close Air Support. Working in cooperation with ground forces to strike targets on the battlefield.

CCF: Chinese Communist Forces.

Chandelle: An aircraft maneuver. The chandelle was a steep climbing turn.

Division: U.S. Navy term for a formation of four aircraft. A division usually consisted of two sections of two aircraft.

Element: U.S. Air Force term for a formation of two aircraft. Two or three elements comprised a flight.

FAC: Forward air control.

FAR: Fighter air regiment (Soviet).

FBW: Fighter-bomber wing.

FEAF: Far East Air Forces (UN).

Fifty: Term used for .50-caliber machine gun.

Flak: Anti-aircraft fire.

Flight: A U.S. Air Force term for a formation of four to six aircraft. The Navy's equivalent was the division. Each flight consisted of two or three elements.

GI: Term referring to member of U.S. armed forces, but often restricted to enlisted members of U.S. Army.

IP: Initial point. This was the navigational point at which a bomber formation began its final run to the target area. During that period, the bombers had to maintain a steady course and speed.

LCVP: Landing craft, vehicle, and personnel.

LSO: Landing signal officer.

Lufberry Circle: A tight, 360° level turn used by one or more aircraft to avoid attackers.

MIA: Missing in action.

mph: Miles per hour.

NK: United Nations term for North Korean troops.

NKPA: North Korean Peoples Army.

NKAF: North Korean air force.

Ops: Abbreviation for operations.

Poopie Suit: Cold weather suit worn by Navy Pilots.

POW: Prisoner of war.

ROK: Republic of Korea.

rpm: Revolutions per minute.

SAR: Search and rescue.

Section: A U.S. Navy term to describe a formation of two planes. Two sections composed a division.

Six: The position directly behind an aircraft. Derived from 6 o'clock.

Sortie: A mission by a single plane.

Split-S (split-essed): A maneuver used by aviators to escape from attack or to launch an attack of their own. The pilot made an inverted roll, then pulled back on the stick. The subsequent dive eventually put the plane on the opposite heading from the one maintained before the maneuver.

TARCAP: Target combat air patrol, a U.S. Navy term used to describe a fighter pilot over an area about to be attacked by Navy bombers.

TF: Task Force. A group of naval vessels charged with a specific task.

Thach Weave: A World War II fighter tactic designed to provide a section or element with a mutually protective maneuver. Starting almost side by side, two fighters turned toward each other. Any hostile aircraft behind the weaving fighters would be subjected to a head-on pass by the wingman of the plane that the hostile aircraft was following. The maneuver was also sometimes called a "scissors."

UN: United Nations. Members of the UN who sent air units into Korea included the United States, South Africa, Great Britain, and Australia.

USAF: U.S. Air Force.

VA: U.S. Navy designation for attack squadron.

VC: U.S. Navy designation for a composite squadron.

Vee: A flying formation used by nearly every nation during the Korean War. Primarily used by bombers, a vee usually consisted of three aircraft positioned in an upside down "V" formation.

Vee of vees: A squadron-sized formation composed of several flights in vee formation. The squadron's flights were then arranged into a larger, overall vee.

VF: U.S. Navy designation for fighter squadron.

VMF: U.S. Marine Corps designation for fighter squadron.

VMF-(N): U.S. Marine Corps designation for night-fighter squadron.

VT: U.S. Navy designation for torpedo squadron.

VT Fuses: proximity fuses.

Notes

Chapter 1. The First Jet Kills

1. Robert F. Futrell, *The United States Air Force in Korea 1950–1953* (New York: Duell, Sloan and Pearce, 1961), 8.
2. Ibid., 8–10.

Chapter 2. The Birth of Combat SAR

1. Because of the F-80C Shooting Star's relative short range, FEAF had reconverted six of these jet squadrons to F-51 Mustangs in July 1950. With much longer endurance than the F-80, the F-51 could loiter over the battlefield for extended periods, thus making it much more effective in the ground attack role. The Mustang's liquid-cooled engine proved extremely vulnerable to small-arms fire, however, which resulted in the loss of many planes and pilots. By December, almost all of the F-51 squadrons reconverted to F-80s, then later to Republic F-84 Thunderjets.

Chapter 3. Fighting 53 Goes to War

1. Richard P. Hallion, *The Naval Air War in Korea* (Baltimore, Md.: Nautical & Aviation Publishing Co., 1986), 38.
2. Malcolm W. Cagle and Frank A. Manson, *The Sea War in Korea* (Annapolis, Md.: United States Naval Institute, 1957), 45–47.
3. Ibid, 46.
4. Ibid, 47.
5. Ibid, 53.
6. Though well-armored and generally able to withstand heavy battle damage, the Corsair had an Achilles heel in its oil system. The oil cooler was located under the cowling in an unprotected area. After a hit in the oil cooler, the Corsair pilot had only seconds either to bail out or to crash-land his plane as the engine overheated and seized. More Corsairs were lost than any other type of Navy aircraft during the first six months of the war as the result, in large measure, of this weakness.

7. Lawson, "A Tour in Hell," p. 38.
8. Although USAF and USN pilots flew in formations of four, their nomenclature was different. A pair of aircraft was called an *element* in the Air Force and a *section* in the Navy. A four-plane formation was called a *flight* in the Air Force, but the Navy called the same group a *division*.
9. This was the information received by Charles Darrow and other members of the squadron. Somehow, Hanton's remains were recovered. He is buried in Arlington National Cemetery.

CHAPTER 4. INTO THE TIGER'S JAWS

1. Hallion, *Naval Air War in Korea*, 49.
2. Cagle and Manson, *Sea War in Korea*, 66.
3. Most secondary sources say that the plane was a Tu-2; however, VF-53's own records state that it was an Il-4. Ed Laney doesn't recall exactly what it was but believes the squadron records are probably accurate. The author is inclined to believe that it was an Il-4, as the Tu-2 had twin rudders—a most distinctive feature—and two dorsal machine-gun positions. Certainly, if guns in two positions had fired at the Corsairs, the pilots would have noticed and reported that fact. On the other hand, the Il-4 had a single dorsal turret equipped with one 12.7-mm machine gun.
4. Hallion, *Naval Air War in Korea*, 61.
5. Cagle and Manson, *Sea War in Korea*, 55–56.
6. Hallion, *Naval Air War in Korea*, 63.
7. In a 1998 interview, Ed Laney stated that Ben Brown's last message was carved in a cell somewhere in North Korea that was later overrun by UN troops. Whether it was a cave or a prison cell, the message was Brown's attempt to provide evidence of his survival following the shoot-out at his crash site.
8. Quoted in Bevin Alexander, *Korea, the First War We Lost* (New York: Hippocrene Books, 1986), 289.
9. Quoted in ibid, 290.
10. Ibid, 288–91.
11. Quoted in Cagle and Manson, *Sea War in Korea*, 225.
12. Ed Laney, telephone interview with author, 26 January 1998.
13. Cagle and Manson, *Sea War in Korea*, 227.
14. Ibid, 227.
15. Hallion, *Naval Air War in Korea*, 75.

CHAPTER 5. HOME BY CHRISTMAS

1. Alexander, *Korea, First War We Lost*, 316.

CHAPTER 6. THE FINEST KIND OF HONOR

1. Quoted in Hallion, *Naval Air War in Korea*, 84.
2. Captain Thomas Hudner, letter to author, undated.

CHAPTER 8. THE BRIDGE BUSTERS

1. Futrell, *United States Air Force in Korea*, 286.
2. Don van Slooten, letter to Commander Harold Carlson, undated.
3. Cagle and Manson, *Sea War in Korea*, 231.

CHAPTER 9. THE BATTLE OF CARLSON'S CANYON

1. Cagle and Manson, *Sea War in Korea*, 231.
2. Quoted in ibid, 235.
3. Hallion, *Naval Air War in Korea*, 94–95.
4. Ibid, 95.

CHAPTER 10. THE DAM BUSTERS

1. Cagle and Manson, *Sea War in Korea*, 240.

CHAPTER 11. NIGHT INTRUDERS

1. Futrell, *United States Air Force in Korea*, 421.
2. Quoted in Kenneth N. Jordan, Sr., *Forgotten Heroes* (Atglen, Pa.: Schiffer Publishing Ltd., 1995), 214.
3. Quoted in Wally McDannel, *Fly Till You Die* (Paducah, Ky.: Turner Publishing Company, 1994), 67–77.
4. Quoted in David Rees, *Korea: The Limited War* (New York: St. Martin's Press, 1964), 353.
5. Quoted in ibid, 357.
6. *Washington Times*, February 21, 1999.

CHAPTER 12. A FIGHTER PILOT'S HEART

1. Quoted in Futrell, *United States Air Force in Korea*, 280.
2. Quoted in McDannel, *Fly Till You Die*, 98–101.

CHAPTER 13. PRELUDE TO BLACK TUESDAY

1. Futrell, *United States Air Force in Korea*, 374.

CHAPTER 15. DEATH RIDE TO NAMSI

1. Quoted in Yefim Gordon and Vladimir Rigman, *MiG-15 Design, Development and Korean War Combat History* (Osceola, Wis.: Motorbooks International Publishers & Wholesalers, 1993), 122.

CHAPTER 16. HORIZONTAL FLAK

1. After their rescue, the surviving members of the crew compared notes and concluded that this must have been the case. He was seen getting out of the airplane, but he never deployed his chute.
2. Douglas K. Evans, *Sabre Jets over Korea: A Firsthand Account* (Blue Ridge Summit, Pa.: Tab Books Inc., 1984), 101.

3. Ibid, 101. Evans also recounted this scene to the author during an interview.
4. *4th Fighter Wing's Unit History* (Maxwell Field, Ala.: Air Force Historical Research Agency, 1951), "F-86E Versus MiG-15 in Korea."
5. Ibid.
6. In a 1997 interview with Doug Evans, Evans recalled that several of his fellow pilots came down with the *Twitch*, a World War I term for a flyer whose nerves were shot and who was basically used up as a combat pilot. Small wonder that happened. FEAF's entire effort to achieve air superiority had rested on the small group of fighter pilots assigned to the 4th Fighter Wing until the 51st Fighter Wing began flying missions in December 1951.

CHAPTER 17.   PAYBACK

1. Evans, *Sabre Jets over Korea*, 156.
2. Ibid, 156–57.
3. Marshall's account of this mission comes from two sources: Gene Gurney, *Five Down and Glory* (New York: Ballantine Books, 1958), 197–198; Joe Foss and Matthew Brennan, *Top Guns* (New York: Pocket Books, 1991), 270–75.

CHAPTER 18.   MORE GUTS THAN THE LAW ALLOWS

1. Interview with author.

CHAPTER 20.   THE EDGE OF DISASTER

Interview with author.

CHAPTER 21.   THE SOVIET RIDDLE

1. Quoted in Gordon and Rigman, *MiG-15 Design*, 137.

Bibliography

Alexander, Bevin. *Korea, the First War We Lost*. New York: Hippocrene Books, 1986.

Brady, James. *The Coldest War: A Memoir of Korea*. New York: Orion Books, 1990.

Cagle, Malcolm W., and Manson, Frank A. *The Sea War in Korea*. Annapolis, Md.: United States Naval Institute, 1957.

Clark, Mark W. *From the Danube to the Yalu*. Blue Ridge Summit, Pa.: Tab Books Inc., 1988.

Evans, Douglas K. *Sabre Jets over Korea: A Firsthand Account*. Blue Ridge Summit, Pa.: Tab Books Inc., 1984.

Foss, Joe, and Brennan, Matthew. *Top Guns*. New York: Pocket Books, 1991.

4th Fighter Wing's Unit History, Maxwell Field, Ala.: U.S. Air Force Historical Research Agency, 1951.

Futrell, Robert F. *The United States Air Force in Korea 1950–1953*. New York: Duell, Sloan and Pearce, 1961.

Gordon, Yefim, and Rigman, Vladimir. *MiG-15 Design, Development and Korean War Combat History*. Osceola, Wis.: Motorbooks International Publishers & Wholesalers, 1993.

Gurney, Gene. *Five Down and Glory*. New York: Ballantine Books, 1958.

Hallion, Richard P. *The Naval Air War in Korea*. Baltimore, Md.: Nautical & Aviation Publishing Co, 1986.

Hastings, Max. *The Korean War*. New York: Simon and Schuster, 1987.

Hess, Dean E. *Battle Hymn*. New York: McGraw-Hill Book Company, Inc., 1956.

Jackson, Robert. *Air War over Korea*. New York: Charles Scribner's Sons, 1973.

James, D. Clayton, and Wells, Anne Sharp. *Refighting the Last War; Command and Crisis in Korea 1950–1953*. New York: The Free Press, 1993.

Jordan, Kenneth N., Sr. *Forgotten Heroes*. Atglen, Pa.: Schiffer Publishing Ltd., 1995.

Lawson, Robert L. "A Tour in Hell." *The Hook* 14:3 (Fall 1986), p. 38.

McDannel, Wally. *Fly Till You Die*. Paducah, Ky.: Turner Publishing Company, 1994.

Meid, Pat, and Yingling, James M. *U.S. Marine Operations in Korea 1950–1953*, vol. 5, *Operations in West Korea*. Washington D.C.: Headquarters U.S. Marine Corps, 1972.

Montross, Lynn, and Canzona, Nicholas A. *U.S. Marine Operations in Korea 1950–1953*, vol. 2, *The Inchon-Seoul Operation*. Washington D.C.: Headquarters U.S. Marine Corps, 1955.

Rees, David. *Korea: The Limited War*. New York: St. Martin's Press, 1964.

Schaller, Michael. *Douglas MacArthur; The Far Eastern General*. New York: Oxford University Press, 1989.

Sgarlato, Nico, and Ragni, Franco. *U.S. Fighters of the Fifties*. Carrollton, Tex.: Squadron/Signal Publications, 1979.

White, W. L. *Back Down the Ridge*. New York: Harcourt, Brace and Company, 1953.

Index

Abakumov, Boris, 169–70, 178

Abbott, John, 40

AD-Skyraiders, 77–78; as attack craft, 87; Hwachon Dam assault by, 98–101; napalm Dam tunnel, 101. *See also* Douglas AD-1 Skyraider attack bombers

African-American naval aviators, 65

air evacuation from Hagaru-ri, 75, 78

Air Force, U.S.: bombing Yalu River bridges, 47; training program of, 208

Akin, Robert, 171

Almond, Edward M., 45. *See also* X Corps

Amen, William T., 49

"An Analysis of Aerial Engagements over North Korea on October 23, 1951" (Beckwith), 162

angled-decks, aircraft carrier, 209

armed reconnaissance missions: Task Force 77, 39–40

Atkinson, Tex, 87

B-29. See Boeing B-29 Super Fortress

Badoeng Straits, USS, 40; Kunsan attacks by 42

Baker Flight, 4th Fighter Interceptor Wing, 135, 137, 138; loses contact with

Able Flight, 140; in Lufberry Circle, 139; shoot at MiG-15s, 143–44

Banks, Ralph, 136–37

Barton, Ray, 169, 174–75, 179; Davis aids, 176; MiGs pursue, 175

Beckwith, Art, 162

"Bedcheck Charlies," 117

Beissner, Fred, 153–54, 157, 158–59

Black Day for FEAF's Bombers, 132

Blue Flight, 4th Fighter Interceptor Wing, 135, 136, 137–38

Boeing B-17 Flying Fortress, 15–16

Boeing B-29 Super Fortress, 47; attacks on MiG Alley airfields by, 129–32; bridges west of Sinpo and, 84; daylight raids suspended, 163; delayed-fused bombs for bridge EA1622 and, 90–91; MiG-15s attack, crew bails out of, 145, 147; MiGs hit, 120, 146; Namsi Airfield mission, 151–53; night escorts for, 190–91; raids on Hwachon Dam, 98; returning to Kimpo battle-scarred, 160–61; Shoran guidance systems of, 133, 151; Yalu bridges and, 48

bogey (unidentified aircraft), 6

Booker, Jesse ("Davy"): on photo run, 34–35; as POW, 35–36

Booker, Lil, 35–36
Boxer, USS, 40, 42
bridge EA1622, 88–91
The Bridges at Toko-Ri (Michener), 92
British Fleet Air Arm, over Kimpo Airfield, 7
Broadway, Jack, 118–19
Brown, Daisy, 66, 72
Brown, Jesse, 65–66; Chosin Reservoir reconnaissance mission, 67; crash lands/trapped in burning Corsair, 68–71; early career, 66
Brown, Russell J., 47
Brown, William Ben ("Bill"): aborts rescue of by helicopter, 44–45; F4U catches fire, 26; TARCAPs for, 27–28
Burke, John, 174, 176
Bush, George, 64
butterfly bomb, 108

C11 catapult, 209
C-47s, 107–8, 109
Cardarella, Vince, 4
Carlson, Harold ("Swede"): assesses Marine chances at Hagaru-ri, 75–76, 87; attack on bridge EA1622, 89, 91; bombing bridges west of Sinpo, 84–85; Hwachon Dam assault and, 98–101; lessons from Chosin Reservoir retreat, 81; von Slooten and, 77
Carlson's Canyon, 89, 92
Carlson's Tigers, 103–4. *See also* VA-195
Carrier Air Group 2 (CAG), *Boxer*, 42
Carrier Air Group 3 (CAG), *Leyte*, 51, 63
Carrier Air Group 5 (CAG), *Valley Forge*, 23; combat air patrols (CAP) by, 34–35; Sinuiju bridge strikes and, 49–50, 51, 53–54; stateside for R&R, 55; VF-53's experience, 42
Carrier Air Group 11 (CAG), *Philippine Sea*: crew inexperience before Inchon

landing, 42; Sinuiju bridge strikes by, 49, 51
Carrier Air Group 19 (CAG), 88–92
Carter, Jimmy, 64
catapults, steam *versus* hydraulic, 209
Cevoli, Dick, 68–69
Chance-Vought F4U-4B Corsair fighters, 23, 24–25; air support mission, July 1950, 31–33; losses among, 87; ordnance load of, 39. *See also* Vought F4U-4B Corsair fighters
Chandler, Ken, 137–38
Charlie Flight, 4th Fighter Interceptor Wing, 135, 139, 145
Chinese: attack after Hwachon dam busting, 102–3; attack at Chipyong-ni, 94; attack ROK 1st Division, 46; logistical support weakness, 83; MiG-15s attack F-80s, 47; open Hwachon Dam, 95–96; retreat to regroup/resupply, 93
Chinese 113th Division, Gauntlet ambush by, 58–60
Chinese IX Army Corps, weather hazards for, 80–81
Chinese Ninth Army Group, attacks at Chosin Reservoir, 60
Chipyong-ni, battle at, 94
Cho Byung Kwi, 28
Chongchon River valley: Chinese attack Eighth Army in, 57–58; "The Gauntlet" ambush, 58–60
Chunchon, Operation Ripper against, 95
Clark, Mark, 201
Cleveland, Charles, 183
close air support (CAS) missions: night-time limitations on, 78; Task Force 77, 39
Coberly, Theodore S., 184–85
Collett, USS, 43
combat air patrol (CAP) mission, 26; target (TARCAP), 27

combat search and rescue (SAR), 11–13, 209. *See also* Wayne, Robert E. ("Bob")

communists: on American "germ warfare" campaign, 114–15; on bomber squadrons, 164; evacuate Seoul, 95; push toward Seoul, 98; Soviet air divisions in Antung area, 129; supply/transportation lines interdiction against, 47–54, 83–92, 211

Conley, Francis J. ("Joe"), 148; Thunderjets' reliability and, 133–35

Corsairs. *See* Chance-Vought F4U-4B Corsair fighters; Vought F4U-4B Corsair fighters

Costello, Ray, 13

Craig, Clement L., 88

Creighton, Dick, 136, 168, 185, 189

Cross, Sergeant, 155, 157

Curry, Nate: downed into Sea of Japan, 36–38; on photo run, 34–35

Curry, Robert, 34

Curry, William, 34

Darrow, Charles, 23–24; crash landing onto *Valley Forge*, 26–27; escorting photo aircraft, 25–26; pre-Inchon strikes by, 43; on Sinuiju bridge strikes, 50–53; tactics argument with FAC team, 33; TARCAPs for, 27–28; Thomson's difficulty and, 31–32; Wonsan Oil Refinery Factory bombing raid and, 28

Davis, George A., Jr., 164, 168, 179; after MiGs, 183; aids Barton, 175–76; attacks Tu-2s, 173–74; dead-stick landing, 178; as deflection shooter, 183; as dogfighter, 182; and Dymock on tactics, 181–82; as fighter pilot, 180–81; four-kill missions of, 183–85; last mission, 186–88; Medal of Honor for, 188–89; MiG Madness of, 185–86; to Taehwa-do, 169

The Dawn Patrol, 196

Dean, William F., 30

"Dentist" control, 120–21, 122

Detachment F (helicopter unit), 12–13

Dewald, Robert ("Slick"): chases IL-10s, 8–9; early life of, 3–4; finds wrecked IL-10, 10; Kimpo Airfield defense, 5–6; learns war has begun, 3

Dignity Able Flight, 4th Fighter Interceptor Wing, 135–36, 137, 138, 148–49; in Lufberry Circle, 139; MiGs engage, 140–41, 145

Dignity Able Flight, 334th Fighter-Bomber Wing, 169

Dignity Baker Flight, 334th Fighter-Bomber Wing, 169

Dignity Red Flight, 4th Fighter Interceptor Wing, 135, 136

Dignity Special Flight, 336th Fighter-Bomber Wing, 169

Dignity William Flight, 335th Fighter-Bomber Wing, 169

Dog Flight, 4th Fighter Interceptor Wing, 135, 138–39, 146

Douglas A-20 Havoc, 107

Douglas AD-1 Skyraider attack bombers, 23, 24–25; crash-lands onto *Valley Forge*, 26; Namson-Ni highway bridge attack by, 49–51; ordnance load of, 39

Douglas AD-4N Skyraider night-attack bomber, 78

Douglas AD-4 Skyraider attack bombers: Carlson's, 75; VA-195 faith in, 77–78

Douglas AD-4W Skyraider early-warning aircraft, 78

Douglas B-26 Invader, 105–6, 122; blown tires at K-2 Airfield in Taegu, 113; dedicated flare-dropping, 110;

mark VI flares for, 109–10; night raids by, 107; Operation Tack and, 107–8

Douglas F3D Skynights, 191

Downs, Dick, 24, 32, 40–41, 44–45

Dymock, Alfred W., Jr., 181–82, 184

Easy Flight, 136th Fighter-Bomber Wing, 144, 147

Eighth Air Force: over Berlin (WWII), 15–16

Eighth Army: Chinese strike on, 55, 57–62; Hwachon Dam and, 96, 97; improved morale in, 95; past Pusan Perimeter up peninsula, 45; seeks Navy air support, 30; Seoul evacuation by, 93

8th Fighter-Bomber Wing, 2, 133, 135

802d Engineer Battalion, NKAF bombing of, 117

Eisenhower, Dwight D., 193, 201

Eisenhower, John, 201

Elwood, Clare, 199

energy fight, 187

Enoch, Kenneth, 114–15

Essex, USS, 23–24, 92

Evans, Douglas K. ("Doug"), 159–60, 167–68, 179; attacks Tu-2s, 171–73; on Davis, 181, 187, 189; to Taehwa-do, 169

F4U-4Bs. *See* Chance-Vought F4U-4B Corsair fighters

F4U-5P Corsair photo aircraft, 25–26

F-51 Mustangs, 2, 158; combat-ready for South Koreans, 4; ordnance load of, 39

F-80 Shooting Stars, 4; The Gauntlet and, 59; *versus* MiGs, 163; ordnance load of, 39; protect Kimpo Airfield, 6; Sinuiju Airfield raids by, 120. *See also* Lockheed F-80C Shooting Stars

F-82 Twin Mustangs: intercept Yak-7s at Kimpo Airfield, 5–6; meet NKAF fighter, 5

F-84 Thunderjets. *See* Republic F-84 Thunderjets

F-86 Sabrejets, 127–28; attack on Taehwa-do, 168; attack support on MiG Alley airfields by, 130–31; *versus* MiGs, 162–63, 164, 204–5; NKAF bombing of, 117; shape similarity to MiGs, 145; Sinuiju Airfield raids by, 120

F-94 Starfires, 190–91

FEAF (Headquarters Far East Air Forces), 2; B-29 losses and, 161; Black Day for FEAF's Bombers, 132; documents Soviets in MiG Alley, 201; The Gauntlet and, 59; Korean War readiness of, 11; logistics/communications campaign by, 83–92, 211; MiG Alley stalemate and, 191–92, 194; night raids by, 106–8; North Korean airfield attacks by, 117–18; against Soviet 151st, 204–5; truce talks and, 193, 209; Weyland commands, 127; Yalu River strikes by, 47

Fifth Air Force, U.S., 1, 4; evacuating wounded from N. Korea, 11–12; night raids on bridge EA1622, 90; Rescue Liaison Office, 12–13

51st Fighter Interceptor Wing, 120, 164

Fighting Four, 23–24

Fighting Nine, 23–24

"Fireflies" (C-47s as flare-droppers), 109

1st Cavalry Division, 58

1st Marine Division: at Chosin Reservoir, 60; from Hagaru-ri to Koto-ri, 78–79; from Koto-ri to Chinhung, 79–81

509th Bomb Wing, 150

535th Soviet Fighter Air Regiment (FAR), 206

flak traps, North Korean, 112

Flying Midshipmen, 65

Ford, John, 24, 36; gunboat attack, Sea of Japan, 37; pre-Inchon strikes by, 43;

Seoul/Sariwon armed reconnaissance by, 44–45; TARCAPs for, 27–28

Ford, William L., 109

Fortner, Farrie D., 146–47

49th Fighter-Bomber Wing, 131, 133

forward air control (FAC) parties: Eighth Army allocations of, 30

Foulkes, James, 153–54

452nd Bomb Wing, 109, 110, 118

4th Fighter Interceptor Wing, 120, 128, 133, 164; attacks Taehwa-do, 167, 168; attack support on MiG Alley airfields by, 130–31; Baker Two grilling after Davis's crash, 188; MiGs attack in MiG Alley, 135–41; on unit's performance, 162

4th Ranger Company, 96

Fox Flight, 136th Fighter-Bomber Wing, 147

Frainier, Al, 33, 44

Franz, Leo, 40

Freeland, Dave, 169, 171–73

French Battalion, at Chipyong-ni, 94

Fuentes, John, 13, 19–20

Gallery, William, 99

"The Gauntlet" (Chongchon River valley ambush), 58–60

George Flight, 136th Fighter-Bomber Wing, 135, 143

Goldbeck, Emil, 150–51, 155, 156, 157–58; Namsi Airfield mission, 151–53

Green, Pat, 159–60

Grumman F7F Tigercats, 122, 191

Grumman F9F-2 Panthers, 24

Grumman F9F-5 Panthers, 195

Grumman SA-16 Albatross, 157, 158

Hagaru-ri, 60, 61–62; air evacuation from, 75–76

Hall, Ralph ("Smiley"): Kimpo Airfield defense, 5–8; and NKAF IL-10s, 7–8

Hammond, Buford, 171

Han River, North Korean/Chinese assault on, 97–98

Hanton, Arthur ("Art"), 32, 36

Harris, Hap, 82, 84–85

Harris, William, 96

Headquarters Far East Air Forces. See FEAF

Hedlund, Harry, 113–14

Helena, USS, 64

helicopters, search and rescue operations and, 12, 209

Hellfire Valley ambush, 60–61

Heyman, Dick, 105–6, 111, 122–24; anti-aircraft fire and, 112–13; on butterfly bomb, 108; cables across valleys and, 113; chases Po-2, 120–22; on M-46 fire-bombs, 109; searchlights for night raids and, 110

Hodson, N. D., 28

Holister, USS, 38

Holm, Stan, 196

"Home for Christmas" offensive, MacArthur's, 57–62

Honaker, John, 177

Horner, John J., 159

Hudner, Tom, 63–72; Brown rescue attempt by, 68–72; early career, 64–65; Medal of Honor for, 72

Hudson, William ("Skeeter"), 6

"Hunter-Killer" tactics, by 452nd Bomb Wing, 110

Hwachon Dam, 95–96; Carlson's Tigers torpedo, 99–101; Chinese offensive at, 97; strength of, 98

Il-2 Sturmovik, 1

Ilyushin Il-10 Sturmovik ground-attack bombers, 1, 7

Inchon landing, 40–45

Inchon refugees, 8th FBW and, 2

Iron Triangle, Chinese military in, 95, 97

Japanese Kawasaki Ki-61 Hien, 180
Johnson, Gerald E., 159
Johnson, Lyndon, 209
Joint Chiefs of Staff, MacArthur and, 47
Joy, C. Turner, 48–49

Kalmus, Stu, 118–19
Karelin, Anatoli, 205–6
Kelly, Joseph, 130, 131, 161
Kim Il Sung, 203
Kimpo Airfield: 35th Fighter-Bomber
    Squadron defends, 5–10; abandoned/
    retaken, 93
Kincheloe, Iven, 183
King, Tom, 119
Kinsey, Ray, 179
Korean names, pronunciation of, 30–31
Koto-ri, 60, 61
Kozhedub, Ivan, 142, 205
Krumm, Robert, 153, 159
Kuhlman, H. C., 43

Lamb, William, 54
Laney, Ed: on MiGs at Sinuiju bridge
    attacks, 54; on politics in war, 56; on
    Sinuiju bridge strikes, 49–50, 54; and
    Soviet bogey during Inchon landing,
    40–41; Thomson's difficulty and, 31–32
Lavochkin La-9 piston-engine fighters,
    170, 172; Marshall engages, 177
Lavochkin La-11s piston-engine fighters,
    190, 205
La Woon Yung, 117
LeMay, Curtis, 150, 161, 162
Leyte, USS, 40, 59–60, 63, 66
Line Utah, 97
Lobov, Georgy, 142, 148, 149, 161, 205
Lockheed F-80C Shooting Stars, 2, 47.
    See also F-80 Shooting Stars
Long, E. B., 122
Lowe, Edwin, 19–20
Lufberry Circle, 139, 198

M-46 firebombs, 109
M-81 fragmentation bombs, 108–9
MacArthur, Douglas, 46–47, 57
Mahurin, Walker ("Bud"), 115
maps, accuracy of, 31
Marines: retreat from Hagaru-ri by,
    75–76
Mark VI flares, 109–10
Mark XIII torpedoes, 99
Marshall, Winton ("Bones"), 168,
    176–78, 179, 183, 185
McConnell, Joseph, 183
McDaniel, Wally, 118
McPhail, Bob, 200
Mercury Blue Flight, 136th Fighter-
    Bomber Wing, 147
Mercury White Flight, 136th Fighter-
    Bomber Wing, 147–48
Merook, Leonard, 171
Merrick, Andy, 168
Merrick, Dick, 99–101, 104
Messerschmitt Bf-109s, 16
Michener, James A., 87, 92
Middleton, John, 199–200, 201
Midway, USS: Hudner transfers to, 63
MiGs, Chinese: Sinuiju bridge attacks
    and, 52; Tu-2 high cover, 170, 171;
    VF-52 shoot down, 54
MiG-15s: against B-29s, 132, 151–54;
    buildup in Manchuria of, 127; Davis
    and, 183; horizontal flak from, 152;
    inexperience of, 140; radar omitted
    from, 190; similarity in shape to Sabre-
    jets, 145
MiG-15s, Chinese, 47; attack CAG-11
    near Yalu river, 49; inexperience of,
    140; Sinuiju bridge attacks and, 53–54
MiG-15s, Soviet, 120; .50-caliber
    machine gun against, 146; Baker flight
    shoots at, 143–44; dogfight with Row-
    lands, Williams and Middleton,
    197–200; losses of, 206–7; protect

Namsi Airfield, 142–49; *versus* Sabre-
jets, 204–5
MiG Alley, 127–28; attack on N. Korean
airfields in, 129–32; MiGs trap F-86s
in, 135–41; new airstrips in, 128–29;
Soviet presence in, 204; UN fighter-
bombers return to, 190
MiG Madness, 186
Mitchell, C. C., 209
Mitson, Claude ("Charlie"), 182, 184–85
Mitsubishi A6M Zero, 180
Moscow Radio, 114
Mosquito pilots, 97. *See also* North
American T-6 Mosquito
Muccio, John, 2
Mulkins, Bill, 110
Murphy, Joe, 36, 40
Mustangs, Air Force, The Gauntlet
and, 59

nails, dropped on key crossroads, 107–8
Namsi Airfield, 130, 133; B-29 crews after
mission to, 154–59; MiG-15s against
B-29s, 151–54; Soviet MiG-15s protect,
142–49
Nashville, USS, 75
Navy, U.S., carrier upgrades and, 209
night raids, 178; anti-aircraft fire and,
112–13; B-29 escorts for, 190–91; on
bridge EA1622, 90; cables across valleys and, 113; by communists, 116–17,
178; deterrent selections of, 107–9;
flare tactics of, 110; on MiG Alley airfields, 129–32; 3rd Bomb Wing and,
106–8
19th Bomb Wing, 47, 130, 131, 132
IX Corps: Operation Killer and, 94–95;
ROK 6th Division collapse and, 97
97th Soviet Fighter Air Division, 205
98th Bomb Wing, 130, 131
Nixon, Richard, 209
North American B-25 Mitchell, 107

North American F-86A and E Sabrejets,
127–28. *See also* F-86 Sabrejets
North American T-6 Mosquito, 19–20
North Korea: flak traps of, 112; nighttime bombing raids by, 116–17;
railroad damage repair in, 89–90; T-34
tanks, 2
North Korean air force (NKAF): attacks
Kimpo Airport, 5–10; attacks Seoul
Airfield and Kimpo Airport, 1. *See also*
communists
North Korean People's Army (NKPA),
22; Task Force Smith, 24th Infantry
Division and, 29–30. *See also* communists

Ofstie, Ralph, 88, 90–91, 98, 99
O'Neal, Julius, 152, 155, 156
116th Fighter-Bomber Wing, 127
136th Fighter-Bomber Wing, 131, 133,
136, 143, 146
151st Soviet Fighter Air Division, 204
154th Fighter-Bomber Squadron, 146
176th Soviet Guard Fighter Air Regiment (FAR), 205
187th Regimental Combat Team, 95
196th Soviet Fighter Air Regiment,
169–70, 205
Operation Killer, 94–95
Operation Piledriver, 103
Operation Ripper, 95
Operation Roundup, 93
Operation Rugged, 95
Operation Strangle, 106
Operation Tack, 107–8
Operation Thunderbolt, 93
Oriskany, USS, 195, 196, 199

P-47 Thunderbolt, 180
Panthers, 24, 42, 195
Parker, R. E., 54
Penninger, Roger, 152, 155

Pepelyaev, Yevgeni, 205, 206
Philippine Sea, USS, 40, 42, 59–60
photo aircraft, Marine-piloted: Darrow escorting, 25–26
"Pisscall Charlies," 117
Pittman, Bill, 24, 56; first combat air patrol mission, 26; gunboat attack, Sea of Japan, 37; Sinuiju bridge attacks and, 51–52; TARCAPs for, 27–28; Thomson's difficulty and, 32; Wonsan Oil Refinery Factory bombing raid and, 28
Plog, Leonard, 24
Polikarpov Po-2 biplanes, 1; airfield raids by, 116, 120; Heyman chases, 120–22; night-heckling by, 178
Port Arthur cemetery for fallen Soviet fighter pilots, 204
Preston, Ben, 168, 169, 170, 176, 185–86
Price, John M. ("Jack"), 2
Princeton, USS, 77, 83, 88
prisoners of war, torture of, 113–15
Puller, Lewis B. ("Chesty"), 78

Quinn, John, 114–15

Radford, Arthur W., 201
radio channels overloaded early in war, 30, 31
Radio Pyongyang, 114
reconnaissance RB-26, 106
Red Flight, 336th Fighter-Bomber Wing, 169
Reeter, William, 153
Republic F-84 Thunderjets, 127, 131, 132; effectiveness against MiGs of, 133–34; MiG-15s against, 142–43; *versus* MiGs, 163–64; returning to Kimpo battle-scarred, 160
Republic of Korea (ROK), 2; 1st Division, Chinese attack, 46; 6th Division collapse at Iron Triangle, 97; air force, Mustangs for, 4

Rescue Liaison Office, Fifth Air Force, 12–13
Rhee, Syngman, 2, 4
Ridgway, Matthew B., 93, 94, 95, 96
Riebeling, Herb, 27–28, 29, 43
Rowlands, David, 201–2; debriefing, 200; dogfight with Soviets and, 195–96, 197–99; Eisenhower and, 201; flak batteries hit, 196–97
Russian language on transmissions, 129, 203, 204
Ryan, John, 150

Saamcham Airfield, 128, 130, 131
Sabrejets. *See* F-86 Sabrejets
Schillereff, Ray: chase IL-10s, 8–9; Kimpo Airfield defense, 5–6
searchlights, 3rd Bomb Wing, 110
2nd Infantry Division, 57, 58, 59
Seoul, 93, 95, 98
7th Cavalry Regiment, 96
Seventh Fleet, 30, 42, 55
7th Infantry Division, 60, 61–62, 75
7th Marines: from Hagaru-ri to Koto-ri, 78–79
Shields, Thomas ("Tom"), 150–51; Namsi Airfield mission, 151–53; Silver Star for, 158; to Yellow Sea, 154–55
Shooting Stars. *See* F-80 Shooting Stars; Lockheed F-80C Shooting Stars
Shoran guidance system, 133; Namsi Airfield mission and, 151, 152
Sicily, USS, 40
Sikorsky H-5As, 12, 15
Sikorsky HO3S-1 helicopter, 69–71
Simmons, Al, 169, 170–71
Sinuiju Airfield, raids on, 120
Sinuiju bridge strikes, 49–50, 51, 53–54
Sisson, Thomas V., 71
606th Aircraft Control and Warning Squadron, 116
64th Soviet Fighter Air Corps, 206

67th Tactical Reconnaissance Wing, 128

Skalla, Darryl: bombing bridges west of Sinpo, 84

Skyraiders. *See* Douglas AD-1 Skyraider attack bombers

slashing attack, 187

Smith, Carl E. ("Gene"), 24; Wonsan raid and, 29

Smith, Ted, 155, 158

Soviet Union, 203–7; air fighter divisions in Korea, 204–6; early precautions for, 204; Fighter Air Divisions of, 142–49; Inchon landing and, 40; TF-77 plans defense against, 42; VF-53 shoots down bogey of, 41

Spencer, Robert V., 108

Stalin, Joseph, 203–4

Starfires, 190–91

Stinson L-5 observation planes, 12, 30

Stockdale, James, 64

Strategic Air Command (SAC), 150

Stratemeyer, George E., 46–47; logistics/communications campaign by, 83–88

Struble, Arthur D., 31

Superforts. *See* Boeing B-29 Super Fortress

Suwon Airfield: communists' night-time bombing of, 116

Taechon Airfield, 130, 131–32

Taehwa-do, 167–69

Taejon, South Korea, 30

target CAP's (TARCAP), 27

Task Force 77, 22; bombing bridges west of Sinpo, 83–85; bombing eastern rail lines, 86–87; east of Wonsan, 36–37; The Gauntlet and, 59; Inchon landing and, 40–45; *Leyte* joins, 66; night raids on bridge EA1622, 90; off combat line, 27; Pusan Perimeter battles and, 39–40; reconnaissance in Carlson's Canyon, 89; truce talks and, 193; Yalu bridges and, 48; in Yellow Sea, 23

Task Force Drysdale, 60–61, 75

Task Force Smith, 29–30

tetrahedrons, 108

Thach Weave, 25

3rd Air Rescue Squadron, 12

3rd Bomb Wing, 106; deterrent selections of, 107–9; double night sorties by, 113; flare tactics of, 110; night raids on truck convoys, 108–9; Operation Tack and, 107–8

III ROK Corps, 95–96

35th Fighter-Bomber Squadron, 2; C Flight defends Kimpo Airfield, 5–10

Thomson, Keith, 27–28, 31–33, 35

303d Soviet Fighter Air Division, 140, 142, 149, 205

307th Bomb Wing, 129–32, 135–40, 153, 161

319th Fighter Interceptor Squadron, 190–91

324th Soviet Fighter Air Division, 140, 142, 149, 205

334th Fighter-Bomber Wing, 168, 169, 173–76, 180–81

335th Fighter-Bomber Wing, 168, 169, 176–78

336th Fighter-Bomber Wing, 168, 170–73

351st Soviet Air Regiment, 190, 205

371st Fighter-Bomber Squadron, 151

372d Fighter-Bomber Squadron, 151

385th Bomb Group, Eighth Air Force, 15–16

Thunderjets. *See* Republic F-84 Thunderjets

Thyng, Harry, 168

training program, USAF, 208

Triumph, HMS, 40

truce talks, strategic air campaign and, 193, 209

truck convoy attacks, 107–8; lit-up convoys, 109; North Korean flak traps and, 112

Truman, Harry: integrating military, 65; MacArthur and, 47

Tu-2 bombers, Chinese, 167, 169–70; 334th attacks, 173–76; 335th attacks, 176–78; 336th attacks, 170–73

Turkish Brigade, 57–58

23rd Infantry Regiment, 58, 94

24th Infantry Division, 29–30, 98

25th Infantry Division, 98, 103

29th Soviet Fighter Air Regiment, 203

VA-55 (attack squadron), 28–29, 49–51

VA-195 (attack squadron): accomplishments of, 104; AD-Skyraiders and, 77–78; assess Marine chances at Hagaru-ri, 75–76; attack logistics/communications lines, 83; bombs bridge EA1622, 89; bombs bridges west of Sinpo, 83–87; torpedoing Hwachon Dam, 99–100; van Slooten bombs too low, 77

Valley Forge, USS, 22; air support missions by, 30; CAG-5 briefing on, 23; crash-landing on, 26; Curry medical treatment on, 38; Thomson's difficulty and, 32; Wonsan Oil Refinery Factory bombing and, 28–29

Vandenberg, Hoyt S., 47, 128

Van Fleet, James A., 92, 201

van Slooten, Don, 77, 84, 85–86

VC-35, 90, 99–100

VC-61, 99–101

veterans, Korean War, 211–12

VF-32 (jet fighter squadron), 63, 67

VF-51 (jet fighter squadron), 23, 24, 51–52

VF-52 (jet fighter squadron), 23, 53–54

VF-53 (jet fighter squadron): accomplishments, 55; close air support missions, July 1950, 33; experience of, 51; first mission briefing for, 23–24; flak suppression for Yalu strikes, 49; gunboat attack, Sea of Japan, 37–38; Hungnam mission, 29; Inchon landing support by, 40–44; loses first Corsair, 26; replacement pilots for, 33–34; retaking of Wonsan and, 45–46; Sinuiju bridge attacks and, 53–54; TARCAPs of, 27–28; Thomson shot down, 31–33; Wonsan Oil Refinery Factory bombing and, 28–29; Yalu bridges constraints on, 48–49

VF-54 (jet fighter squadron), 23

VF-111 (jet fighter squadron), 49

VF-781, 195, 201

Vietnam, helicopters in, 209

VMF-513, 191

von Boven, Paul, 13; as POW at Stalag Luft 3, 17; rescues Wayne, 18–20; shot down in WWII, 15–16

Vought F4U-4B Corsairs: armor plating for, 63. See also Chance-Vought F4U-4B Corsair fighters

Walker, Walton W., 45. See also Eighth Army

Walmsley, John, 110–11

Ward, Charlie, 69–71

Wayne, Penny Sue, 5, 14, 20–21

Wayne, Robert E. ("Bob"): delivers F-51 to South Korea, 4; early life of, 3; evacuated to Japan, 20–21; helicopter picks up, 19; Kimpo Airfield defense, 5–8; learns war has begun, 2–3; waiting for rescue, 17–18; wounded in N. Korean rice paddy, 13–15

Weyland, Otto P., 127–28, 129–32, 164

White, Stan, 18–19, 20

White Flight, 4th Fighter Interceptor Wing, 135, 136

Wild Weasels, 50–51

Williams, Royce, 200, 201; dogfights with Soviets, 195–96, 197–99

Wonsan Oil Refinery Factory attack, 28–29

X Corps: ashore at Wonsan, 45; Chinese strike on, 55, 57; Hungnam evacuation for, 81; at Hwachon Dam, 95–96; onto Hagaru-ri, 61–62; Operation Killer and, 94–95
X-Ray Flight, 335th Fighter-Bomber Wing, 169

Yak-18, 1
Yakovlev Yak-3, 1

Yakovlev Yak-7, 1, 5–6
Yakovlev Yak-7B, 1
Yakovlev Yak-9, 1, 25–26, 123
Yalu River: Joint Chiefs counter-order on, 48; MacArthur's advance to, 46; MiGs south of, 128–29; Turner's concerns about attack on, 48–49; U.S. strikes on, 49–54
Yellow Sea, Soviet pilot limitation over, 204
Yongyu Airfield, raids on, 120
Yorktown, USS, 23–24
Yudam-ni, Marines at, 62

About the Author

John Bruning is a historian, writer, and designer of combat flight simulators and educational CD-ROM products. A graduate of the University of Oregon, he lives in Independence, Oregon, where he served as a city councilor and a school board member.